SPITFIRE
ODYSSEY

© C. R. Russell & Kingfisher
Railway Productions. October 1985
ISBN 0-946184-18-6

Typesetting by:
Aquarius Typesetting Services
New Milton, Hants.

Printed by:
Netherwood Dalton & Co.
Bradley Mills,
Huddersfield,
Yorkshire.

SPITFIRE
ODYSSEY

C. R. Russell

Published by

Kingfisher Railway Productions

188 Bitterne Road, Southampton SO2 4BE
Tel. (0703) 222032

Aerial view of the Woolston Works after the extensions just before the War.

Vickers

For my two sons, Geoffrey and Steven, and in memory of all the Supermariners whose sacrifices in the air-raids of the 24th and 26th September 1940 contributed to the peaceful lives they have enjoyed to date.

LEST WE FORGET

15th September 1940

This day is Battle of Britain day
He that outlives this day and comes safe home,
Will stand a tip-toe when this day is named
And rouse him at the name of Britain.
He that shall live this day and see old age
Will yearly on the vigil feast his neighbours
And say: 'Tomorrow is Battle of Britain day'.

Old men forget, yet all shall be forgot.
But he'll remember with advantages
What feats they did that day; then shall their names
Familiar in his mouth as household words
Dowding the Chief, Park and Brand,
Johnson and Tuck, Townsend and Deere,
Be in the flowing cups freshly remembered.

This story shall the good man teach his son
And Battle of Britain day shall ne'er go by
From this day to the ending of the world,
But we in it shall be remembered;
We few, . . . we happy few.

Spitfire of No. 288 Squadron here being flown by F/O B. Hicks, early 1946.

Contents

Page

Chapter One
Opening Gambit 7

Chapter Two
A Handy Lad 13

Chapter Three
Stranraer Hull Building 19

Chapter Four
The Facts of Life 24

Chapter Five
Spitfire Production Commences 28

Chapter Six
Growing up and Going up............... 35

Chapter Seven
Panelbeating and Wheeling 40

Chapter Eight
Prelude to War 47

Chapter Nine
Into War 55

Chapter Ten
The Battle Begins 58

Chapter Eleven
Sunday September 15th 1940 67

Chapter Twelve
The Tuesday Air-raid 72

Chapter Thirteen
The Thursday Air-raid 77

Chapter Fourteen
Castle Bromwich 85

Chapter Fifteen
Dispersal 89

Chapter Sixteen
Production Facts and Figures 98

Chapter Seventeen
Trowbridge and Air Ducts 102

Chapter Eighteen
**Salisbury — High Post Airfield
and Wessex Motors** 109

Chapter Nineteen
Return to Trowbridge 119

Chapter Twenty
Post-war Changes 133

Chapter Twenty-one
Decline and Fall 147

Chapter One
Opening Gambit

It took just two and a quarter years from leaving school at 14 years of age, through a series of blind-alley jobs as errand boy, store boy, and baker's van boy before, through the good offices and kindness of Mrs Read, one of the baker's customers, that I achieved my ambition to be something — anything almost — in the world of aviation and aeroplanes. Mrs Read's husband was the Chief Gateman at the Supermarine Aviation Works at Woolston, Southampton; already a name renowned worldwide for the achievements of its Schneider Trophy successes and the genius of its Chief Designer, Reginald J. Mitchell.

After an interview at the gatehouse with a white coated foreman, I was told to start on Monday, 9th March 1936.

It was to be a long journey together — hence the 'odyssey' in the title — spanning twenty-one years all told, with only two relatively short breaks; years that covered that part of our country's history instantly pinpointed by the word 'Spitfire', until after the war years with the gradual demise and disappearance of that other equally famous name 'Supermarine' from the aviation world. What happened in those years and why?

So far as the flying and wartime fighting is concerned for both the Spitfire and the ubiquitous Walrus, they have been adequately covered by book and film many times — if not always as accurately as they might have deserved — and to these there is little I can add except to redress where possible some of the errors that are extant, and contribute a few anecdotes of a personal nature where the paths cross.

Historians and Engineers have probed and delved in great length and depth into the relevant matters of their particular concerns — the former coming up quite often with some real schoolboy 'howlers', no doubt due to the unmistakable disadvantage of being far too young to have any personal recollections to draw upon, a condition which for me is not applicable, and that being an admitted aircraft enthusiast since the age of ten I have not only accumulated a fairly modest library of pre and post-war books and magazines on the subject, but, most fortunately, have somehow retained the wartime diaries I kept and, perhaps even more fortunately for the purpose now intended, all of the notebooks I kept at work of the actual job details and locations.

Let me establish, if I may, the validity and my own credibility with a recent example.

Within the past two years a book was published which had been long awaited by those interested in the Spitfire. It was the autobiography of Jeffrey Quill, a Test Pilot of rare quality, and quite possibly the only man who flew every single prototype of the many variants and mark numbers of both Spitfire and Seafire, not to mention the Spiteful and early post-war jets.

In its own way it is the definitive book on flying the Spitfire, and yet when I read it with avid interest I was amazed to find a few errors that I knew personally were not as he had stated. The simplest one is sufficient to make my point. Jeffrey Quill had stated quite unequivocally that K5054, the Spitfire prototype, first flew on 6th March 1936. Now Jeffrey Quill is a man who I happen to respect and admire very much. To me, especially in my younger days, he was a hero figure; a pilot, a test pilot, and furthermore a test pilot who was entitled to wear the little gold silkworm shaped tie pin that was only given to those who had been compelled to take to a parachute from an aeroplane no longer capable of staying in the air. In his case it was a Vickers Wellesley and fairly early on in his test flying career.

Supermarine Works at Woolston in the early 1920s.

Vickers

The Baker's Boy, 1935.

All this posed a dilemma. I did not want his book to be wrong, or to be used in future references with information I knew to be incorrect; whilst at the same time how does one attempt to tell a person who is a legend in his own lifetime that he has made a mistake — however small?

In the end I wrote to his publisher — it was the only contact I had — who forwarded my letter on to him. To my surprise, and relief, he wrote back to me personally accepting the other amendments I had put forward but quite rightly querying my source reference regarding the 5th March date that I had submitted. He made a point, that so often dates and other matters were perpetuated by repetition from an original source being inaccurately reported yet always referred to — a statement that contributes very largely to my writing of this mainly autobiographical account — and in an interchange of letters I was able to satisfy him that 5th March 1936 was the correct date, which I am delighted to say he conceded very graciously.

It was this event, and the publication of more blatant accounts of events and people, that were, in my humble opinion, just rubbish that decided me to set down for the record, not only the facts as I knew them to be, but to also tell the story of Supermarines and the Spitfire as I experienced it, first as a lowly 'handy lad', starting but four days after 'Mutt' Summers had first lifted into the sky the aircraft that was to dominate nine years of my life, then as an apprentice 'tinbasher' in the shop where the flying boat hulls and Spitfire fuselages were produced, into the War and how it was to be working in an obvious Luftwaffe target, the bombings and subsequent dispersal, of years being 'directed' to different workplaces, and often different and new work, denied the right and desire experienced by many young skilled men (as I had become) because of the laws applicable to 'Restricted Occupations' to join the fighting Services; some, if not all, of the lifestyle in which we lived and worked, and how boredom, distress, and sometimes tragedy were offset by the will to win, our self-made recreations and the help of others.

It is a part of the Spitfire story that, to the best of my knowledge, has not been told in such detail before, curtailed only as it must be by the extent of my personal experiences and knowledge. Some amplification has had to come from research, and in this I am indebted to many old colleagues whose numbers sadly diminish each year, and also to the generosity of a fellow author who, in compiling his book about the Luftwaffe Erprobungs-gruppe 210, was referred to me for certain details he required and, as a result, was able to supply me with information that I needed from his personal contacts with the 'enemy'. To them all, my thanks for their help, and not least of all their encouragements.

The final chapters about post-war Supermarines are included mainly because I have seen an account which, in my opinion, is so terribly at variance with the truth that I felt they must be incorporated whilst it is still within my capability to do so, and from the 'special' positions I was in at the pertinent times.

Having explained my purpose and its reasons, I sincerely hope that readers will find something informative, as well as entertaining, on the journey that occupied over half of my working life, and turns now back to the day in March 1936, when a tall, skinny lad entered the land of his boyhood dreams, little realising where, and to what, those dreams would lead.

For me personally, the induction into factory life was a large and unknown step, not without risk; especially when there were two and a half million unemployed. None of my family had any experience I could draw on for guidance, and up to the moment I had been interviewed in the factory yard I had not even had a glimpse of what I had let myself in for, as my previous jobs had either been pushing a carrier-bicycle around in all weathers with all too infrequent spells in the shelter of the shop, and latterly delivering bread from a van.

'Walrus' hull line at Woolston in 1939.

Vickers

Supermarine Walrus amphibians 'bombing up' on aircraft carrier.

Vickers

As someone with little or no known mechanical skills, it was a challenge — a fresh start — and a major change in content and environment so that having presented myself to Mr Read at his little green-painted wooden gatehouse, and parked my bicycle in a rack as directed, I then had to wait the few moments to 7.30a.m. when, as soon as the factory klaxons sounded, the metal folding gates were closed and those who had not made it in time were shut out.

It was explained to me that provided their foremen agreed, these latecomers would be let in at 7.40a.m. but would lose a quarter hour's pay. One also lost a 'quarter' if one failed to clock-in at your shop time office no later that 7.32a.m.

Having satisfied himself that the gate closure procedure was properly attended to, Mr Read detailed an assistant to see to the latecomers and bade me follow him into the work-sheds. He led me through the whole length of it, as the 'shop' I was destined for was at the furthest end, adjacent to the Floating Bridges.

I clearly remember my first impressions. The wonderment of seeing and being close to seaplanes and flying boats in their varied assembly stages, the Machine Shop with its whine, the comparative calm as we passed the Wing Shop and then into a gangway to a small wooden and glass office in the middle of a sea of benches, with men banging and hammering pieces of silver coloured metal, and all down the wall backing on to the floating bridges was a row of metal girder structures within which were seaplane and flying boat hulls in varied stages of assembly.

The noise from the hammering men supplemented by what I later found to be rivet guns was deafening to my unconditioned ears and the subsequent form-filling and verbal information passed in a daze. My raincoat and coat jacket I hung on a rectangular frame with coat hooks all round which, to my astonishment, was a few moments later hauled up into the roof girders. Somehow I found myself placed into the care of Bill Peckham, who led me to a bench alongside another boy about my own age to whom he gave a chit of paper, and who in turn led me up some stairs to a balcony store where I received a wooden mallet, two files of differing roughness, a funny shaped piece of plate which was called a template, and two sheets of 6ft. x 2ft. of the silver metal.

'Sign here', said Harry Jay, the storeman, indicating a card for the tools now mine on loan, 'and here', he indicated another card for the template, and yet again on the chit for the two sheets of metal. The boy with me said, 'He'll need an eighth drill and some nuts and bolts', which Harry duly dispensed, and so with all this gear we descended the stairs and back to the bench.

The remainder of that morning passed in a whirl of noise, with people having to yell at me so that I could hear, instructions on how to set a foot operated guillotine, the way to use a small bandsaw, a pillar drill, and cutting and filing to the template. I had to borrow a screwdriver.

The Time Clerk came and showed me my clocking on card and how it had to be used, and across the top he had written, C. Russell, K175. At midday the klaxons sounded for lunch time and I took my sandwiches outside to the river front and slipway area and tried to get my bewildered self back to some sense of normality. My head was still full of the sounds of hammers, rivet guns, and the screech from bandsaws; my mind was a confusion of instructions, the unfamiliarity of it all, and an underlying fear that nagged at me wondering whether I had made a mistake in changing jobs, or bitten off more than I could chew.

Slowly munching my sandwich lunch I pondered these things in my mind and, after twenty minutes or so, I screwed up the empty paper lunch bag and tossed it into the river, stood up and looked along the factory river frontage and, for the first time, saw a Seagull Amphibian there. I walked over to it and touched the metal hull and floats and smoothed my hand along the taut fabric covered wing. This was different, this was the real thing, and for me it was the first time I had ever been so close to any aircraft. The remaining half hour or so of the lunch break was joyously spent inspecting this object of my greatest interest, and when I went back to my bench there was now a fresh resolve to somehow overcome the initial difficulties.

That evening, when I got home, my parents and younger brother were all keenly interested in my account of the day. My father pointed out that I needed some overalls as my clothes at the front were covered with silver filings and bandsaw swarf, and lent me a pair of his for the next day, as well as a screwdriver. Mother wanted to know how much pay I would get and I had to admit I had forgotten to find out.

Looking back in time now I realise how the seed for what was to follow was sown. As a child, my mother used to push my younger brother and me by pushchair from our home in Whites Road in Bitterne, via the floating bridge at Woolston, to the markets at Kingsland Square in Southampton. Not being overblessed with this world's goods, these journeys enabled her to save a few pence of her meagre housekeeping money.

It was the free trip on the now sadly long defunct floating bridges that provided my first glimpses of Supermarine seaplanes, either floating in the River Itchen, or better still taxi-ing to or from take-off. When the then Prince of Wales visited the Supermarine Works in the 1920s, it was my mother who took me with her to see the occasion of this rare Royal visit, and holding me up on the window ledge of the newsagents shop, I saw the slim dapper figure of the man who later created an historic event of his own. Little did I dream then that one day I would be lying face down in the gutter outside that same shop, as German bombers swept in to attack.

From such little beginnings my future hopes and love of flying and aircraft evolved.

Chapter Two
A Handy Lad

After that first day, things rapidly improved. Bill Peckham the chargehand was a great help, picking out the simple jobs first and then over the weeks gradually leading me into jobs requiring more skill and differing tools. He chastised just once, and that was because I always 'sirred' him, as he said 'he felt he was unlikely to receive the Royal accolade'.

From then on he was always Mister Peckham. The funny thing is that later in life I could not bear being 'sirred', and object to it still forty and more years on.

My curiosity was boundless; I watched how other people worked, the tools they used, and of course lunch hour was the great exploration time. No sitting to eat sandwiches, they were devoured whilst I went over every part of that works that I could enter without query. To me it was a veritable wonderland, and one lunch time in that first week we were told that the Spitfire would fly over the factory for all to see, and there I saw, for the first time, the prototype of the aircraft that was to become a legend.

After two weeks I found all of a sudden that the noise did not bother me any more, and that I could hear and speak much more normally, and this coincided with my first week's pay packet, as they paid a week in arrears. The sum total was eleven shillings, with a deduction of stoppages which was National Insurance and twopence for membership of the Sports Club which I had unknowingly contracted during my first morning. This was of little importance as during those two weeks I had found out that every job was timed, and if you did it in less time than allowed you were paid for half of time saved at a bonus rate, which was a little lower than your basic hourly rate. It did not take me long to take advantage of this, but it took a little time for the payment to work its way through as it was dependent on the job being inspected and passed satisfactorily, being cleared in the Time Office and then via the Ratefixer, to the Pay Office and thus eventually to my pay packet. Just to complete the record, this bonus was always shared equally with my mother until the day I left home.

A few weeks later, during which time I had been shown how to operate a nibbling machine, folders, and rollers, Bill Peckham came up to me and said that when I had finished my next job he wanted me to go as 'the boy' with a man on the metal skinning of the flying boats. This was great news!

Incidentally, I should clarify that by this time I had found that I was employed as a 'Handy Lad', as were the majority of my contemporaries at that time. As formal apprenticeships were somewhat rare and costing money, but having formulated no plans for my own future, and being quite happy doing what I was doing, my horizons at that time were no further than the next job from Bill Peckham's pile of job cards.

This particular 'next job' was in its way significant, it meant that I had overcome the initial vetting from my shop chargehand, which was quite something during a period when it was not unknown for men, and/or boys, to start work at Supermarine's at 7.30a.m. and be back out on the dole by 10a.m. This particular activity was so prevalent at the Woolston works that the local Labour Exchange used to waive the usual three day waiting or qualifying period before one became eligible again for dole money. It sounds pretty horrifying in these Welfare State days, but it had its benefits and safeguards, as many a man desperate for a job would 'talk' his way in, as say a sheetmetal worker, but when he turned up for work one look at his toolbox told all and sundry that this was just not so.

The 'Spitfire' prototype after it had been brought up to combat standard. Note the Diaper Brothers (riveters) and the Eastleigh hangar in the background.

Side view of K5054 after modifications.

'Handy Lads', like myself, sometimes could not stand the early days, or failed to grasp the simple essentials of factory life, and soon were weeded out and shown the gate. It was tough but many years later, after successfully being selected as one of five required out of over 200 applicants, I asked my new boss why he had chosen me. His reply was 'that you came from pre-war Supermarine's and with that experience you can get a job anywhere!'

I finished off my bench job, part-numbered it with the aid of metal type numbers, put it on the Inspector's bench with its labels, etc. and presented myself to Bill Peckham. He led me over to the Seagull jigs (this was the Australian name for what eventually became more famous as the Walrus), and introduced me to Joe Colvin. Joe looked like, and I believe probably was, an ex-boxer, with a flat cap and brown smock and nearly always a matchstick in his mouth, which had the dual purpose of stopping him smoking and serving as a tooth-pick. He was also the Leadinghand of the Seagull shell platers.

Perhaps it might be opportune to mention now how 'K' Shop functioned. The 'K' came from 'keel', a throw back from earlier ship or boat building local connotations, and, with fly-ing boat hulls, the first job was to lay the keel.

Mr Heaver, as Foreman, was in complete overall charge with Bill Peckham as full time chargehand. Supervision was then sub-divided to the Leadinghands — one to each of the many sections such as Scapa Flying Boat hull structural framework and shell plating, simi-larly for the Seagull Amphibian. Then there were the Riveters, Angle and Section bending, Panel beating, a small Mould Loft up on the balcony, the Shipwright and men who were responsible for replacing the wooden profile plates that used to provide the top and bottom centre line surround, as well as superintend the removal of all completed hulls from their jigs, a Finishing and Water Test line, and a Detail Section mostly staffed by boys. Not under Mr Heaver's jurisdiction were the Inspectors, the Ratefixer and the Time Office staff.

Leadinghands were working chargehands and for their additional supervisory duties used to receive an extra twopence an hour.

Joe Colvin was the first of these that I was to know, and what appeared to me at the time to be over-awing was the information he imparted, that I was to be 'his boy'.

Like so many, Joe's bark was worse than his bite and during the next eleven years with Vickers Supermarine I found almost all the people I met or worked with kindly, patient, and never failing in satisfying my wanting to know.

In the course of this narration of events I shall name some of them, but of course it would be too great a task to mention them all, so may I say now, named or unnamed, in one way or another I owe you all my very sincere thanks for whatever you did for me.

In compiling this book, it has been my intention to keep as far as possible away from tech-nical content — other people better qualified have already done that side. There are, however, certain jobs with which I was involved that can be explained relatively easily so the average non-technical reader can follow, and where this does not suffice I have included either illustrations or maps as applicable.

Some of these semi-technical descriptions apply to aircraft building techniques that are very little changed in their basic principles, even in this high technology age — but some, particularly the Stranraer seaplane hull erection, have now disappeared in the mists of time, and therefore only have a minor historical or nostalgic interest.

Shell plating, or skinning as it was more commonly known, meant covering the structure, i.e. the frames, stringers, longerons, etc. with light alloy plate. This plate comprised a series of panels, some flat, and some shaped in accordance with the structure to which they were to be fitted. To start with, the structure members had to be marked off for attachment holes, which varied in diameter and pitch to meet the subsequent riveting, and strictly in accord-ance with the design drawings. If memory serves me correctly, I believe we were obliged to work within plus or minus thirty thousandths of an inch.

Joe and I started the bottom forward plating which went from the nose to the step longitudinally, and from the keel plates to the chine angles port and starboard in width.

This area is known as the 'planing bottom', and for take-off from the water, the pilot has to get sufficient forward speed and lift so that the amphibian rides up on to this area forward of the step, just prior to lift-off into the air. The two front plates were pre-shaped by the panel beaters, and it was our job to trim the keel edge first so that a proper fit was achieved of the panel to the contoured structure. Having met that requirement my job was to sit inside the structure and drill a hole through, where indicated by Joe, from selected ones that we had pre-drilled in the structure earlier. Joe would use a mallet handle to force the panel into position, and after my drilling he would secure panel to structure with a Parker-Kalon self-cutting screw. The attachments would average out at about nine inches apart, and on Keelsons (that is the longitudinal members between frames from keel to chine) were relatively easy as their vertical Z section did not impede the drill's access, but on frames where often the channel section flanges went the same way, it meant using a six inch long ⅛in. diameter drill, and pressing on it so that it bowed into the section to present a square face to the drilling surface. I must confess that I broke a few drills in learning to master that technique, but Joe was very patient with me, and as a leadinghand he could sign a store chit for a replacement so no one but us was any the wiser.

Once the temporary attachment was completed, I drilled all the remaining holes, while Joe marked off the cut lines from the chine angles and the frame where the next panel would be placed underlapping the one we had fitted. When this was done we would fit the remaining panels each side that took the plating to the step frame using the same procedure, but with ease as there was much less shape in them. Having completed that, all the panels would be removed and whilst Joe did the final cutting and trimming to size, my job would be to deburr all the holes in panels and structure and remove all drilling swarf.

Before replacement, both structure and panels had to be inspected by the shop inspector who at that time was a genial red haired giant of a man named Conrad Mann (known to all and sundry as 'Con' and later to reach the top of his department). When I think back to those early days and remember how Con and only one assistant did all the inspection required by all those sections that I earlier enumerated as the composition of 'K' Shop, I realise how well they earned their salaries, and it serves a useful measure to assess how far we have sunk in productivity per man when compared with today's standards.

With Inspection's clearance, I would then hold the panels whilst Joe set in the 'joggles' around the panel's peripheries to align with the keel plate, chine angles and lap joint edges. The panels would then have to be anodically treated, after which we would apply to structure and panels, an anti-corrosive compound wherever panel met structure or overlapped other panels — this was to assist in an eventual water-tightness and to combat the fierce corrosive effect of salt water — then finally we would bolt them back to await the riveters.

I have deliberately explained this plating process in some detail because, in essence, a similar procedure applied to all shell plating, and apart from one or two changes in material specifications of the metals used and improved anti-corrosives, the job is done in much the same way today.

I stayed with Joe or was loaned to other members of his squad for a number of weeks, during which time I helped to fit every shell plate over the whole hull. There were two incidents of note that I recall, and each is a tale against myself.

I have mentioned the balcony or gallery that was on three sides of 'K' Shop, the river end being Harry Jay's store, and the opposite end holding the small mould loft as well as Ted Gardiner's section which was a part of 'P' Shop (the wing shop, 'P' being for Plane) but the whole side between the two ends was a sub-assembly section of women and girls also belonging to 'P' Shop. There was a central stairway to this where, at lunch time, the girls used to suffer (or enjoy) the banter and wolf whistles from some of the 'K' Shop personnel.

It was also used by many of us lads to go to the stores, and, one day, Joe having sent me for something, I found myself in conversation with one of the girls who was also using the store. The trouble was that our chat carried on long after we had both been served. Suddenly I felt a hand grasp the back of my collar and another the seat of my pants and I was propelled along the gallery in front of all the laughing females and then by one ear down the stairs. Joe did not have to say anything — we both knew he had made his point and for weeks after I avoided that gallery like the plague, and I did not waste any more time either! But there was a reverse side to the coin.

One day, after we had replaced a front bottom panel, I saw, as I thought, four holes that I had omitted to drill from a small support bracket which was a reinforcing member for a towing attachment. I promptly drilled them and having completed the job climbed out of the hull where to my shock and horror I found another four holes in parallel, just ⅛in. away. A row of double holes! In those days no repair scheme was permissible, the panel would have to be scrapped and it was more than likely one would get the sack. I got hold of Joe and showed him; he looked very grim and said, 'I'll have to get Mr Heaver on this.' So off he went and I sat there looking at what I thought would be the end of my career. Presently I was aware of Joe and the white coated Foreman bending beside me to see the two ominous rows of holes. Mr Heaver asked if I had done it and how it had happened. I told him and he paused for a moment, looked at me as well he might as I had only ever spoken to him previously when I had applied for the job. I could see the panel was going to be scrapped and that a new one would have to be provided and fitted, no mean expense in those days, and I thought I had had it. Gradually I became aware that Joe was saying to the boss that he did not really think it was my fault and that he was sure that he had inadvertently knocked the bracket off line when he was setting the structure into what we called 'a fair line'. Mr Heaver looked at him and, without doubt, knew what he was doing, so with a curt 'I'll give you a scrap note' to Joe, and 'Do not do it again' to me, he turned and walked away. Joe Colvin was to me then 'a man', and I still hold the same respect for him now as I did on that fateful day.

The result of working with other men, especially what could be called the 'Young Lions' of the shop, other interests gradually infiltrated their way into my life. The 'Young Lions', as I have chosen to call them, were all ex-'Handy Lads' but had reached the ages of 21 to 25 or thereabouts. All of them were unmarried and many a tale was told that apparently they felt could be told with me present, of their previous evening or weekend's amorous adventures, some of them uproariously funny.

They must have realised that in matters of sex I was as innocent as a babe — and I was. Incredible though it may seem in this day and age, no one had ever explained even the most basic facts of life to me, and by now I was 16½ years old. The sequel to that state of affairs comes later.

One of the constant arguments between these young men was whether or not Al Bowly or Rudy Vallee was better than Bing Crosby.

They would recount the latest recordings or radio programmes of their respective idol, and one, who I was assured by one of his backers, could give a fair imitation of Crosby would often do so. With the normal racket of the shop he would only be audible to those very adjacent to him. At home I began listening to the radio and then later to recordings, and for me Crosby was miles in front, but the peculiar thing was that I found I could make an even better imitation than the other chap, although as the junior I was not disposed to display this talent to my 'Young Lions', but on occasions when no one could hear me I would give full bore to quite a few of the early Crosby numbers. Later on in life this was to prove very useful to me, and very nearly had me launched on a completely new career.

The dear 'Old Groaner' died at the latter end of 1976; I was in hospital at the time listening to a music programme on the radio when they broke into it to announce his death. I believe everyone else in the ward was either reading or watching the television and until the nine o'clock news came on the television none of them knew why I had suddenly laid back with tears streaming down my face. Dear old Bing, I only wish I could have given the world, in my lifetime, just a fraction of the pleasure and entertainment that he had. There must be hundreds of people all over the world who were inspired or comforted at some time or another by his life and voice.

Other influences of less commendable value were 'picked up' as the early couple of years progressed. 'Factory language' became an accepted way of speaking, although half the time I was using words that I did not know the proper meaning of. This was brought home very forcibly to me quite early on when, quite innocently, I told a man he was a 'silly bastard'. His quick and violent grip on my throat was so unexpected that I could do nothing about it. As my face began to change colour from red to blue other men pulled him off and it was some little time before I convinced him that I did not realise its implications, until one of the chaps spelt it out for me, and so I went back to apologise. Charlie Standish was only a short wiry man but he taught me a lesson I've never forgotten.

That 'faux pas' on my part was an avoidable error, but 'K' shop, in common with all other engineering works, had other hazards. One contemporary of mine was careless enough to leave a fingertip under the cutting edge of the foot guillotine he was operating, and sliced it off. Bandsaws would snap and spring out on the unwary sometimes leaving nasty gashes. I was foolish enough to come up under a wing profile plate on the Stranraer jigs which necessitated a trip in the firm's car to hospital for stitching. During the factory extensions a roofing contractor fell through one of the asbestos corrugated sheets and smashed his head on a bench vice near the end of his fall, which killed him instantly. Thankfully I did not see it.

Apart from such occurrences these formative years were mostly influenced by the impressions left by others like Bill Peckham, Bill Heaver and Trevor Westbrook.

Chapter Three
Stranraer Hull Building

The side of 'K' Shop parallel to the floating bridges, as I have mentioned, was the location of the seaplane hull building jigs, and when I first started working there in March there were four or five jigs for the Australian Seagulls and two still being used for the building of the last two Supermarine Scapa flying boats which were much bigger. There had most likely been more Scapa jigs but, as the contract ran out, unused jigs would quite properly have been removed.

In the meantime, quite unbeknown to me, or I suspect anyone else in the shop, momentous decisions had been taken in Ministries and Boardrooms that were to affect us all.

I imagine the sequence went as follows; first the Fleet Air Arm decided to purchase some amphibians which were similar to the Seagull but henceforth to be known as the Supermarine Walrus; Coastal Command of the Royal Air Force decided to have a replacement for the Scapa to be named Stranraer, and in June 1936 the Royal Air Force ordered 310 Spitfires.

The first indication I had of any of this was that a new jig began to be erected at the end of the shop almost underneath the gallery where the mould loft was. Enquiries soon provided me with the information that the Stranraer was about to be built.

By now I had also found out what the mould loft was doing, as part of its duties were to provide big screive boards that showed the precise full scale contours of all the new frames that the new flying boat required. Also by now I thought that repetition of Walrus or Seagull shell plating would not teach me anything more useful, so having ascertained that the leadinghand for the building of the whole of the Stranraer hull was one Bill Kerslake, I went up to him and asked him if he would be wanting a boy on his new job.

There was the usual question and answer procedure and in the end he said 'If Joe Colvin will release you and Mr Heaver agrees, I will give you a run.' I tackled Joe and told him honestly why I wanted the change to get the greater experience, and like the man he was he said, 'OK, with me nipper, but you will have to convince Mr Heaver.' This seemed quite daunting to me as the last time we had spoken was a few weeks earlier when I had scrapped the panel, so I decided to have a night's sleep on it.

The next morning, unknown to me, Bill Kerslake had chatted to Joe Colvin to get his opinion of me, and the next thing I knew was the pair of them confronting me and wanting to know what I was 'hanging about at'? I told them how I did not relish tackling Mr Heaver, so having assured themselves that I was still keen, Joe with his usual blunt directness said 'Come on' and before you could say 'Jack Robinson' there we were in front of the boss once again, and Joe was doing a very nice line in sales talk on my behalf, so much so that I felt myself blushing like a big schoolgirl.

I stammered when asked, that I felt there was more to be learned on the new Stranraer, and that as Bill Kerslake was going to be responsible for the whole build, I would gain experience on structures as well as plating plus some subsequent fitting out operations. There was a slight softening of Mr Heaver's stern but cherubic features and a little twinkle in his eyes as I falteringly gave my reasons. Later on I learned he had a son of his own only a few years younger than myself.

He gave his approval and the next Monday morning, I transferred to the Stranraer section. I never worked for Joe Colvin again, except for a minor service I later was able to do

Stranraer flying boats at anchor in the River Itchen at Woolston.

for him, but I am still very conscious of the guidance and help he gave me and the quiet but blunt directness of his manner, which to me seemed so effective and which I must confess in later years I adopted with equal success.

On the Monday, Bill Kerslake took me under his wing and introduced me to the only other member of the section, Fred Rashley. It transpired that the Stranraer order was only for seventeen, with a view to an eventual build under licence in Canada, so there would only be two jigs erected and additional labour would be allocated to Bill Kerslake on an 'as and when required basis'. In a way this was a wonderful piece of luck for me because it meant quite literally having to build the new flying boat hull from the floor up.

The metal jigwork provided was in two unconnected parts, one which determined the main wing attachments and the other, some thirty feet away, which catered for the tailplane attachment fittings. Wooden profile boards for the fore and aft centre line profile were provided from the Woodshop from the information and lines from the Mould Loft, but before they were positioned Bill, Fred and myself scratched on to the concrete floor what would be the actual centre line, using the two jig parts for reference, and then with a plumb-bob from the halfway measurement between the jig port and starboard attachment fitting locations.

A scratch where the plumb-bob point hovered gave us four markings, with thirty feet between each pair. Add to this approximately twelve feet forward of the wing position that would be the area for the cabin and the front gun position, and also something like three feet aft of the tailplane where the rear gunner position would be, and we were going to have to produce a straight line scratched on to the concrete of some fifty feet.

This was achieved by using a length of string wound round six inch nails at each end. An over length position was selected at each end and with Fred on one end and me on the other, Bill checked its relationship to the four basic marks we had already scribed between the two jig areas, and on his instruction we hammered the nails into the flooring and then adjusted by packing until our string was accurately positioned to pick up all four points.

From the string we scribed (the proper name instead of scratched) points at about three feet intervals, and then with six feet long metal straight-edges (really six feet long steel rulers) we connected all points up so that we ended up with a straight scribed line of about sixty feet long. Using this line and the jig positions, the shipwrights then moved in and positioned the centre line profile boards on triangular support struts so that at its lowest the profile would be no less than two feet six inches from the floor. Finally, they would position a datum line of piano wire, tautened by screw adjusters at each end, until it ran the whole length of the hull to be built and longitudinally exactly to the line we had scribed on the floor, but its height would be approximately equivalent to the middle of the finished hull.

Back came Bill, Fred and myself once Inspection had cleared the shipwrights' work and checked that frame positions marked by pencil lines on white paint at both top and bottom of the profile outline were in accordance with the design dimensions. Using a plumb-bob from the datum wire, we first laid the inverted 'T' angle section that formed the basis of the keel, fixing it with a screw into the wood at each frame position and packing it with metal pieces equivalent to the thickness of the keel plate or other strengthening doublers that were to be fitted later.

Fred and I fitted the vertical keel plates between each frame position from the wing position aft, whilst Bill and another 'borrowed' boy did the forward portion. After this there were diagonal channel members to be fitted, and then long lengths of lipped angle sections back to back so that the completed keel was approximately twelve inches in height, with the solid keel plate taking up the lower third and the channel and angle members looking like lattice work for the remainder.

After this part was fully drilled and then riveted we began to erect the frames that had been made as separate sub-assemblies elsewhere. The biggest and heaviest were those that would take the wing attachments and for them, and the tailplane, the metal jigwork had strong metal pick up points and pins that simulated the actual wing and tailplane attachments, so that apart from their weight their fixation did not present any real problems.

It was the fixation of the remaining frames that intrigued me, and when one sees the present day elaborate (and expensive) jigging for very similar components, it makes one wonder whether we have progressed or, more importantly, have we not by removing basic trade skills, generally deprived our country of a vital economic element, and by so doing let loose masses of unskilled and semi-skilled labour that so dominate the politics of today.

Whilst the keel was being laid and riveted, the shipwright and a labourer had been chipping away behind us, and between each frame position had set a wooden block into the concrete floor about a yard or so from each side of the centre line scribed on the floor. These blocks, about 9in. x 2½in. and 3in. thick, were set in concrete so that they presented a flush surface with the floor. Each frame was identified by its drawing number and the procedure to fit was as follows.

Once identified we would, by measuring, find its top centre and into the outer channel flange drill an eighth of an inch diameter hole having due regard to the design requirement of 'landing' from the edge. The bottom of the frames were joined on the centre line with angle members which were service bolted only (the rest of the frame angles and stiffeners, etc. being already pre-riveted).

By removing the service bolted angles we were able to 'spring' the bottom halves over the keel, and whilst one steadied the frame the other climbed up on to trestles or staging and aligned the back outside of the channel section with the pencil line on white paint mentioned earlier, and also positioned the pre-drilled hole in the centre of the profile plate thickness; a quick push into the wood with a 'podger' and then in went an inch long woodscrew of the appropriate diameter. The frame would then hang, allowing for packing pieces to be pushed in to simulate eventual plating thicknesses, and also allowing us to set correctly the bottom angles in relation to the keel, and drill off and service bolt.

So far, so good, but these frames were often four feet in width each side of the keel, and it was essential before proceeding further to set each side at both top outer corner and bottom chine line. Using trammels on a length of one inch square spruce, and working from the scribed centre line at the mark indicated as the frame position (known as the datum), we used the well-taught schoolboy geometry method of bisecting a line at right angles from a given point. This gave us two sets of intersecting arcs approximately four feet or so from the centre line which, when connected up with straight edge and scribe line, gave us a datum line to which we could plumb-bob down from top or bottom of the frame to set its outer vertical alignment. The setting was achieved by using ordinary mild steel one inch flange angle iron, cutting away an inch or so of the vertical flange, and bending these ends so that they presented a flat face to the frame in the region of the most convenient tooling hole (or if necessary drilling out one of the rivets) and at the other end to the wooden block set in the floor, so that looking side on, one would see the vertical frame, and from it, at the bottom on each side, a diagonal mild steel angle to the floor block; then drill a hole in the angle iron at each end, a nut and bolt at the frame and woodscrew to the floor once the plumb position was correct.

The method at the top was similar except that the iron angle was screwed back to the wood profile boards. Simple but very cheap and effective, particularly as the frame scribe lines needed only refreshing with a straight edge and scriber after being used for one complete hull.

Apart from the jig-positioned frames, most others were fitted as described, except for a few smaller ones each side of the tailplane main pick-up frames, and with these it was considered satisfactory to fix at centre top and bottom as described, but a half inch square length of spruce batten each side would be used to space them with clamps, the design datum dimension for spacing being pencilled on the spruce.

After all the frames had been installed, we then began to fit the longitudinal members. These would be Keelsons from keel to chine each attached by angles already riveted to the frames, then up the side would be lengths of stringer section extending over six to ten frames and fitted into slots and on to brackets on the frames. After three or four rows of stringers would come a row of intercostals similar in style to Keelsons, and then a stronger, heavier type of stringer known as longerons until, by this progression, one went over the top surface generally with stringer and dorsal longerons.

Of course it all had to be fitted in so that a suitable surface would be available to the shell platers, and this involved using battens on curved areas, and just six inch steel rulers at frame joints, and of course the first hole drilled at any fixation point had to be right otherwise all the others at that joint would be equally wrong.

Eventually, the whole birdcage-like structure was completed, the riveters following closely behind as soon as each section we had done had been cleared by inspection.

At the nose, upper middle, and at the tail end, we had to set and attach metal rings of some two feet diameter. These eventually became the mounting position for the Scarff mountings which held the machine guns and enabled them to be swivelled.

There was a sliding hatch over the cabin, and window and windscreen members to be catered for and, by now, our original three was more like thirteen in number.

The shell plating was very much the same as that described earlier. Some of the panels were bigger and thicker; a torpedo rail had to be fitted, not for the dropping of same, but so that the flying boat could transport it, perhaps to a submarine way out in the ocean.

After the plating and its riveting there were towing attachments to be fitted at the bow end, and along some fifteen feet of the starboard side a walkrail to facilitate entry when afloat. This rail of 1/8in. thick one inch diameter tube of anodised duralamin was located about four inches from the hull's side by machined brackets that were bolted at every other frame position along its length. Water tightness and strength was essential, and these brackets were attached on points where frame and intercostals met, and their oval attachment surface used four holes at the 90 degrees positions which, when drilled, had to be subsequently reamed to take specially-machined raised countersunk bolts, and involved us in the messy business of making grommets from caulking materials then soaked in caulking compound (a dark brown sticky treacle-like substance) that had to be fitted under the bolt head outside, and under the nut and washer inside.

By the time we had almost completed this first Stranraer hull, the jig builders had completed the second jig behind us and Bill, Fred and I moved across to start the procedure all over again.

By now, I was much more confident, and very often I would be allowed to proceed with some jobs on my own, which would previously have been done by either Fred or Bill.

Naturally this pleased me immensely, and I can quite honestly say I really enjoyed going to work, but then, as I look back now over forty years, I have always considered that chance gave me a job that I would not have missed for anything.

Chapter Four
The Facts of Life

My stay with the Stranraer section lasted until February 1938, but lest the reader becomes bored with the technicalities, or even worse begins to think that I was a dedicated goody goody, this would seem the opportune moment to give some account of other happenings, both inside and outside of work, that occurred over this period.

Previously, I mentioned that I was absolutely ignorant of the 'facts of life', and when the second Stranraer jig was completed, Fred Rashley and I were given the task of getting it up to the 'keel laid and frames erected' standard as detailed earlier, whilst Bill Kerslake and the newer members of the team completed the first hull.

Laying the keel involved Fred and I working face to face with barely a foot distance between us and naturally as we worked we chatted. Fred was a deep thinker, read a lot, was quiet and unassuming. He and his wife had one child, a daughter who in 1936 was about thirteen years of age. Somehow, and I have no idea how, I must have given my chaste and uninformed state away to him and he asked me a question which I could not answer. He then said, 'Are you kidding or do you not really know what I am talking about?' I told him it was the latter, and for ten minutes or so Fred mulled this over in his mind and cast quick glances at me whilst he weighed the matter up.

Finally he said, 'Would you like to know?', and I answered 'yes', and so he told me over the next hour all that which everyone else had knowingly or unknowingly kept from me. Not only that, but it was so beautifully done. In simple terms, without coarseness, ribaldry, embarassing me, or any insincerity on his part, this humble, intelligent man did me a service for which I can never repay him, but which in the fullness of time in so many ways has helped me to help others. Our paths were later separated by the actions of war, and after 1940 I never saw or heard of him again, but now, however belatedly, I offer him this tribute he so richly deserves.

Of course the effect on me was profound. Suddenly, things that had puzzled me since I was about thirteen began to fall into place. I had walked the odd girl home from Sunday School and even kissed one, and two girls during the time I was on the bread round had made me welcome in their homes, but I could never discuss them at my home as it was absolutely taboo. Naturally this one sided arrangement did not make for very long friendships, although one, whose father was a tug skipper, understood the predicament I was in and with her family I had some very enjoyable days at the seaside. Girls around my age were about five years ahead of me with their knowledge of life, and soon realised that the basic impulsion of the male was singularly lacking in me.

The knowledge now gained not only explained why I failed to laugh when some of the exploits of the 'Young Lions' were told to their evident enjoyment, it also clarified one or two 'peculiar' experiences I had had with some girls whose actions on occasions I failed to understand.

Fred's explanation of the basic facts were encompassed with an equal insistence that all that he had to impart was within the context of love, respect, and definitely marriage, and to his teaching I remained faithful until my own marriage.

I also indicated earlier that, unbeknown to most of us, an order for 310 Spitfires had been placed with the Company within three months of the prototype's first flight in March 1936.

Looking back on it now with the benefit of a long and not entirely undistinguished Production Management career, I can more readily appreciate the immense problems that faced the Design Office, Works Management, and all their various supporting staffs. The sheer quantity of 310 aircraft must have seemed daunting as previously orders would be for 10, 12 or even as high as 40, but 310; and for a high speed fighter which no one except that special few who had worked on the prototype had any idea of the production problems involved, but there it was, and behind it lay the growing shadowy threat of the 'Third Reich'.

My first awareness came when I saw the factory itself being extended. The end of 'K' shop did not reach the river's edge. Before that there were the 'drawbenches', where flat coils of metal would be drawn by power-operated jaws through a series of shaped rollers, so that at the end of the process one had thirty foot lengths of whatever sectional shape was required. Further on came grinding wheels, buffing machines for polishing, small power presses, mostly belt-driven, long baths for softening metal prior to forming, and other baths for the anodising process so necessary to reduce corrosion. This was the Process Shop, and beyond its end wall was the gents' lavatories, but to reach them one had to go out of a door in 'K' shop, level with the commencement of the Process Shop, which was only half 'K' shop's width, and across the yard.

The procedure for using these toilet facilities was archaic but effective. A man was in charge, complete with a book (a ledger actually), and if one did not wish to use the stand up urinals which were made of unwanted aircraft sheet metal (and it was possible to vary the sound on impact depending on how high or low one went), then use of the separate closets would be entered in the book, name, shop number, time in and time out recorded, and should you exceed seven minutes in any one day your shop foreman would be informed. As smoking was prohibited in the works it must have been a work of acquired skill for those smokers to have their need for 'a drag' coincide with their bowel actions.

Fortunately I did not smoke, but one other endearing aspect of this long-departed establishment should be recorded for, if you will forgive the pun, posterity.

There were six or eight closets all made from discarded aircraft metal sheets, with only the actual seat being made from wood. Below this seat was a channel-shaped trough about a foot wide at the top with six inch sides, and approximately a seven to eight inch flat bottom, and it was a continuous length so that at number one end it was right under the seat but at the other end it would be eighteen inches lower. Each closet had its own normal flushing arrangement, but boys being boys we soon discovered that if you flushed at the highest end (number one) and sent down some floating burning newspaper it caused all sorts of havoc right down the line.

The tactics used were very simple, leave flushing until you were properly dressed to walk out, flush, ignite paper and smartly retire to the urinal position to await developments. Of course if you were caught you would get a belt round the ear, but in this respect I never got caught, luckily I feel in retrospect, and mainly due to that facility being better accommodated in the new building going up, and the old site space shortly being used for an extended Process Shop. Prior to that time it became standard drill to stand as soon as one heard a chain pulled.

One other matter of great importance to me occurred in September 1936. Another handy lad joined us on the Stranraers and, being contemporaries, we used to tend to get together whenever we could at meal breaks and sometimes during work. An item of unfailing amusement was to get up on the staging at the bow end of the hull which, being closest to the wall, provided us with a magnificent view of the loading and unloading ramp for the floating bridges. In those desperate days of unemployment, to miss a bridge in the morning might well mean to lose a job, and to see some of the antics of those caught as the bridge drew away may have been funny to us, but disturbing and sometimes very wet to those whose leaps, very often with a bicycle, were unsuccessful.

However, this other lad had a brother-in-law who worked in the Drawings Library, and it was through this connection that I learned of a vacancy in that library. At that time, to me, it appeared to have the attractions of a staff job (with sick pay), later start, and clean clothes, so I applied and was interviewed by the departmental head (John Bull) who accepted me subject to release by Mr Heaver. Later that afternoon I saw the familiar white coated, cherubic featured foreman heading for where I was working.

Kindly and patiently he explained how the proposed move was really a blank end job and, further to that, he said if I would drop the idea he would personally see that I should have an indentured apprenticeship at no cost to me.

He was as good as his word, and in September 1936, the Company Manager and my father duly signed the indentures which were back-dated to the very first day I had started in the previous March. There were two minor hiccups, one that the period of apprenticeship had to expire on my attaining majority age (then twenty-one years), and as I was exactly sixteen and a quarter years when I started, the period of apprenticeship was typed in as four and nine twelfth years. The other was that it categorised me to be trained as an Aircraft Fitter, but my heart lay in becoming a good Sheet Metal Worker, so the one was crossed out and Sheet Metal Worker typed above it.

Again I realise how much I am indebted to the interest and care of yet another person who strayed across the path of my life, and influenced it far more than I or they could ever have imagined.

Another person who I only saw on three occasions was R. J. Mitchell, whose name is forever imperishably linked with the Spitfire. The first time I saw him was when I was working with Joe Colvin, who told me who he was, and then twice more when he came down to see the progress of the Stranraer.

There was something about him that immediately left an indelible impression, a fine forehead, fair hair brushed straight back, a strong featured face, and an aura of quiet unassuming confidence. Those who have seen the Leslie Howard film portrayal of R. J. can take it from me he was not at all like that.

Over the latter years of my own career, I have met and worked with quite a few Chief Designers of aircraft. Some adopted lofty poses and needed to be handled like touchy prima donnas, others had different flaws, but the only one I have met who impressed me in the same way as R. J. did, because he too with all his brilliance had not lost the 'common touch', was John Fozard, then Chief Designer of the Hawker Harrier. But I digress, so back to 1936/7.

Each group of people, working or playing together, in one way or another, allow their individuality to shine through.

Joe Colvin and Fred Rashley I have mentioned, but there were others whose personalities are still well remembered and for a variety of reasons.

Bill Kerslake adopted a pseudo-aggressive manner but at heart was really kind and thoughtful. One time when we were working together he told me of his experiences in the Army of Occupation in Germany after the First World War, and I clearly remember how he told (to my astonishment) of a German woman who offered her body to him for food for herself and child.

Some of the agony of those helpless defeated people came over clearly from his words, and his subsequent help to that woman without availing himself of her offer was transparently obvious and true .

Then there was Jock, a tousled-haired, small, wiry, but very tough native of Glasgow. He was the first to tell me of life in the Gorbals which at the time seemed to me to be unbelievable. He also used to give me instruction in the Glasgow 'dirty' fighting techniques which, although I became an apt pupil, I fortunately never had cause to use. Part of the reason was that before I had left school I had been a member of the Bitterne Boys' Brigade, where I had not only received instruction in First Aid, playing both flute and bugle, but also gymnastics and boxing. It was this latter with which I desired to become proficient, and with the aid of Mr Jones, ex-Navy P.T.I., I soon learnt some of the rudiments of the noble art. Being tall, five feet ten inches and skinny, I could easily get into the lightweight category, and my public debut (which is far too grandiose a description) took place when I was about sixteen years old in a display put on for a Boys' Brigade parents' evening.

My mother was horrified, telling me afterwards 'that I looked as though I was out to kill the other chap', but as he was bigger than me, and we were pulling our punches, she was quite wrong. During my brief stay at Edwin Jones' store, I chanced upon George, the goods liftman, who had been a welterweight divisional champion in the Navy, and as his lift was about twelve foot square, we used to stop it between floors so that further lessons could be imparted.

Funnily enough, he was the only person that has ever knocked me down in a fight, and this was pure reflex action as I caught him a beautiful right to the angle of the jaw which must have hurt, and he let go one equally as good catching me square between the eyes and on the bridge of the nose, which sent me reeling back against the lift side where I slithered down to the floor. Poor George, he was full of apologies, but I knew it was not done in malice. Nevertheless, weeks late, following successive nose bleeds, I had to go to hospital and have some broken blood vessels cauterised.

This brings me to Patrick Maloney who was as Irish as his name, and whose nose and ears clearly showed that he too had been 'a gentleman of the ring.' Paddy joined us first on the Stranraer team and, like Jock, was soon giving me the benefit of his experience during lunch breaks and any other odd moment we might find convenient. Paddy was good, and although I had learnt the basics from others, it was Paddy who taught me the real skills. How to punch with either hand, but with all one's body weight behind it — sounds simple and obvious, but watch the boxers on television and see how many punch just from the shoulder only, and with no body weight behind it. All the fancy stuff with the rhythmic use of the punch ball is all right for light divertisement, but you really learn to punch properly with the heavy punch bag, and if you do not get it right you will soon crack a knuckle joint. It is to Paddy and the others, that apart from one or two exceptions I have enjoyed a relatively peaceful life, and on the exceptions shall we say I was hardly inconvenienced.

Boys Brigade night was always on Fridays, and mention must be given to the Shergold family who devoted most of their time to us lads and the Wesleyan Church, and also to Mr Aveson who was a proper St. John Ambulance instructor and member of the Docks' First Aid Team, who gave us first class instruction that enabled nearly all of us to get our St. John's Certificate and our own Boys Brigade First Aid badge. Also to Mr Wilson, who although he was the leader of the Docks and Marine Brass Band, gave many a Friday evening to teaching us how to play a bugle. Sometimes we would persuade him to play the Post Horn Gallop on his trumpet, and a very nice piece of triple-tonguing it was!

The saying 'that no man is an island' is borne out by the many and varied influences and effects the actions, or even just the impression, of others have on all our lives.

It does seem to me today, that somehow since the end of the 1939-45 war we have lost some of the community spirit of free help to others, and have replaced it with materialistic, selfish, money-grabbing attitudes, leaving us all somewhat the poorer.

Chapter Five
Spitfire Production Commences

With the Stanraer hulls fast reaching completion, it was not a great surprise to me to be told to report to the Spitfire fuselage section on 7th February 1938. My very first Spitfire job was to help complete the rear, top, bottom and sides plating on No. 24 production fuselage.

Above: The Itchen Works fuselage assembly lines. At one time upwards of 100 Spitfire fuselages were at this stage due to wing supply problems. The production numbers in the front row are in the 270s, indicating a 1939 date.
Vickers

Right: View of Spitfire fuselage framework and skin plating. *Vickers*

Early production Spitfires at Eastleigh.

Vickers

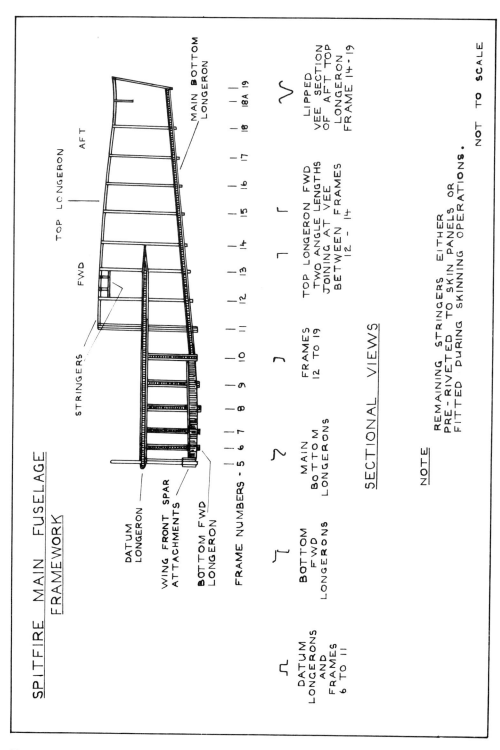

SPITFIRE MAIN FUSELAGE
FRAMEWORK

TOP LONGERON

AFT

FWD

STRINGERS

DATUM LONGERON

WING FRONT SPAR ATTACHMENTS

BOTTOM FWD LONGERON

MAIN BOTTOM LONGERON

FRAME NUMBERS - 5 6 7 8 9 10 11 12 13 14 15 16 17 18 18A 19

BOTTOM FWD LONGERONS

DATUM LONGERONS AND FRAMES 6 TO 11

MAIN BOTTOM LONGERONS

FRAMES 12 TO 19

TOP LONGERON FWD TWO ANGLE LENGTHS JOINING AT VEE BETWEEN FRAMES 12 - 14

LIPPED VEE SECTION OF AFT TOP LONGERON FRAME 14 - 19

SECTIONAL VIEWS

NOTE

REMAINING STRINGERS EITHER PRE-RIVETED TO SKIN PANELS OR FITTED DURING SKINNING OPERATIONS.

NOT TO SCALE

Although there were a number of detail part problems to overcome, the assembly of the main Spitfire fuselage was relatively simple. The first frame in the jig was also the front wing spar attachment pick-up, and this, frame five, was located by simulated wing spars but with undersize holes for location pins, these holes to be subsequently opened up to be reamed full size much later on. This same frame also had the pick-up points for the engine mounting structure, and served as well as a fireproof bulkhead between engine and fuel tanks, and provided the eventual rear fastening positions of the detachable engine cowling panels. As can be seen by this, it was by far the most important and heaviest of all the fuselage frames.

Frames six to ten inclusive were all of sturdy, hard-cornered, 'U' shaped flanged construction, but only roughly half height, compared to frame five, as between five and eight would be the well for the upper fuel tank, and after that the cockpit coaming framework. Frame eleven was the pilot's rear bulkhead; the one he leaned back on to the circular cushioned headrest. This was the last of the 'U' flanged channel frames, from thereon going aft up to frame nineteen they were all simple and thinner channel section, with both flanges forward facing so that there were no acute angles. Frame nineteen was slightly more robust, and its web had holes around its periphery with reinforcings for the later attachment of the tail unit. This frame was bolted firmly to a jig plate that simulated the mating unit to come. All frames except five and nineteen were reduced in weight by flanged lightening holes in their webs.

To these frames were fitted five longeron members; two bottom longerons; two central or datum longerons of flanged channel section that, at the front would have engine mounting fittings attached and were tapered down at frame thirteen and finished at frame fourteen; and the top longeron that began behind frame eleven as two angled members approximately six inches apart, but also tapered together at frame fifteen, and then continued to the end at frame nineteen as a tight 'V' shaped lipped flanged channel.

There was a small upper half frame inserted between frames eighteen and nineteen, and the front bottom longeron was made from two separate flanged plates riveted at right angles to each other between frames five to ten on each side, and from ten to nineteen by a more open 'V' flanged section in one length per side. All these frame-longeron attachments were riveted together after the attachment holes had been drilled from pre-positioned brackets already riveted to the frames.

Once this was done and cleared by Inspection, the shell platers moved in. The front end plating was from frame five to twelve on the sides, and from five to eleven on the bottom, the latter being in two halves with a buttstrap joint at the centre and aft line.

The remainder, known as the top, bottom and sides, comprised three top panels from frames twelve to nineteen, three bottom panels from eleven to nineteen, and panels on each side from frames eleven to nineteen upper half, and twelve to nineteen on the lower half. The side and bottom panels already had their stiffening stringers riveted to them when we received them, except where the side panels overlapped each other, and where they met the top panels, we had to fit this total of ten stringers at the appropriate stage, plus some stiffeners and the door frames for the radio hatch and battery access.

All the rear plating was done by pairs of 'handy lads' and apprentices, and the front plating by the slightly older boys or young men.

The first established pairs of rear platers were 'Ossie' Scott and 'Kid' Barker, and 'Joker' Newland and myself; others were added as production increased, but initially the two squads were in friendly rivalry, right from the start. 'Joker' Newland and I were paired from No. 27 production and I left him almost a year later on 11th January 1939, when we commenced No. 217.

Wing assembly and jigs in Woolston 'P' shop, 1939/40. *Vickers*

Out of jig fuselage assembly. Note the engine mounting structure with the Oil Tank fitted.

Vickers

During that time we completed rear fuselage plating on sixty-three fuselages, and from my notebook I see that our first together, No. 27, took us one hundred and fifteen hours, but by No. 40 we were down to seventy-six and a half hours, and by the end of our spell together we were comfortably averaging fifty hours.

This period was a very happy time; 'Joker' was an extremely nice fellow to work with, quiet in manner, deceptively adept at working fast, and with a marvellous sense of humour — hence his nickname. We got on well together as did 'Ossie' and 'Kid'.

Nos. 48 and 49 fuselages were both selected for the High Speed Development Aircraft in which it was hoped a new world's air speed record would be attempted.

These two had specially-strengthened structures, and some of the panels were of thicker gauge material. We were instructed to take extra care to achieve a good finish.

'Ossie' and 'Kid' did No. 48 and 'Joker' and I, No. 49. In the end, they only completed No. 48, and it appeared in the Paris Air Show static display in July 1939.

Some accounts say the idea of going for the world air speed record was abandoned because a German, Ernst Udet, pre-empted us and had raised it to just over 400m.p.h. However, I can recall early one morning hearing a very fast aircraft in the direction of Eastleigh, and I was later told that a timed run each way over the measured mile was attempted using the straight stretch of the railway line between Swaythling and Eastleigh, where every fourth sleeper had been whitewashed as a guide for the pilot. What I can vouch for is that a few days later, at the bottom of the front page, the *Daily Express* headlined a small report that a 'British aeroplane had flown over 400m.p.h.', but it did not specify which or where. Very recently Jeffrey Quill confirmed for me that trial runs were made to check the 'position error' of the pitot head and stop watch synchronisation.

I mentioned previously that the Spitfire fuselage assembly was relatively easy. Jig positions provided locations for each frame at the top and bottom, panels were pre-shaped with stringers already riveted on, pre-drilling of the panels was much in evidence, and one only had to draw a pencil/centre line down the frame's outer flanges to line the panels and frames together. Templates with a handle, not unlike a shield, enabled the apertures to be scribed and cut where the radio and battery access doors were to go.

The riveters followed the platers as soon as either front or rear was finished, and then after the usual inspection procedures, about eight of us would lift the finished fuselage out of its jig and on to trestles for its fitting out operations done by 'K' shop. There was one out of jig operation that each fuselage had to undergo, and that required it to be lifted yet again into a cradle type jig, in which the wing attachment holes would be drilled and reamed to size, and the location holes drilled to set the nut plate attachment points for the wing to fuselage fillet panels, thus ensuring interchangeability. This jig was in the tender care of my old Stranraer colleague, Paddy Maloney.

Other operations that I particularly enjoyed doing were, fitting the cockpit coamings, the windscreen, a hinged door on the cockpit's port side for pilot access, hood runners and finally the hood itself.

At that age imagination played no small part in pretending to be the pilot, snugly ensconced in the closed cockpit, even if there were no instruments or controls, and my seat an old apple box.

Apart from 'K' shop's one-half commitment to the Spitfire, the Walrus was still in full production, and as the Stranraer and its jigs departed, the space they left unoccupied was soon filled with the fuselage jig for R. J. Mitchell's four-engined bomber.

Other shops began simultaneously to take on their increasing quota of Spitfire work — in particular 'P' shop, without whose Leading Edge sub-assemblies for the Mainplanes, the whole project could so easily have foundered, with a result that does not even bear contemplation today.

The 36th production Spitfire at Eastleigh, circa August 1938. Delivered to No. 66 Squadron, Duxford, it subsequently crashed and was wrecked on 6th June 1939.

Vickers

Spitfire K9876, the 90th production at Eastleigh, probably in the Spring of 1939. Note the 3-bladed propeller, whip aerial, the bulged canopy for better view, and the tailwheel replacing the original tailskid.

Vickers

Chapter Six
Growing up and Going up

Altogether this was a very pleasant period amongst people who worked hard but with skill and always a sense of humour.

The variety of people and personalities never failed to interest me; one smoked a German Meerschaum pipe, another was a member of the British Union of Facists, and one in particular, I recall, was training as a pilot under the Air Training Scheme brought in by the Government. After war was declared, the Facist member was called to report to the gate-house one afternoon and we never saw him again, and sadly our young pilot was killed on flying operations.

Outside of work, I had started to take dancing lessons in the then new Peartree Hall and also attended the Saturday evening dances there. Inevitably I met a girl and spent a fair proportion of my free time with her, and having reached the eighteen year old limit, duly resigned from the Boys' Brigade.

By far the most important thing for me was that since I had become an apprentice it was obligatory for me to attend evening classes, taking at first, English, Mathematics, and Workshop Drawing, for which I managed to obtain a pass in each, with a distinction in two. That was in the September 1937 to April 1938 session, and for September 1938 to April 1939, I was able, by virtue of the previous session's work, to take Southampton University Evening Technical College classes for Mathematics again, and a new course on Mould Loft Laying Off, which I believe was the first time this subject had been on any British educational curriculum and, so far as I can gather, has never been repeated since.

It was very appropriate to seaplanes, aircraft and shipbuilding as it involved taking an off-set sheet from the designer which was his best estimation of the full size dimensions at various fixed points, and drawing them out to the full dimensions and, with batons of spruce or lengths of ⅛in. thick perspex strips, making sure that when each point was connected it was 'fair line', i.e. it did not bulge or sink in. If either of the latter occurred, we would alter to suit and amend the designer's dimension.

Naturally, at evening classes, we could not cope with a full scale flying boat, but we did complete a half scale Walrus Float which gave us plenty of problems as it had both concave and convex surfaces and included a 'cant' frame which, as its name implies, leaned from the vertical. It was a very interesting subject.

Curiously, the tutors in both subjects were members of Supermarine's staff; Len Gooch was taking Mathematics and by day was a member of the Works Engineers Department, and Don Snooks was in charge of the Mould Loft. That they both applied themselves diligently to these evening activities is shown by the fact that even an elementary school education such as mine, plus the previous year's evening classes enabled me to gain a first class pass in both subjects, and I still have the letter from the Executive Officer of University College, Southampton, saying, 'I beg to inform you that you have been awarded and Exhibition to the Evening Technical Classes for the session 1939-40.'

This meant I could go without payment of the usual term fees, and I felt quietly very proud of that, but when the time came, the War had started and it was overtime and production that had precedence over education; thus ended my scholastic training.

However, back to 1938. My courting was a continual on/off affair; she was an only child, spoilt by her father and dominated by her Irish mother. The father and I got on very well together and it was he that disposed of another flaw in my make-up. At the church I attended it was taught that drinkers were sinners and pubs were dens of iniquity, and I believed this. One Sunday morning her father asked me if I would like to come with him to meet his father. Now all I knew was that the older man was a seaman, then aboard a dredger, and that he was a tough old nut who I was told had belted the daylights out of Joe Beckett, no less, in a pub fight. We cycled into Southampton together and met the older man near the dock gate. We walked our cycles with him and went to the nearest pub.

I swallowed hard on my so-called principles and went in with them, trying as best I could to look as though this was nothing new. On previous outings at various times when they pulled up at a pub I had always worked it so that someone would bring me out a shandy.

On this occasion, when asked, I said, 'lemon shandy please' and settled down at a table and listened. The old man was really a character from a Conrad novel; weather-beaten leathery face, with sharp bright eyes under bushy brows, and his hands gnarled, big and strong. Although a couple of inches shorter than me and nearly fifty years older, I would not have liked to have taken him on as an opponent. He was, and still remains, probably the toughest man I have ever met, but his voice was low and gentle, and when he walked you could see the smooth tiger-like movement and sense the coiled up energy of his whole body.

When I could get a word in between father and son I tried to work the conversation round to the Beckett business, but the old man brushed it aside with the pithy comment that Joe Beckett was not as good as his (Beckett's) brother. To me it was a privilege to meet a non-professional who had won a bare fist rough and tumble over Britain's one time heavy-weight champion. All I could get him to add was that the Frenchman, Georgés Carpentiér, had proved that in less than one minute. I got to know and like this old man over the next four years, but apart from seeing him handling ropes when his dredger docked, I never saw him other than polite and almost self-effacing.

However, this and subsequent meetings certainly made me question the prejudice that I had been taught regarding pubs and the people who frequented them. I remember mentioning this much later to my girl friend's father, and he said that as long as I kept an open mind I would find that life was not all either black or white but every shade of grey in between. How right he has proved to be!

There is one other day that stands out for me during the period under review and that was Empire Air Day on a Saturday in the summer of 1938.

This Air Day was a nationwide event and the nearest display for me was at Hamble Aerodrome within easy cycling distance, and although the day was not the brightest weather-wise, for me it still shines with a brilliance of unforgettable memories.

At this time, the Royal Air Force fighters were fabric-covered bi-planes, and displays generally consisted of aerobatics by single aircraft and formations of three or four aircraft at the most, culminating most often by three aircraft 'tied' together by ribbons. It was all thrilling stuff at the 'fabulous' speed of 180-200m.p.h.

I had purchased a programme which constituted the entrance fee to the airfield, and my afternoon was a delight in being with and seeing the various aircraft being displayed in the air and in the static park. One item on the flying programme was down as 'Surprise Item', and just before the stated time I moved to the front of the spectator line. The previous item had finished, and a mainly silent expectant crowd waited — for what we did not know.

Suddenly, and it was just that, with a rush and roar and seemingly at incredible speed, a Spitfire flashed very low in front of us all. Before it had reached the end of the airfield it went straight up like a rocket, rolled over and within seconds had dived back and made another high speed run before the crowd. 'Surprise Item' was aptly named as the aircraft had come up from Eastleigh, flown low down the Itchen River and Southampton Water and then turned behind Hamble hangars, lined up, and virtually hopped over the hangars and there we were, completely surprised.

I believe it was piloted by George Pickering, one of the Supermarine test pilots, and he brought home to the assembly there that day what vast changes were being brought about by this new generation of aircraft now being built — the fabric covered bi-plane fighters looked almost prehistoric by comparison.

Although this display was a great thrill to me because of my own association with its manufacturing origins, how can I possibly explain how I felt when I heard over the tannoy soon after, that my programme had the number which had been drawn for a free flight. My cup of joy truly overflowed. I could not get to the officials' stand quick enough and was informed that if I would report there at the end of the flying display I should receive my flight in one of the Flying School's aircraft. These were all Avro bi-planes, mainly Avro Tutors, wood and fabric, open cockpits and a single radial engine with a top speed of around 100m.p.h. In fact it was very little different from the aeroplanes that were in use at the end of the First World War.

I have no recollection of what the remaining flying display was, as my thoughts (and fears) were concentrated on this unbelievable luck.

After the show was completed, an official led me over to one of the 'Tutors', introduced me to the pilot and departed. The helmeted and leather-coated figure with his goggles pushed up, seemed to be like a figure from one of today's U.F.O. stories.

He asked if I had flown before and I gabbled out that I had not, but that I knew quite a bit of the various controls and I asked if I could possibly have the aircraft under my own hands and feet once he felt the situation was appropriate? I suppose some of the youthful enthusiasm so earnestly displayed penetrated as he said, 'O.K., I will tap the back of your head and lift both hands, which you can see in the rear view mirror, but do not try anything too ambitious'.

I climbed into the front cockpit and he strapped me in, asking me to show him how I intended to work the ailerons and rudder. If I had not been telling the truth, that would have caught me out, but I carried out both functions with slow deliberate movements. Those hours reading of flying and the theory of flight were now about to pay off.

The pilot then settled into the rear cockpit and the familiar starting interchange between him and the mechanic who was to swing the propeller took place.

Soon, with a cough of blue smoke, the engine burst into life, the revolving propeller sending back a mild hurricane, and I put my head further down behind the small half-moon windscreen to escape it, whilst the Tutor vibrated more and more as the pilot ran the engine higher and higher. After a minute or so he throttled back and gave a thumbs up to the mechanic who withdrew the wheel-chocks, and then withdrawing himself to one wing tip, gave the pilot a thumbs up in return to signify all was clear for taxi-ing. The engine began to open up and soon we were trundling away with the wheels transmitting to our bodies the little humps and bumps of the grass field. At the edge of the airfield the pilot turned the aircraft round and I looked to see if the yellow windsock was being blown towards us so that we would take-off against the wind. It was, and in my mirror I could see the now goggled pilot looking towards the airfield controller's position, way over the other side. Presently a steady green light from an Aldis lamp was directed to us and, with that, the pilot gently, but firmly, pushed the throttle handle into the fully open position.

The old plane leapt into life, the grass passing under me faster and faster; the tail came up and then suddenly the wheel trundling noise was gone and the ground seemed about twenty feet below; a position the pilot held momentarily to build up the speed. Then I could feel the backward inclined angle of my seat and also saw the joystick in my cockpit moving back towards me. I looked over the side and saw the hangars pass well below and soon Southampton Water was underneath. Still we climbed and I sought out the altimeter on my instrument panel; it showed 500 feet and climbing. This was wonderful, this was flying, this for me was what it was all about.

If I am ever asked what crystalised my devotion and never failing interest in aircraft for the rest of my life, this must be it, without any doubt.

Overhead were lowering clouds which had threatened rain during the afternoon's show and now the first spots appeared on my windscreen but were immediately dispersed by the airflow coming back from the propeller and our forward speed. I stuck my head gingerly over one side of the cockpit, the wind force was like a blow being struck on my cheeks, my hair went all haywire, and the rain spots felt like air gun pellets — I soon reverted to the safety and comparative comfort of the windscreen. I say comparative because it was blowing a minor gale in there, and every time we changed direction I soon knew as the wind hit the side of my face when we turned.

I would not have cared if it had snowed, for I was flying and, although in later life I had many more flights in many types of aircraft, I was never to fly again in an open cockpit, and it is as different as riding a motorcycle compared with being in a bus.

The altimeter was reading 1,200 feet and we had levelled off as well as turned back towards the airfield when I felt the tap on the back of my head. In my excitement I had almost forgotten it, but quick as a flash I simultaneously put my feet on the rudder bar, and grasped gently but firmly the joystick, which I then wiggled. A look in my mirror confirmed the pilot understood, and I felt his feet come off the rudder controls and saw both his hands held aloft — it was all mine; an indescribable moment.

I looked forward and the horizon was about a third of the way down the radial engine and the altimeter was steady at 1,200 feet — so far so good — now let us try nose up and nose down, a gentle pull back on the joystick and the horizon slipped away below the engine, slowly forward and back it came. Now I thought, there is one thing I must try, as I knew I might never get the chance again and which I knew from my reading was regarded as a reasonable test of skill and co-ordination of hands and feet — a banked turn without losing height. The banking was easy as that meant moving the joystick to one side, and the ailerons brought one wing up and the other down but, at that angle, some lift was lost and to correct this, one had to use the rudder, but this time as if it were the elevator. That was successfully accomplished although I noticed I had lost nearly 100 feet in height, but the rudder soon regained that for me. Then came the awkward bit, using the elevator now as a rudder to turn; this meant keeping the joystick still very slightly to one side but gently pulling it towards me. A quick look in my mirror told me my pilot did not seem concerned, so back came the joystick and round we went in a complete circle. I only knew this because the westerly light from the cloudy sky was in front when I had started this manoeuvre and was in the same position when I had finished and brought the aircraft back to straight and level. That done, I felt I had done enough so I wiggled the joystick again and removed my feet from the rudder bar. In the mirror the pilot gave a wave and retook control.

We went up the Hamble River as far as Bursledon Bridge, where he banked and turned left and set the nose down for the airfield. I was looking at all the familiar sights I knew, but from this new vantage point, and it was just wonderful. Soon the airfield seemed to be racing towards us and then with a lovely three point touch down, the wheels began their trundling sound, and the pilot throttled the engine back to a tick-over until we lost speed enough to turn and taxi back to the hangars. Once there he switched off, the engine died and the propeller gave a last kick, and silence prevailed.

I let the pilot get out first, and a mechanic who had placed wheel-chocks in position came up on to the wing and undid my safety straps. Then I climbed out and jumped from the wing to the ground, where my pilot had peeled off his helmet, goggles and gloves.

I went to him to thank him and he modestly brushed this aside and said, — 'Did you say you have never flown before?' I assured him this was so, but I do not think he really believed me as his next words were, 'Well, if that is true you are the only chap I have ever known who could do a circular banking turn without instruction'. He asked me where I worked and finally said, 'You ought to try and get into the Air Force Auxiliary Reserve', something with which I agreed wholeheartedly, but unfortunately was never to be.

I have often wondered how that young man fared in the holocaust that was to come. I never knew his name, but because of him, and that lucky day, my course was set for the remainder of my working life.

Somewhere among my papers, possibly up in the loft of my home, there is that very programme with the lucky number torn off from the top corner of the front page. I do not suppose I shall ever see it again as it must be buried beneath all the other 'junk' that my wife keeps reminding me I am hoarding, but if it were found, I think I would frame it as a lasting reminder of one of the highlights of my life, and an unforgettable experience.

Author at 18 years of age.

Chapter Seven
Panelbeating and Wheeling

Back at work, despite the fun, rivalry, and comradeship that I enjoyed on the Spitfire fuselage production line for nearly a year, it dawned on me that, after sixty-three top, bottom and side platings, I was hardly likely to learn any further skills of the trade which I had decided on. By this time I had realised that although assembly work was important, the real skills lay in the two basic sections of 'K' shop where the flat sheets, coils, or drawn sections were manipulated to the required shapes.

The angle and section bending section was under a leading hand named Peter Wallis, and the panel beating section under Jack Rolf. Observation of both these sections over some weeks led me to the conclusion that the panel beating section, if achieved, would be the most rewarding and hardest to succeed in. This in no way implies that the angle bending was not very skilled — it was, but it did not appear to me to have the depth and scope of panel beating. There was one other important factor in that as a bread delivery boy I used to deliver to Jack's house, and so at least he knew me by sight.

I approached him one afternoon and asked him if he would consider me joining his squad. This squad consisted of three men who generally used the wheeling machines (one other machine was unallocated) and one man who did mallet or hammer forming work on the bench, using sandbags and various shaped metal heads for planishing, as well as other tools. So, all told, including Jack, it was a squad of four, and I had never seen a boy working there since I commenced work in 'K' shop.

Boys were always present in the angle bending section and I wondered why not in the other. When I spoke to Jack that afternoon he told me that three years previously, two young men of over nineteen years of age had been tried out but it had proved a failure as they could not master the wheeling techniques. He was considerate enough to show me how the wheeling machine worked, the sheet metal being stretched by compression between a ten inch diameter three inch wide flat-faced upper wheel, and a variety of smaller diameter but curved surface wheels that could be inserted on their extended axles into the socket mounting below, and then adjusted by a foot-operated, screw-threaded shaft against the underside of the panel. The operator (or wheeler) then pushed and pulled the sheet of metal over the area in which he wanted it to stretch. The important thing Jack explained was that if you were putting shape in, it was essential not to stretch each side edge but, conversely, if you needed to take shape out, it was the edge you let go first.

This brief explanation fascinated me as I could see it was a matter of 'feel' that was essential, and I said so. Jack looked at me with a slightly puzzled look and his eyes gazed directly into mine as though he was trying to decide whether I really meant what I had said, or had by accident chosen those words without fully appreciating their meaning. In the years that lay beyond that first chat, I got to know Jack Rolf very well, probably better than anyone else in Supermarine's. A lot of people did not like him, mainly, in my view, because they were jealous of his particular skills which they could never achieve, and others perhaps because he was sometimes very pithy in his remarks about other people who he considered 'empire builders' and 'credit seekers'. He certainly did not seek popularity, but whatever others may say or think, I can say from my own experience, and long personal working association with him, that he was the best 'wheeler' bar none that I have met in the whole of my aircraft-building life. To that I must add that it was his trust in me and his guidance and instruction that made me what I know he used to say was his 'best man'. That has been the finest accolade I ever needed.

40

Above: Charlie Chapman and 'Mac' Mutten, the other two wheelers.

Left: Jack Rolf and his Hillman car just prior to the War.

C.R.R. with the 'little beast' Spitfire panel 30027-363.

Following that chat, he said he would have a word with Mr Heaver and, a couple of days later, the shop office boy came and told me that Mr Heaver wanted to see me in the office.

Poor old Bill Heaver must by now have been wondering what does one have to do to keep this young Russell quiet. His first words in that familiar hoarse, gruff voice were. 'Rolfy tells me you want to go and work for him'. I said that was true. 'Why?' he said, 'you are getting good bonus where you are'. I said that it was not a matter of the money but that as an apprentice I should be learning all I could whilst I had the chance. He countered by saying that he had tried two young men before and it had failed (which I knew was so) and said, 'Give me one reason why I should try it again?'

But this time, although I still had a lot of respect for him, I had lost the awe which I had in my earlier days, and now felt more confident of myself and more at ease with him, so I replied with two reasons. One was that if he would give me three month's trial, and I failed, he could of course take me off the section, and secondly, as the work load on that section from the Spitfires was far more than that on angle bending, he would be obliged to increase the numbers there anyway, so why not start with a willing horse.

I think he was taken aback by the sheer effrontery of the latter part coming from this now nineteen year old apprentice, and he dismissed me with a snort and 'I'll think about it', and back to the Spitfire fuselage line I went. He did think about it, and it was not until the Wednesday of the following week when I happened to be passing the office and he was standing outside the door that he caught my eye and jerked his head indicating that he wanted me. I walked over to him and I will never forget his actual words. 'You can report to Rolfy tomorrow, and don't you bloody well let me down'. On Thursday, 12th January 1939, the panel beating squad increased from four to five.

Jack, the leading hand I have mentioned, and my other new workmates were a Scot, Mac Mutten, a diminutive slightly stooped Charlie Chapman and, on the bench, a gentle and kindly Fred Waygood. I was allocated the opposite side of the bench to Fred, and to its drawer I transferred the tools and other bits and pieces that I had accumulated over almost the last three years.

Rolfy (I will stick with that as he was always referred to in that way, just as, later on, I was always known as Russ), started me off with possibly the easiest piece of work there was involving using the wheels. The keel plates on the Walrus ended with the furthermost one aft being a very shallow trough section, which one formed in the big folding machine (hand-operated), and having got the section correct to templates supplied, the back end two foot or so had to be stretched in the wheels by compressing and working back and forth on each side of the trough section, only until it would lay correctly curved to a wooden jig supplied.

The folding was easy, as I had learnt that in my first few weeks, so having completed that on six lengths I was ready for the wheels.

My new leading hand set up the spare wheeling machine and, to my amazement, gave me some rags and a tin of metal polish. He explained that all wheels needed to be polished at least once a day, and more if there was any pick-up of dust or dirt or even slight scaling being shed from the aluminium clad metals we were using, and on Friday nights they all had to be oiled all over to eliminate rust and the corrosive effect of the salt-laden sea breezes from outside.

Having polished everything to his satisfaction, Rolfy then demonstrated how to shape one of my keel plates.

'Not too much pressure, and work in from the edge of each side', he explained, 'and it will probably need five passes between the two wheels, and as you move in towards the fold this will decrease four, three, two, one.'

The track made by the bottom wheel which was contoured would be about ⅜in. flat at its only point of contact. He took only three or four minutes and then placed it on the jig and it lay there exactly to profile.

In that simple demonstration which he had explained in detail, as he went along, was the real key to being a good wheeler; clean wheels, correct contact surface width for the job in hand, the pressure judgement which you could only feel as one pushed and pulled, the grading of the compressed area so that the maximum stretch was where it was needed to be without leaving the area adjacent to it too under-stretched thus creating inner stresses, and finally the master touch of being able to put the finished job on to the jig so that it lay in its correct position untouched.

That last item is the hardest of the whole lot to achieve, and although on this simple keel plate the Inspector would always pass them if only a gentle hand pressure would take it to the required shape of the jig, much later there were to be some very tricky shapes, some of which only Rolfy and I were able to achieve the desired result.

But let me not run before I can walk, I first had to now copy this demonstration as best I could with the other five keel plates. Rolfy said nothing but watched, and I knew somehow that this was the crunch. It would be nice to say I did it, just like that, but I did not and if these recollections of mine are going to be of any use to anyone, then they must show me warts and all.

I had correctly deduced earlier that I thought the 'feel' was important, and Rolfy had just confirmed it in his explanation, but I had no idea what the feel was at all, and in the back of my mind I had visions of another 'scrap note'. My palms were wet with nervous perspiration, and my head was full of flashing thoughts seeking some inspiration. Flying that Avro Tutor was a piece of cake compared with this, and all the while Jack Rolf just stood, watched, and waited.

Suddenly I had an idea — I think Rolfy thought I had quit — but a few yards from where we stood was a small metal cutting guillotine and behind it the box that collected the off-cut scrap pieces.

It was to this box I went and picked out three of the biggest pieces I could find of the same gauge thickness as the keel plate. Returning to the wheels I practiced pushing and pulling as well as increasing and decreasing the pressure. I can only guess that this must have taken all of twenty minutes but Rolfy watched and waited, his face showing none of his thoughts.

However, I now had some idea of the feel and after using the three pieces of scrap I picked up a keel section and, with a pencil, marked how far down its length the bend started, put it into the wheels, set a gentle pressure and began pushing it backwards and forwards. I did this on one side then on the opposite, and I could see it begin to bow, and so by alternating each side, and not increasing the pressure, it kept each side in balance and oh so slowly went in the desired direction.

I laid it to the jig and the front portion of the bend was all right, but at the very back end there was at least an inch gap. I marked again with a pencil the spot where the correct bow ended, and returned to the wheels and repeated some more passes over this shortened length. Another try to the jig, much nearer now, only half an inch at the back to go, so back again and again, until suddenly all it needed was the merest additional application, and it was there. I stood back and looked at that simple strip of metal, now a keel plate, as though it was a Rodin sculpture. Rolfy came over and said 'Finished?' I said, 'I think so.' 'Good lad', he replied, 'give it a little more pressure and it won't take so long' and with that he turned and walked away.

As I write, I have beside me my notebook which I started when I first went on the Spitfire fuselages so that I knew how long each job had taken, the job card number and the bonus time, and under a new underlined heading of 12th January 1939, six off, keel plates No. 8 took me five and a half hours. The official time allowed was six hours which meant to get time and a half they had to be completed in three hours, but that was the time allowed for a man, so I knew I would get some small allowance for being an apprentice.

This timing business was the province of the Ratefixer, in 'K' shop, Jack Beavin, whose job it was to assess the value of each job in actual time taken, add 10 per cent for 'contingencies', e.g. going to the stores for material or parts, personal toilet time (the famous seven minutes) and, in our particular case, polishing or oiling the wheels each day.

That time would then be doubled, and if his estimate was correct, the doubled time which would be the one printed on the bonus card would be exactly halved by the operator and the other half saved, shared between him and the company. Thus six hours allowed, three taken, equals one and a half hours bonus, so without any allowance my five and a half hours would have brought me just a quarter of an hour bonus.

I was not really bothered, my reward lay in the fact that having been inspected by Rolfy, the keel plates now stood part numbered and labelled awaiting the proper Inspector, and already Rolfy had sorted out my next job.

There was no doubt that he intended 'to sort me out' once and for all, as the next job he gave me was Walrus Keel Plate No. 1. This was completely at the other end of metal forming — no wheeling — but a pair of cast blocks bolted together at each end, the lower one being the inside profile for all three faces of the trough section, the upper block holding only the bottom width of the trough, and the finished shape of the trough being about one sixth of the circumference of a circle which, if projected on, would have been something like four feet in diameter.

Probably the best way to explain this to the uninitiated is to say; take a length of paper twenty-eight inches by six inches, fold it along its length so that the fold lines divide it equally into a trough section, then see what happens when you try to curve it inwards on to the cut edges. You will get a series of tucks and creases which in paper or cardboard can be eliminated by vee cuts.

My problem was to form that same shape by using a wedge shaped mallet to compress the surplus material into the material adjacent to it, with no cutting allowed. In effect what you do is establish a firm heel line as soon as the metal has been softened in the normalising bath, and then deliberately make the tucks appear, and by working back and forth on each side, gradually force the surplus metal into a greater thickness.

It sounds more complicated than it was, once you have been taught how to 'tuck' or 'draw' or 'spoon' as it is variously called; it is something you do not forget.

Having 'bashed' the two sides down to the bottom block surface, and ensured that the drawing width of the sides was met, one could leave all the little surplus tucks outside of this width, and cut them off.

It was then a matter of planishing the malleted surface smooth with specially-faced hammers and light touch, try it to the jig, adjust to suit, and then mark off and cut to finished length, finally checking the angular set of each side as it varied along the length by roughly fifteen degrees.

Fred Waygood was a great help to me at this bench job, and kept a fatherly eye on me until he was sure I was going along in the correct manner. This was also in a batch of six, and man's time allowed was fifteen hours, and on this first batch I had taken nineteen hours. Once again it was the sense of achievement that gave me the greatest pleasure, and Rolfy was already showing signs that he thought perhaps his young protegé 'might have the makings'.

It would be boring and tedious to go on with each individual job, but over the weeks and months, to his eternal credit, Rolfy kept me at top stretch by varying the types of work he gave me, and later I was to find out just how good a job he had done.

I must also revert for a moment to one other person already mentioned, but not yet credited here for his proper due. This was Jack Beavin the Ratefixer who, during the time I was going through this long learning phase, made my bonus up to time and a half. Such was his belief and trust, which, in due time, I was able to acknowledge and demonstrably repay.

When I first joined Rolfy's squad, not only was I the youngest member but the other three men were all older than him. Fred Waygood was always on bench jobs and Mac and Charlie were the only other wheelers. Whether the fact that the latter two were supervised by a younger man got under their skin or not I am not sure, but at odd times, perhaps when I might be working with them or in Rolfy's absence, an undercurrent of some form of discontent was made known to me.

With the benefit of hindsight, I can now see it was just 'sour grapes', and a little envy of his skill. One occasion comes readily to mind which brings this point right to the fore.

The top rear panel on the Spitfire fuselage was part number 30027-363, and it was a little beast. At its front end it was 'U' shaped about ten inches deep by ten inches wide, then it narrowed down to almost a Vee section, but its top profile reversed from the natural slope down of the main fuselage to the upward curve to meet the fin attachment frame. Now a reverse shape is the hardest to achieve, as it means it can only be met by stretching the edges of the panel in that area, and thus making the middle collapse, so that on this one panel of fairly thin gauge material (24G or .022in. if I recall correctly) one half went one way and the other half the other — in and out shaping to be blended in one panel barely three feet in length, and a constantly changing section.

Originally, it was considered that this panel for production could only be a power press job, and Woolston, in those days, did not have anything in the machinery line that could handle that class of work. In fact, Woolston never did have a rubber press, and not until late 1938 did it have its first 'Ceco' stamping machine which was based on the drop hammer principle. Whoever pressed out the early 363s, did not make a very good job of it, and our section was left with the task of altering these pressings to get some sort of fit. Not an easy task, and probably expensive as well, so, early in 1939, it was decided to make them in our squad from the flat sheet.

By this time I had established a rapport with Rolfy, and one afternoon he beckoned me to him and told me that this job was coming on the section the next day, and that on that day he would not be in. He intended to allocate this little job late in the afternoon to one of the two other experienced wheelers, and he whispered, 'I'll bet you there will not be one made when I come in on the following day.'

True enough, the next day was one of great confusion and frustration, not only for the person to whom the job had been given, but also to the other wheeler as well who came to assist his colleague in distress and, although they tried many various ideas, by the end of the day our section was littered with goodness knows how many twisted, bent, and battered shapes, but nothing that was in any way like that required to fit the jig.

The following morning Rolfy turned up from his 'day off' and nonchalantly enquired if all was well. Of course the truth had to come out as not only were there no 363s, but also several sheets of scrap material to be accounted for, plus of course the time booked for which there was nothing useful to show.

Rolfy went off to the Foreman to explain the scrap and difficulty, and having obtained a new job card by the withdrawing of the original, he drew a fresh supply of sheet material, cut out his blank shapes, rolled each into a half circle as a commencing section, then began wheeling and, to cut a long story short, three hours later, there on the jig sat one perfectly-shaped 363 panel.

He did not make any snide remarks, neither did he take any of the other advantages that were open to him, but by example, skill, and confidence in his own ability he had demonstrated not only was he the section boss — but why!

I remained with Rolfy and the panel beating squad even after the bombing during September 1940 and, after the War, returned to him at Eastleigh Airport and right up to the moment I left Vickers Supermarine. He never ever let me down in any way, and I think he feels similarly about me despite all the changes of life that have affected us both ever since. His marriage was childless and perhaps none too satisfactory, a matter he bore with great stoicism, and I suppose in a way I may have been in his eyes, the son he possibly may have wished to have had. If this assumption is correct, I am glad that now in the autumn of his life he will know that all he did for me was not wasted, but was greatly treasured, and still a matter of fond memory.

Just as I had anticipated, the production requirements to meet the new impact of an increasing programme of Spitfires and additional Walruses necessitated the strengthening of the squad, and it proved difficult to find the right people. Our first new recruit was Hilton Duxbury who had come all the way down from North Yorkshire to seek work.

Also the success of Mr Heaver's experiment with me led to other young fellows of similar age being tried; some fell by the wayside but later, under the pressure of war, one or two were retained, even if their skills were limited to the more mundane jobs. Even today the skills of a competent panel beater are still in demand, particularly in the motor and aircraft industries, where their services are often required prior to mass production tooling. In these prototype or early adjustment phases Jack Rolf excelled. It was a fascinating thing to watch — a master of his craft demonstrating his skill like an art form — and I knew then I would not be satisfied until I could do the same panels, although I was all too aware it would be some time before that became even a matter of serious consideration.

My jobs ranged from Walrus keel plates, bow panels, all its float panels, Spitfire flare tubes, cockpit coaming channels, and assisting Rolfy with the long skin panels for Mitchell's bomber, and the modifications to the nose shape on the Sea Otter necessitated by its refusal to take off from the sea, and the reshaping of its engine nacelle from its straight forward conical form to something that eliminated the fin buffeting it was suffering. Once these faults were corrected the Sea Otter became another useful amphibian, although it never eclipsed the Walrus in its popularity.

At this stage, the Walrus forward bottom and side float panels provided me with enough to get my teeth into, as both involved, in part, the same wheeling techniques that the Spitfire 363 panel required, in that they had to have shape taken out, and the side panels being similar in gauge to the 363, would coil up on themselves if proper attention was not given to the distribution of the wheeling pressures.

By the time I had chance to get my hands on 'the little beast' as Mac always referred to 363, the international situation had deteriorated and the ominous clouds of the coming struggle had begun to accumulate.

So that the reader can follow the events that were now imminent, it is appropriate to give more details of the Supermarine factory layouts and the departmental locations, together with some of their staffing complement, as well as the functions performed.

Chapter Eight
Prelude to War

In addition to the two plans of the Woolston works herewith, which are, as best as I can recall, the building changes from 1936 to 1940, the following information will, I trust, add flesh to the bare bones of the layouts, and introduce some of the other personalities involved.

My own shop, 'K', at the southern end adjacent to the floating bridge dry dock and hardstanding, has already been mentioned including the balcony that belonged to 'P' shop, Harry Jay's store and Ted Gardiner's section occupying the three sides at balcony height and, under Harry's store, the Process section, etc.

'K' shop's northern side abutted with 'P' shop; the 'P' designation being derived from the word 'planes' as wings used to be called. The shop floor was not quite the width of 'K' shop and for the first 20 feet its width was overhung by a girder-supported office complex.

Under these offices, in 1936, were assembled the structures for the various flying boat tailplanes, elevators, rudders and ailerons, but once the order for the Spitfire was placed, these items were moved out, and the whole length beneath the offices became the site for the Spitfire's most important component — its leading edge assembly, under Bob Randall as chargehand; a name that will return again as part of my own story.

This leading edge component was effectively a torsion box made up by two pressings of 14 gauge .80in. thick for the top and bottom skins, with inter rib 'Z' section stiffeners riveted to them and joined at their leading edges by a riveted internal buttstrap. These skins, which not only provided the leading edge elliptical curve, also included the bend about 15 inches from their root attachment ends that gave the wing its dihedral. They were made by the Pressed Steel Company.

The other remarkable item in the torsion box was the spar booms. The design requirement for these spar booms was for square section tubes, four in number, but each one had to be a close fit inside the other, the final square hollow remaining, roughly an inch and a half, to be filled with a machined steel bar at the inboard end where the wing to fuselage fixing bolts passed through. This boxed sectioning was then cleverly reduced in its lengths so that only the outer one went fully to the tip, whilst the others were progressively shortened in accordance with the design strength requirements, but cranked to produce the dihedral as the skins. These square tube assemblies were made by Reynold Tubes.

The top and bottom tube assemblies were assembled into the spar jigs and the spar webs fitted, followed by the rib assemblies, after which the leading edge skins were added.

This assembled torsion box is, by common consent, acknowledged by aircraft designers and engineers as the key to the Spitfire's success, and the long development programme it was able to sustain throughout all the demands of the changing fortunes of war, hinged very largely on its small chord height.

Although the overall responsibility and credit for the Spitfire design is quite properly attributed to R. J. Mitchell, I feel sure that he would have been the first to acknowledge how much this wing design owed Beverley Shenstone, a Canadian who joined R. J.'s team after working in Germany. This fact raises the question of that beautiful elliptical wing shape. Was it one of Mitchell's inspirations or, as I believe possible, the outcome of seeing the Heinkel 70 that Rolls-Royce purchased as the flight test bed for the engine that eventually became the 'Merlin'? Drawings, still in existence today, show the cranked wing Spitfire to Specification F7/30, which so disappointed Mitchell, and his improved version to the

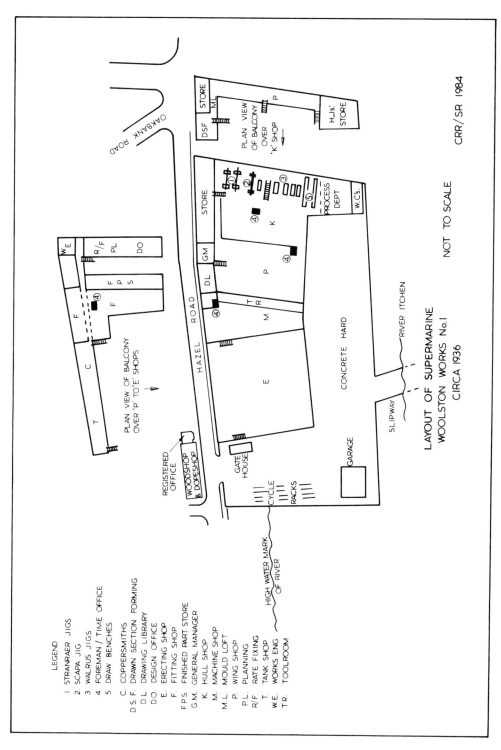

LEGEND

1. STRANRAER JIGS
2. SCAPA JIG
3. WALRUS JIGS
4. FOREMAN / TIME OFFICE
5. DRAW BENCHES

C. COPPERSMITHS
D.S.F. DRAWN SECTION FORMING
D.L. DRAWING LIBRARY
D.O. DESIGN OFFICE
E. ERECTING SHOP
F. FITTING SHOP
F.P.S. FINISHED PART STORE
G.M. GENERAL MANAGER
K. HULL SHOP
M. MACHINE SHOP
M.L. MOULD LOFT
P. WING SHOP
P.L. PLANNING
R/F. RATE FIXING
T. TANK SHOP
W.E. WORKS ENG
T.R. TOOLROOM

LAYOUT OF SUPERMARINE
WOOLSTON WORKS No.1
CIRCA 1936

NOT TO SCALE

CRR/SR 1984

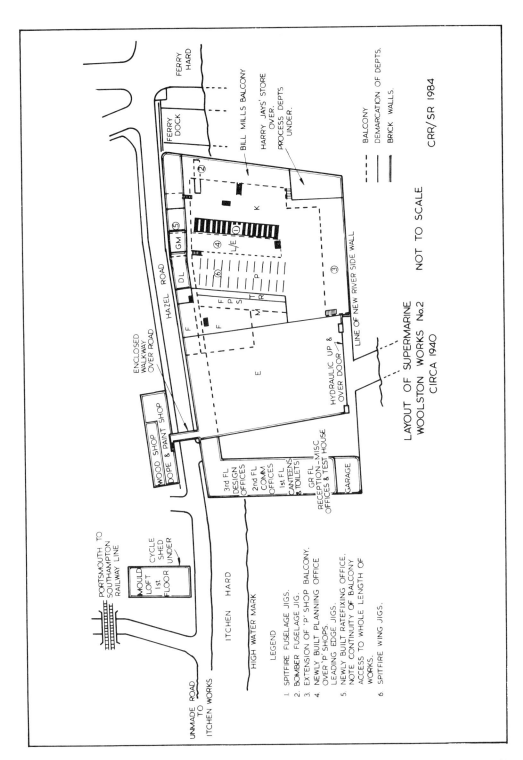

LAYOUT OF SUPERMARINE
WOOLSTON WORKS No.2
CIRCA 1940

NOT TO SCALE

CRR/SR 1984

LEGEND

1. SPITFIRE FUSELAGE JIGS.
2. BOMBER FUSELAGE JIG.
3. EXTENSION OF 'P' SHOP BALCONY.
4. NEWLY BUILT PLANNING OFFICE
   OVER 'P' SHOPS.
   LEADING EDGE JIGS.
5. NEWLY BUILT RATEFIXING OFFICE.
   NOTE CONTINUITY OF BALCONY
   ACCESS TO WHOLE LENGTH OF
   WORKS.
6. SPITFIRE WING JIGS.

- - - - BALCONY
- - - - DEMARCATION OF DEPTS.
──── BRICK WALLS.

BILL MILLS BALCONY
HARRY JAYS' STORE OVER.
PROCESS DEPTS UNDER.

FERRY HARD
FERRY DOCK

HAZEL ROAD

ENCLOSED WALKWAY OVER ROAD

WOOD SHOP
DOPE & PAINT SHOP

LINE OF NEW RIVER SIDE WALL

HYDRAULIC UP &
OVER DOOR

3rd FL DESIGN OFFICES
2nd FL COMM OFFICES
1st FL CANTEENS & TOILETS
GR FL RECEPTION—MISC OFFICES & TEST HOUSE
GARAGE

PORTSMOUTH TO SOUTHAMPTON RAILWAY LINE

MOULD LOFT 1st FLOOR
CYCLE SHED UNDER

UNMADE ROAD TO ITCHEN WORKS

ITCHEN HARD

HIGH WATER MARK

38A-74

A German Heinkel 112. The earlier civil type HE70 was purchased by Rolls-Royce to test the engine that eventually became the 'Merlin'. Note the elliptical wing shape.

same specification both having straight leading and trailing edges, yet, suddenly in 1935, they are transformed to that familiar ellipse. I wonder?

There is a poetic justice if R. J. seized the opportunity and the basic shape was 'borrowed', for the design and detail adaptation for the Spitfire was still nothing short of brilliant.

There must be a moral somewhere that the end result rebounded so successfully on its originators, but there is some balancing equity if we remember that both the prototypes of the JU87 Stuka and the Messerschmitt 109 were originally powered by British Rolls-Royce engines.

However, back to 'P' shop. The foreman was Jim Weedy, to whom chargehands like Bill Mills on the balcony over 'K' shop, Chris Parker on the draw benches, and leading hand Ted Gardiner, were responsible, although away from 'P' shop proper.

Jim Weedy, who was not physically unlike Robert Newton's character as played in the film of Shaw's, *Major Barbara*, was not a popular man. In my opinion I think he saw himself acting in the image of Trevor Westbrook, but he tended to overdo the rigid disciplinarian control and, consequently, was more feared. Many years later, after the war, when I was at British European Airways, he turned up there as Chief Maintenance Engineer and when he knew of my Supermarine background he was always agreeably affable to me. Strangely enough, Beverley Shenstone also did a stint at B.E.A. whilst I was there.

At the Hazel Road end of 'P' shop was the Drawings Library, responsible to the Chief Planner, Johnny Bull, who operated as did the Ratefixers, Planners, etc. from the offices situated over the southern boundary between 'P' and 'K' shops, all of whom were in turn responsible to Mr Butler, the Production Engineer. Again, at the Hazel Road end under this office complex was the brick-built office of the Works Manager. It was a dingy office, the two relatively small windows facing on to Hazel Road and too high to really see out of. Permanently under the shadow of the offices overhead, and leading straight out on to the noisy 'yammering' of rivet guns on the Spitfire leading edges, not to mention the close proximity of 'K' shop's noise, it has always seemed to me incredible that Trevor Westbrook was able to work in it. However, he did, and to some purpose, for he was the man who, despite what others may claim, steered and implemented the productionising, tooling and sub-contracting for the Spitfire. I have read and heard how this was attributed to Leonard Gooch, but not only was he a draughtsman in the Works Engineer's office at the time but, as I shall relate later, he did not then or ever have the experience necessary to do such a task.

The Works Engineer's office was over the top of Westbrook's office at the balcony height. It too was quite small and run by Jack Knowles, who always looked at one through pebble glasses, which made his eyes appear a lot larger than they were.

Just to complicate matters further, the northern Hazel Road corner of 'P' shop held the jig in which the Walrus main spar frame was assembled. This, the most important frame in that aircraft, was worked by 'K' shop personnel and, for a while, I was 'the boy' for Reggie Saunders and Tommy Quick who worked there. I must confess that what little part I played, on reflection, seems to have been stealthily going up to Ted Gardiner's balcony where cigarettes and chocolate were dispensed by the inestimable Ted during working hours at the risk of his job if discovered. He never was, and many a 'Mars' bar found itself into my digestive system from his small attache case stock.

As can be seen from the layout drawings 'P' shop was greatly extended towards the river during 1937/8. Next to 'P' shop was the Machine shop under its foreman Mr Gingell, a busy bustling man of pleasant disposition, whose nephew worked in the company and ended up at South Marston when the Design Office moved there. Mr Gingell's brother was in charge of the company's garage and transport department. The Toolroom, under Dick Earl, was an adjunct to the Machine shop.

The Machine shop was relatively small, mainly because the machined item content of aircraft in those days was considerably smaller than it is today, and its equipment ordinary 'run of the mill' machines, with none of the more sophisticated items that were available even then. It was identified by the letter 'M'.

Its shape was like a truncated right-angled triangle, due to the fact that the works buildings grew together from either end of the total plot area; the floating bridge end being originally square on to Hazel Road, whilst its opposite end came off as a separate building at an angle. As they grew together, the last connecting roofing span gave the shape that became the Machine shop, and so it remained, despite the later extensions to other shops.

Next to the Machine shop came the Erecting shop, E shop, and was the largest area without supporting girders within its span. In 1936 the western (river) side was made up mainly of large sliding doors which opened on to the ample hardstanding and the slipway into the River Itchen. The doors were large, wooden and heavy, requiring two men to crank them open or closed.

For the life of me I cannot recall the Foreman's name, and the only people I knew there were Basil Brown, a fitter-erector who had worked on the Schneider Trophy aircraft, and 'Digger' Pickett, who often flew in the flying boats to render the services necessary in attaching the craft to anchorage buoys, etc.

The balcony, which in 1936 ceased at Ted Gardiner's section, continued after the Works Engineer's Office, right along the remainder of the Hazel Road boundary. In a manner somewhat similar to the overhead offices between 'P' and 'K' shops, there were extensions at balcony height that ran outwards to the 1936 riverside buildings frontage. These places, where the roof trusses were only two or three feet above an average man's standing height, contained, between 'P'and 'M' shops, the Finished Parts Store run by Dennis Webb, and then between 'M' and 'E' shops, the detail fitters shop, 'F' shop, under Mr Camm. Somewhere among those high eyries was the Design Office, my early knowledge of which is solely that from a photograph belonging to Beverley Shenstone, and printed in his contribution to Alfred Price's book on the Spitfire. It shows very clearly the spartan accommodation that Mitchell and his team shared throughout R. J.'s productive years. Tragically R. J. died from cancer in June 1937, and so was not able to reap the rewards he so richly deserved, which would have included a magnificently positioned and equipped office at the river end of the new office block, that was built with the money arising from the contracts awarded for his Spitfire and Walrus designs.

Mitchell's team in those far from ideal working conditions was remarkably small, and yet its design output was prodigious. Some of the names come to mind and deserve to be remembered. Joe Smith of course, Beverley Shenstone, Alan Clifton, Arthur Shirvall, Mr Harris, George Kettlewell, Frank Perry, Frank Holroyd, not forgetting Miss Haines and Miss Attwater (tracers) and, at the flight end, Ernest Mansbridge. Later these ranks were increased by Reg Caunter, 'Deafy' Dickson, Eric Cooper, 'Alf' Faddy, and others whose names escape me and for whose omission I ask forgiveness.

For its last length, the balcony was the location of the Coppersmiths, Pipe Benders and the Fuel Tank builders. Under the benign eye of a Foreman, Harry Collins, whose mustachioed face seldom lost its somewhat mournful look, it was a quietly run and efficient shop. Harry, the Foreman, had a son working with him as the shop boy and, as the poor chap was slightly mentally-handicapped, no doubt his father's face reflected his private grief.

I only had occasion to speak with Harry twice, and I must say his replies and attention to my errands were in marked contrast to the usual grunt, bark or abuse young lads like myself normally received from Foremen.

Beyond the Erecting shop north wall was a yard, containing, at the river end, the garage, the bicycle racks and, just inside the main gate, 'Nobby' Read's gatehouse.

Across Hazel Road, opposite the gates, was another corrugated-iron clad workshop containing the Dope and Fabric shop, and the small Woodworkers' shop under Harry Warren. Abutting this shop Supermarine's owned a bay-windowed house, the last of a terrace of nine of which the other eight did not have bay windows. This house was then the Company's Registered Offices, where the Commercial Manager, Mr Marsh-Hunn, presided over his small departments.

Apart from the one hangar at Eastleigh, rented from Southampton Council to facilitate the new fighter's final assembly and flight testing, that completed the comparatively modest size of the Supermarine organisation. I have not included the Hythe flying boat hangar, as it was soon to be put to other uses and, at the time about which I write, was mainly used as a storage unit.

Once the order for 310 Spitfires was placed in June 1936, and well over 150 Walruses ordered almost simultaneously, expansion and extensions became the order of the day. The old toilets at the end of 'K' shop were demolished and reinstated in greater splendour in the new office block that arose in the northern yard, where the cycle racks had been situated. That end of 'K' shop was then taken right to the end of the site's boundary with the river, the additional space gained from the old hardstanding used to improve and increase the Process Department.

This new line of river's edge wall was extended northwards to a point roughly opposite the Machine shop, and the whole of the space became part of 'P' shop, and included a new balcony that stretched unbroken from Harry Jay's store and round the wall to the column support for the new hydraulically-operated, up-and-over, massive swing door that now provided 'E' shop with almost twice its floor space, now that its riverside boundary had been pushed out to enclose most of the original hardstanding.

The Ratefixing and Planning Offices were rebuilt in more modern materials and the opportunity was taken to connect up the balcony at Ted Gardiner's end so that — with the overhead, over-the-road, covered walkway that was put up for access to the brand new replacement Dope-Paint-Fabric, and Woodshop opposite the main gate — it was possible to walk at balcony height from the Erecting shop door, round three sides of the factory, across Hazel Road, and down into the Dope shop.

The old registered offices in the bay-windowed house were demolished by the new extended Dope shop, and transferred to the magnificent four storey office block that arose in all its sandy cream walls with blue-tiled piping glory.

The design staff had the top floor — a just reward for their achievements in that iron-trussed garret in the roof area of the old buildings. For them the move must have seemed like going to an hotel penthouse suite, after being in a garden shed.

Sadly, by this time, R. J. Mitchell's illness was already in its advanced terminal stage, and he passed away in June 1937 and, to the best of my knowledge, did not enjoy the new accommodation that would have been his right.

The floor below the Design Offices was occupied by the Commercial Offices, including Wages, Cashiers and associated departments. The first floor contained the new toilet facilities where the ubiquitous 'Taffy' Williams, now in a small partitioned office, presided over the 'gents', and provided all his old facilities.

I've often wondered if there was not a conflict of interests in his services, as his wife was the midwife for the Sholing district — however, it was almost universally agreed that 'Taffy' had 'the best business in the business'. This same floor had the canteens and, at the river end, a new innovation — an apprentices' classroom complete with an Apprentice Supervisor, Mr Locke.

The ground floor had the front reception office area which had replaced 'Nobby' Read's little wooden hut and, at the other end, the garage and an enclosed area for Arthur Black's Test House and Metallurgical Section.

To we apprentices our interest was naturally on Mr Locke who, because of his short stature, bald head and general appearance we irreverently dubbed 'Professor Nimbus', after a newspaper cartoon character. For all our youthful insensitivity, he was a good man who did his best to advance our academic grasp of engineering, and as we were his first intake I hope he was able to follow our varied achievements. I shall always remember him best on the morning I had to report to him that the Apprentices' Outing of the previous Saturday was in financial trouble, as the lad who was the Treasurer had spent the monies collected on his own requirements, and we could not pay the coach-owner's bill. Without hesitation, he wrote me out a Company cheque for the amount and as I went off mightily relieved, he began chasing up the dishonest apprentice and his father, from whom he recouped the amount involved.

Further northwards, along Hazel Road, about 100 yards from the main works entrance and on the opposite side, another, smaller building was erected. Its ground floor housed our displaced cycle racks, and above them Don Snooks was provided with a nice clear floor-space, with good window and sky lighting, for his Mould Loft. When this new Mould Loft was firmly established, the responsibility for it was transferred from Bill Heaver to the Design Office, who made Frank Perry their liaison member.

The new Office Block was only one of the major buildings in the expansion programme. Five hundred yards along the unmade dirt road that Hazel Road became, and sandwiched between J. S. White's shipyard and Tagart Morgan and Cole's Timber Yard was built the Itchen Works, a large, airy, simple 'hangar-like' type building with the minimum of vertical girders supporting its high roof trusses. The offices were all built as a single storey unit that lay against its northern wall, so that the large rectangular floor assembly area was not encroached upon. The western wall was practically one large hydraulically-operated door, similar to the Woolston Erecting shop. Beyond the door was a large hardstanding, and a new slipway into the water.

On the eastern side, a large forecourt comfortably accommodated the Canteen building, and at its boundary with J. S. White's, a new Sports and Social Clubhouse.

Beyond the road boundary fence and on the other side of the road lay the Woolston to Southampton railway line, on an embankment some fifteen or so feet high with a ten foot wide arched tunnel running through it to the swampy unused ground beyond. All these, the fence, railway bank, the tunnel and the ground beyond, were to be featured within two years of events tragically painful to recall.

In the meantime, the additional assembly floor space proved a blessing, as with Spitfire wings delayed from the sub-contractors, and Eastleigh's single hangar now dealing with the Spitfires that had been completed and undergoing their test flying, the accumulation of fuselages from Woolston were able to be accommodated at Itchen, where the opportunity was taken to fit all the fuselage systems and equipment, as well as their engines and tail units, thus reducing the turnover time at Eastleigh once wings became available.

At one time there must have been anything up to a hundred fuselages, not to mention the last Stranraer and first Sea Otter flying boats, as well as the two bomber fuselages. In 1936, the total number of employees was in the 500-600 region, and by the time of September 1940, it was probably nearer twice that figure.

Chapter Nine
Into War

As my 19th birthday, Christmas and the New Year came and went, some of the impending events began to cast their shadows before them. Overtime became more necessary, our complement of personnel began to swell, the new Design block was already well in use, and the new Itchen assembly building was coming into use.

Later, and more ominously, air raid shelters were constructed, and A.R.P. preparations were being made and volunteers sought. I opted for the Light Rescue Squad. I suppose its sort of Flying Squad glamour appealed to me, but I am sure I did not pay as much attention to the instruction given as I would have done if I had known what lay in the months ahead.

Late in August 1939, my younger brother who had joined the local Territorial Army unit earlier with most of his mates, received his mobilisation papers. Then Hitler invaded Poland, and with an almost relieving inevitability, my mother, father and I heard the tired, disappointed voice of Neville Chamberlain announce over the radio 'that we were at War with Germany'.

Dad and I dug a four foot deep hole midway down our back garden, covered it with corrugated iron sheets and piled earth from the hole over them, leaving a single narrow entrance at one end by cutting steps down in the earth. A few weeks later an Anderson shelter was delivered to us and our original hole needed very little done to it to provide proper accommodation. This task was also completed by dad and I on a Sunday morning and we fitted it out gradually with bunks and all the other items that we thought might be required if we ever had to use it in earnest.

Monday, 4th September 1939 showed no marked difference in my working life, except for the overtime now essential, other than the fact that gangs of men were very busily engaged in painting the factory's external walls and roof in camouflage patterns and colours.

My story is not the place to recall the phoney war period or the subsequent Norwegian and European campaigns that culminated in the 'miracle' of Dunkirk; these are all far more accurately and ably described elsewhere.

During this period, a considerable part of the Walrus skin panels were passed over to Charlie Chapman and myself, whilst Mac Mutten, Fred Waygood, Hilton Duxbury and, of course, Jack Rolf concentrated on the mounting needs of the Spitfires. Another young man joined us, Fred Veal, and although he had up to then been a trainee butcher, he adapted to this new life very well indeed, and I believe is still to this day pursuing the trade that he began with us.

Reference to my works note book reveals that, despite the Walrus work, I formed and assembled no less than 472 Spitfire flare tube containers required for up to the 700th aircraft; Fred Waygood having made the others. These tubes intended for night flying usage and originally two per aircraft, then later one per aircraft, ended up as ignominious scrap when it was found that the Spitfire's night-fighting capabilities were of little use, and they were deleted in the newer aircraft and eventually removed from the old. No more were made after May 1940, and of course this particular month brought other changes that gave a new sense of urgency to the conduct of the war.

Prior to that, changes much more local had taken place. The Wing Shop ('P') was building Spitfire wings, and completed fuselages were being assembled at the Itchen Works, so that by the end of 1939 the aircraft, including stacked wings, could be transported by low loader 'Queen Mary' lorries to the airfield at Eastleigh for fitment of wings, cowlings, pro-

Above: My Mother and Father in 1939.

Left: Homemade air-raid shelter. The 'hole in the ground', September 1939.

The first Bofors A/A gun on Peartree Green, 3rd September 1939.

peller, then ground test systems, flight test and off to the R.A.F. reception unit. It was not uncommon for the test pilots to make flights on six to nine aircraft each in one day.

Trevor Westbrook had earlier been recalled by Vickers to the Weybridge Works to get the Wellington bomber production programme under way. Later he was to join Lord Beaverbrook where his experience and drive served his country well. I only ever spoke to him twice, the first time was in answer to a question he put to me whilst I was on the Spitfire plating line, and the second time I was having a chat with a planning office clerk I knew, and Westbrook came up on us before we were aware of it. There was just time for my friend to scuttle away to his office, but my way led me towards him.

Now Trevor Westbrook was well known for his directnesss, and he maintained a high standard of discipline, brooked no argument, but had always seemed to me to be firm but fair. He was a bachelor, lived in the Botleigh Grange Hotel, played Rugby, and flew his own small aircraft. He had strong, rugged features and an athletic body. Add to this his open sports car and his position, it was no wonder that many a female heart fluttered in his presence. My heart, however, was fluttering for entirely different reasons on this day. I had been caught chatting, and before the war this could still mean the sack.

'What were you doing?' he asked very brusquely. For a moment I wondered whether I could make up some story to justify the chat, but there was something about those piercing, searching eyes and beetled brows that made me admit that we were discussing the previous weekend's football. Once again came the hard stare and the questions. 'What is your name?' and 'What shop are you from?' Both questions were answered with a sense of resignation on my part. 'Well get back there and don't waste time that someone else is paying for', and with that he was gone. Weeks later it filtered down as these things do that he had spoken to my Foreman, who was not very pleased, and who in turn had spoken to the shop chargehand, Bill Peckham, who told me that it was only that Westbrook believed I had spoken the truth that had saved me. Nevertheless, the memory of the man's patent honesty and fairness, whilst still being firm, remained, and later I was to adopt a much similar approach in my own executive career, and if those who worked for me can think of me as 'firm but fair' I shall not be displeased.

Churchill's appointment of Lord Beaverbrook as Minister of Aircraft Production soon made its effect felt, and our Company was instructed to concentrate on Spitfires only. For me this meant farewell to all the Walrus jobs and I began to get more panels to shape for the Spitfire. Most of them were easy and took little time, but the one I had set my heart on was still denied me. However, by this time we had the front wing to fuselage fillet panels to make, and these were difficult and once again Rolfy proved that at least he could do them. It soon became obvious that he could not solely provide the quantity needed of both different panels. He gave some instruction and help to Mac who after a while could just manage the 363; but only just.

One day, having accumulated some time in hand on my own jobs, I asked Rolfy if I could try a 363, having explained that apart from the piece of metal it would not cost the Company anything. By now he was a good judge of my capabilities and he realised what it would mean to me if the gamble paid off, but he still cautioned me of the difficulty with the particular job, thinking, no doubt, that a failure might undermine the confidence he had so carefully instilled in me. Finally he gave his approval and, as always, his unstinting help and guidance.

That one off took me approximately eight hours to complete but, at the end, there was my own first (and unofficial) 363. I had hoped to have been given a card for a batch of five but three months earlier the sonorous and pugnacious voice of Winston Churchill had broadcast to the nation that 'the Battle of France is over, the Battle of Britain is about to begin.'

Chapter Ten
The Battle Begins

There is a growing myth that the 'Battle of Britain' finished on the afternoon of Sunday, 15th September 1940.

The film of that name, excellent as it is, portrays Air Marshal Dowding, C in C of Fighter Command, as pacing the balcony of his Headquarters on the Monday morning as though the previous day's exertions had finally cleared the skies, and in one otherwise interesting and detailed book, the author provides the reader with a finale that, as best I remember, stated that, 'at 3.20p.m. on Sunday, 15th September, the last of the German raiders crossed the coastline, the all-clear sounded — the Battle of Britain was over.' There must be many, especially in Southampton, who would have wished he was right, but who by 6p.m. that same day could have shown ample evidence of how horribly incorrect he was, and that there were many dangerous days ahead before his assertion would become fact. So for this present and future generations let me try to get one small segment of these events accurately described.

The actual period of the Battle of Britain is arbitrary. There were phases; the Channel convoys and ports, the all out attempt to smash Fighter Command and its airfields, and then the thankfully delayed last ditch attempts to stem the flow of new Spitfire and Hurricanes from their manufacturing factories and airfields.

This story concerns the latter phase as seen from my own and necessarily localised account of the events I witnessed, supplemented by research that I have done since to establish matters that are relevant, and which have incidentally brought some little-known items to light which I trust will be of interest to those, both young and old, who study this period in the life of our country. I have declared my personal interest, and if, whilst trying to be objective, the reader detects the intrusion of feelings of pride, then bear with me, because a voice far mightier than mine did say, 'This was our Finest Hour', and for all my life since then I have felt this to be true.

The official period for the Battle of Britain is from 10th July to 31st October 1940, and even by having as a definition, 'that period when the German Air Force attempted to subdue, mainly in daylight, the Royal Air Force Fighter defences and supply sources', it is possible to extend this at each end, but for the purpose of this narrative the official period will suffice.

It is also necessary to define the localities with which we are primarily concerned and their relationship to each other. These are the Vickers Supermarine Aviation Works, comprising the Woolston works just north of the floating bridge, the Itchen Works approximately half a mile further on and the Eastleigh works, roughly three and a half miles North on the Southampton Airport complex. The first two fronted the eastern side of the River Itchen, and the Itchen works was bounded on its eastern side by a service road and a 15 feet high railway embankment.

When air raid shelters were built, apart from three surface shelters in the Itchen works fence line, the main shelters for both Woolston and Itchen employees were constructed in rows on the far side of the railway embankment, and access to them was through a brick arched tunnel, approximately 10 feet wide. Prior to the Dunkirk evacuation, two dummy test raid warnings were made to see how the air raid shelters would cope, and for those from the Woolston works, it was obvious that it not only took too long, but that the tunnel became a bottleneck. Furthermore, the shelters were in line with possible bombing raids. As

Top: The 58th production Spitfire.

Centre left: The Messerschmitt 110.

Left: A Messerschmitt 109.

Above: A German Do215 bomber.

a result, a number of us resolved not to use them, a decision which subsequently and tragically became all too well founded.

By 10th July, Southampton had already experienced its first few bombs mainly by single aircraft and mostly at night. During both day and night there were also many air raid alarms which caused a great loss of production hours. My diary entry for 16th August says, 'Five raids today — only did five hours work'. That was a loss of five hours. Soon after, instructions were issued for all works to operate a 'delayed warning system'. This meant that public air raid alarms were ignored, and works sirens would be sounded when spotters on the roof saw enemy aircraft approaching.

The real pressure on Southampton began to be felt on 13th August, when, by using a low cloud base for cover, a large and determined German raid was attempted on Middle Wallop or Worthy Down aerodromes.

With a reasonable warning, a colleague and I made our way to Peartree Green. Lying on the grass alongside Peartree Church we could hear, but not see, what sounded like a vast air armada pass over. The sounds gradually faded in the direction of Winchester, then suddenly new sounds intervened, screaming engines straining for maximum power and the sharp chattering of machine guns. The main attacking force was being broken up by our fighters and retreating back overhead, the way they had come.

We were very conscious that at any moment one of the fleeing bombers might jettison its bomb load from above the clouds — a point that was all too clearly emphasised as one bomber pierced the low cloud over Southampton and let go a stick of bombs across the docks area, hitting, amongst other things, the International Cold Store which caught fire and blazed continuously for days and nights as its stocks of butter and other items defied the efforts of the Fire Brigade.

That same night the Germans bombed the Castle Bromwich factory at Birmingham, the largest 'Shadow' factory set up to produce Spitfires. This night raid was by nine Heinkel IIIs of which only four found the target with 11 bombs. Some damage, casualties, and material loss was incurred, but insufficient to halt its production — which is a subject I shall return to later.

On 14th, there was another small raid, and this time the bombs fell in the Manor Farm Road, Adelaide Road, and the St. Denys area, which was getting pretty close to Southampton Airport. My belief is that the airfield was the intended target but the attack was frustrated by rapid raising of the balloon barrage.

The next day, 15th August, the factories' delayed warning sounded, indicating imminent danger, and I made my way to a new vantage point I had found, with the crew of a Bofors gun set on the footbridge over the railway from Lower Vicarage Road to Wharncliffe Road. It was only about 150 yards from the Woolston works and had a magnificent view over the town, docks, and way down Southampton Water, with the added benefit that the gun crew sergeant's conversation on his telephone link and orders could be heard. We saw a group of what looked like Hurricanes flying up Southampton Water just beyond Hythe. The sergeant requested confirmation of identification by telephone but, before he had a reply, the planes turned over Totton and came back over Southampton at roughly barrage balloon height and merrily blazed away. The sight of balloon after balloon going down in smoke and flames soon dispelled identification problems as nine ME109 aircraft swept past, leaving seven balloons as flaming markers in their wake. The Bofors barked as its surprised crew belatedly attempted to extract some vengeance, but they were too late and the 109s flew off unscathed. The gap now apparent in the balloon barrage looked ominously like a pathway to our works. Later that day we heard that Rollasons at Croydon had been bombed and damaged. This apparently minor attack had repercussions far more than was ever thought until more detailed information became available after the war; in fact it may well be the hinge on which the Battle of Britain turned in our favour. Although it means departing from my main theme it may be opportune to insert the details at this stage, as it is mostly information I have gleaned from a variety of sources over the last ten years — some as recent as 1982 and 1983, when the Deputy Editor of the Southampton *Southern Echo* asked if I could help a Lancashire author with some details for a book he was researching.

One result of this was that, in turn, I was able to gain from him information pertinent to my story to which he had obtained from an ex-Luftwaffe Officer, who had actually participated in parts of the account I am about to render.

It concerns a Luftwaffe Group which, although it had a relatively short existence — its active service life lasted only a few months in the summer of 1940 — played a significant role in the German air attacks on Britain during that period.

What is not commonly realised is that with aircraft, as in so many other walks of life, there are 'horses for courses', and in this respect there were major policy differences in the long term thinking of the R.A.F. compared with that of the German Luftwaffe regarding the class, type, and function of the aircraft they ordered. Basically the Luftwaffe was organised and equipped to fight from a territorial, rather than a functional, war footing, and did not take into proper account the circumstances that might (and did) arise in the perpetual changes due to the moves and countermoves of war.

The R.A.F. had clearly delineated Commands applicable to specific roles — i.e. Fighter, Bomber and Coastal Commands — whereas the German Air Fleets were mainly organised for support roles to their armies as they operated on the Continental land mass.

The intricate details of this, and other differences in tactics and strategy, which had a marked effect on the final outcome of the wartime bombing, are explained more fully in *Night Bombing* by Hector Hawton (Nelson 1944).

These different approaches to the problem of bombing, particularly in daylight and over a country with a newly-developed defensive system, plus fighter aircraft superior to their own, instigated a German rethink.

After the fall of France, some reassessment of the activities of the German Air Force's performance took place, and in some quarters the first doubts about the Stuka dive-bombers had led to the formation of Test Group (Erprobungsgruppe) 210, a mixture of Messerschmitt 109s and 110s equipped to carry bombs, the idea being to use their speed to get into the target and their basic fighter capabilities to fight their way out. Under their Commander, a dynamic Swiss-born German, named Walter Rubensdörffer, they trained at Rechlin, near the Baltic, and adopted a low angle dive-bombing technique as distinct from the Stuka's almost vertical dive, and by July 1940 were operationally posted to the Denain airfield as part of Kesselring's Air Fleet 2. They quickly proved their mettle by sinking a ship on their first strike, then went on to make many fast and incisive thrusts against shore-based targets. Manston, probably the R.A.F.'s most exposed fighter airfield, was visited a number of times, the high cliffs effectively masking radar screening, and from wave top height, TG210 would suddenly appear over the cliff edge, guns blazing and bombs dropping. So frightening were these attacks that, sad to relate, a high proportion of Manston's ground staff took shelter in tunnels off the cliff sides and refused to come out for many days, despite pleas and sometimes threats from the Officers.

We now know that 13th August was to be the commencement of the German Air Forces' main attack to obliterate the R.A.F. Fighter Command's opposition, as the pre-requisite to the plan for invasion. To them, this day was called 'Adler Tag' (Eagle Day), and to give them the advantage of surprise, TG210 was detailed to knock out five of the radar stations on the South-East Coast. Despite the skill and execution of this task, no vital damage was done and, of these radar stations, none were out of action on the next day, although another group bombed the southern stations, and Ventnor was put out of action for three weeks.

The next two days were busy ones indeed for TG210. On 15th August, Rubensdörffer's Squadron was ordered to bomb Kenley Airfield but, through some mistake in navigation or information, they bombed Croydon Aerodrome which, being in the Greater London area, was contrary to the express orders of Hitler himself, and there were demands by the Fuhrer for the court-martialling of those responsible for the failure to comply with his instructions. This was subsequently dropped when it was found that Rubensdörffer, and his second-in-command, had both perished when Hurricanes, ironically up from Croydon, caught them just after the raid had taken place and shot them down. Hitler's instruction was a cynical attempt to appear to comply with President Roosevelt's letter to the combatants at the outbreak of War to refrain from bombing centres of civil population. The R.A.F. wasted men and machines dropping leaflets until the Germans bombed Rotterdam. Nine days later, night attacks on South-Eastern London enraged Winston Churchill whose Cabinet instructed that a night raid be mounted against Berlin, and Bomber Command duly obliged on the night of the 25th/26th August.

This action not only discomforted the braggart Goering but enraged his Fuhrer, and right at the moment when the R.A.F. were hard-pressed, the Germans switched to concentrate mainly on London, thus providing just the relaxation the airfields needed. Other targets were not totally ignored.

From then on, in Southampton, it became a matter of increasing alarums and excursions by day and night, and although sometimes the warnings from our 'delayed system' were very short, the enemy action did not appear to be aimed at our works, and from my Bofors gun position on the bridge, I had a good view of the daylight activities. I saw Flight Lieutenant Nicholson and his partner shot down, but did not see the actual deed that made him the only Fighter Command Victoria Cross of the war. His partner baled out but his parachute failed him and death came to him in the back garden of a house next to where one of my workmates lived.

Most of the bombings were by very small numbers of planes, and it was peculiar how much of the effort affected areas more adjacent to the Thornycroft Shipbuilding Yard. One such event took place on the afternoon of 23rd August. The warning was delayed, so that by the time I started up the dirt road, anti-aircraft guns were in action including the one I was headed for. A glance to my right showed a low flying German plane on a parallel course with me, but of much more immediate concern was the winking lights from his upper gunner's position, and the zips and sputs on the road near me, as he ranged his gun along to attempt to silence 'my' Bofors.

A girl, running beside me, screamed hysterically and leaped forward, which was quite the wrong way to go. With a diving rugby tackle I brought her down and rolled her and myself into an empty sandbagged rifle position at the side of the road.

Peering over the top I saw the German plane release its bombs in line with Thornycroft's but they overshot, missing the target completely, but laying a line of destruction up Obelisk Road, and into Archery Gardens and St. Anne's Road. As I began to climb out of the sandbagged haven, the guns started blazing away again and coming up river at a similar low level was another German plane. His line of attack was almost pointed directly at me. I heard the gun crew sergeant yell 'open sights', and the crew ignored the predictor instructions and used the tracer lines from the shells as they winged their way toward the enemy.

As there must have been at least another four Bofors at other sites doing much the same, the intensity of the anti-aircraft fire caused the plane to swerve away toward the river just as he dropped his bombs, which plummeted down in a line which fortunately was mostly water, although one hit the Corporation Destructor in the yard at Chapel on the opposite river bank.

With me, on this day, was a fellow worker named Hilton, and as the first bomber's 'stick' had appeared to go towards the Archery Grove area where his wife and child resided, he asked if I would go with him to see if all was well. We jog trotted up Portsmouth Road, turned down St. Anne's Road intending to go down Temple Road, but a woman rushed out of the corner house, begging for assistance.

Telling Hilton to carry on home, I went with the woman through a door in a wall, where inside on a garden seat was a man with a nasty wound to his right thigh. Other people there had ripped away his trouser leg, and his broken femur was projecting through the gash, strings of torn muscle hung down, but worst of all was the blood gushing from what looked to me like a torn artery. The poor chap was calling 'Mother, Mother!' and it was strange how pathetic this sounded from a big man.

What little first aid I learned years before in the Boys' Brigade and St. John Ambulance came back in a flash. The pressure point in the groin! I got the others to help me lay him down and then with one thumb on the other I bore down until the gushing became just a trickle. However, there was a snag. It took all my weight and strength on those two thumbs to hold back the forcing blood, and after about a minute I knew I would not last very long. I asked a man to go out to the street and get three or four more men. Just as I was almost at the end of my tether they appeared; one fortunately being a first-aider. He took over from me with the thumb over thumb technique, and two others said they would take turns but, 'as I was a warden, would I get help?' Suddenly it occurred to me that having a Service type steel helmet which I had painted black, here was a chance to use it — official or not. That Service type tin helmet served me well. An uncle gave it to me with a Service gas mask haversack (empty) to play with when I was nine years old. They had been his own in France during the 1914-18 War.

I stepped out into St. Anne's Road and stopped the first car I saw and asked the driver to take me to the Woolston Fire Station where there was an ambulance post. As we arrived the fire engine was just coming out, so I hopped on to the running board and told the driver I wanted an ambulance urgently. It speaks well for that driver (a big man who I believe was called 'Tiny') and my tin hat, that, without hesitation, he climbed down, told another fireman to take over and, in less than a minute, he and I were in the ambulance and on our way.

Suffice to say that the man was saved and, years later after the war, when I returned to live in Woolston, I often saw him riding his bicycle. I never did learn his name.

Two days later, an after dark raid which lasted five hours, but was mainly conducted by single German bombers at 10-20 minute intervals, dropped more bombs in the Woolston area, again noticeably more adjacent to Thornycroft's Shipyard than the aircraft factory which, in the light of newspaper reports of the battle for command of the skies, seemed most odd. It was not until 1969 that I discovered that on the German Luftwaffe Intelligence briefing and air crew maps that half of Thornycroft's yard, nearest the Weston shore, was clearly marked as the 'A.V. Roe, Aviation Works?' How this 'intelligence' was fed into the German system I do not suppose we will ever know, but I believe this error probably gave us at least one or two months extra production time, just when it was most needed. It is even more remarkable when one recalls that the German mailplane catapulted from the liner 'Bremen' pre-war used to alight in the River Itchen and used Supermarine's slipway for transferring mail and refuelling. Another interesting fact emerged from the study of the German aircrew maps. They were mostly 'British' Ordnance Survey maps with the German terminology superimposed over the English print.

We now know that early in September, there were meetings of the very senior commanders of the Luftwaffe, including one with Goering, in which a certain amount of acrimonious discussion took place. One set of officers felt that the R.A.F. were finished —

misled by their own statistics that there could only be a handful of fighters left — but the opposite view, led by Air Marshal Von Sperrle, argued that there were still about 1,000 fighters in being as they had not smashed the source of supply — the factories.

Von Sperrle was not quite accurate in his estimate of fighters available to Fighter Command — 600 would have been nearer — but under the driving force of Beaverbrook, the supply of aircraft was not the problem that worried Dowding, C in C Fighter Command; he was running short of pilots.

There must also have been some reappraisal of Intelligence, as prior to September, air attacks on factories had been mainly on those producing bombers — Short's at Belfast and Rochester, etc.

On 4th September, about twenty ME110s went to Weybridge and hit the Vickers Works, but were intercepted by a Hurricane squadron which shot down six, but six got through causing heavy casualties and destruction. This factory was producing Wellington bombers and either the association of the Vickers name misled them or, as I believe, the raid was really intended for the Hawker Hurricane factory on the other side of the aerodrome.

On 11th September, our delayed alarm sounded and I went quickly to my Bofors gun view point. The sergeant told me there was 'a red alert and 50 plus bombers headed in this direction'. In youthful anticipation of action I stayed. Fortunately for us, they went to the north and we had fleeting glimpses of bombers attacking Eastleigh Aerodrome. They hit the Cunliffe-Owen factory killing over 50 people. Once again it seems to me this was a mistake. At the time, Cunliffe-Owen were mainly bringing Lockheed Hudson aircraft, brought from America, up to the standard required by the R.A.F., yet only 400 yards away were the old Southampton Airport hangars from which the main supply of Spitfires was still being made.

Meanwhile, between the two dates, Hitler, infuriated by the raid on Berlin ordered by Churchill, instructed Goering to bomb London by day and night. On 7th September London's long ordeal began, but that is another story adequately related elsewhere. Our interest is that the massive forces of German bomber aircraft used were overnight diverted from the effort applied to the original, and almost successful, strategic aims required to effectively invade this island. It also meant that fighter cover for the German bombers coming in daylight was stretched to their maximum range, and they had little or no resources of fuel to engage our fighters when they flew into the bomber masses and wrought a savage vengeance.

Some experienced Luftwaffe Commanders, whilst complying with their orders, continued to carry on with the strategic plans with whatever resources were available. Into this category came TG210, and also Von Sperrle's KG54. (Note: Kesselring commanded Air Fleet 2, which stretched from Denmark to Le Havre and included TG210, and Von Sperrle commanded Air Fleet 3, from Le Havre down to the border of unoccupied France).

My theory regarding the Cunliffe-Owen raid being a mistake has recently been confirmed by one of the pilots who participated in it. Oblt. Otto Hintze flew his bomb-laden Messerschmitt BF109, E4, (service serial No. 2024, squadron marking Yellow 6) with Erprobungsgruppe 210 in this the first raid on the Southampton area by this prestigious squadron, and via the author I mentioned earlier who is researching for a book on Erpro. 210 and visited Otto at his home in Germany in the Spring of 1983, I learned that the attack was supposed to be on the Spitfire Final Assembly and Flight Hangars at Eastleigh.

This is the raid which Jeffrey Quill attributes to July 1940, but when I drew his attention to the Southampton City Archives which report no raids in July 1940 and my own diary entries, he conceded he must have been misled, and bearing in mind his work load at that time, and his spell of active service in Kent at the height of the Battle of Britain during August, such an error in dateline is excusable. I only wrote to amend his book on minor factual errors, because it must rank as a valuable historical contribution from his unique position of having tested every mark of Spitfire and Seafire that flew.

Oblt. Otto Hintze was shot down and made prisoner on 29th October 1940 by Squadron Leader Barton flying a Hurricane from 249 Squadron, after a raid on North Weald Aerodrome. Ironically, he was also in the raid on Croydon which precipitated the Luftwaffe's major change in strategy.

Otto Hintze who took part in the Me: 109's raid on Cunliffe-Owen factory on 11th September 1940.   *J. Vasco*

Sunday September 15th 1940. The scene on the south side of the 'iron' railway bridge in Woolston after the attack by Erprobungsgruppe 210 led by Martin Lutz.

Southern Newspapers

Above: Martin Lutz who led the raid by Erpro: 210 on 15th September 1940.   *J. Vasco*

Centre left: Alf Fleet and C.R.R. This photograph was taken just two hours before the air raid of Sunday 15th September 1940.

Left: Wharncliffe Road, where the shelter collapsed. The houses behind the rubble heap were damaged in later raids, but the brick heap marks the site of the shelter.

Chapter Eleven
Sunday September 15th 1940

It was now only a matter of time before our factories at Woolston would be attacked. A detachment of soldiers took up discreet residence and set up and manned a machine gun position on the roof of the new office block, whilst other patrolled outside with rifles and fixed bayonets. At half a dozen points inside the factory were positioned conical steel structures. They stood about seven feet high, were about one yard diameter at the base and two feet diameter at the domed top cover. A door, hinging outwards, took up roughly a third of the circumference, and slits of about six inches long by half an inch wide were cut at eye-level at four positions. This was for damage reporting to the factory air raid control centre. Two persons were required (as volunteers) to observe bombing and report, by the telephone installed, to control as and when bombing was taking place.

The two volunteers for my shop ('K' shop), were both contemporaries and friends of mine, and to this day I still think that they were very brave to undertake these unpaid duties. To Frank and Ron let this be a belated, but sincere, tribute, and similarly to all the others who carried out the same task in other parts of the Works.

Sunday, 15th September was a bright summer's day. I worked the half shift until noon and at five o'clock I was having tea with a girl friend and her parents at their bungalow just off Peartree Green — about half a mile from Woolston shopping centre and the Spitfire factories.

The air raid sirens sounded about 5.30p.m. but we continued with our meal. People generally did not show too much concern, as so many times the town's warnings went and nothing happened. Unless one heard aircraft or gunfire, sirens were practically ignored. However, about five minutes later the sharp crack of the bigger anti-aircraft guns were heard, and this noise was followed by the closer, faster bark of Bofors. The Anderson shelter was only about 30 feet from the back door, and we four rapidly made tracks for it. Being last I paused to see what was about, and sweeping in was a rectangular-shaped formation of twin finned aircraft at about 2,000-3,000 feet, and there was no mistaking the intention of their visit. I leapt into the shelter as the whistle of the bombs commenced, the ground trembled and odd bits of earth vibrated down from that covering the shelter. The anti-aircraft fire was now bursting almost overhead and odd thumps sounded in the vicinity, which at the time we thought might be unexploded bombs or anti-aircraft shells, but later turned out to be some of the bricks and debris from the bombs falling half a mile away.

Almost as suddenly as it began, the noise faded away, and we climbed out of the shelter and saw just the top of a settling dust cloud. Alf, my girl's father, and I, were both members of our respective employer's Light Rescue Teams, (everyone had some A.R.P. duty as well as their normal employment in those days), so with our black tin hats on, and gas masks slung, we mounted our cycles and pedalled furiously to Woolston, and in less than two minutes we reached the devastated area.

A steel railway bridge spans Bridge Road just North of the centre of Woolston's main shopping area. A great hole, with flames leaping out from fractured gas mains, spanned the full width of the road. On our left was the railway station goods yard seemingly untouched, but to our right had been a row of shops with residential accommodation over the top, and these were just one long heap of debris, of bricks and broken wood. Apart from the hiss and crackle of the burning gas in the crater there was an unworldly silence and stillness — a stunned effect; but then, to our utter amazement, a figure appeared on the top of the debris,

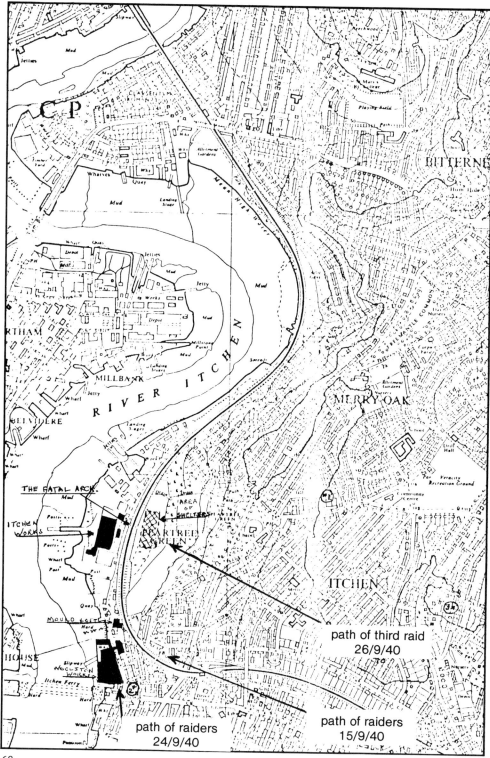

path of third raid
26/9/40

path of raiders
24/9/40

path of raiders
15/9/40

carefully picking his way and testing each forward foothold. What made it all the more remarkable was that he was carrying, piggyback fashion, a woman. We called out to see if he required help, but he shouted back that he could manage, but for us to get 'over there' indicating the road to his left.

The area he indicated was a triangle of small completely residential streets, with Defender Road, Tankerville Road, Shamrock Road, and Ailsa Lane, leading off from Bridge Road (the main road), connecting up to Highlands Road, with Wharncliffe Road forming the curving back road — the whole lot contained in a quarter mile square. No sooner had we gone a few yards into Defender Road that it was obvious that this area had taken a lot of the bombs intended for the Spitfire factory; in fact not a single bomb had struck the factory, as I found out the next day.

Alf and I must have been the first persons from outside the bombed area, but now people began to emerge from their shelters and noises became apparent again. A woman called to me from her downstair broken window. Obviously suffering from shock, she told me she could not open the room door, and that she and her daughter had taken refuge under the table.

The house was standing, but only just. Cracks ran up all its walls and it leaned. The front door had been blown open so I went into the hall to the front room door. Its frame and surrounding brickwork were badly distorted and a quick glance up the staircase showed blue sky. I yelled through the door for the woman and her child to pull the table close to the window and get under it again. Satisfied when this was done, I turned the door handle and pushed as hard as I could with my shoulder. The door burst inwards with me quickly following. Behind me debris started to fall and ominous cracking sounds followed. I jumped on to the table and kicked the remaining pieces of glass out of the bottom half of the window, and then with all the speed possible, got mother and child out on to the road outside.

The poor little house, so recently a home, gave a lurch and leaned over further — like so many in that area that day it was destined for eventual demolition.

Neighbours took the woman and child away, and from almost opposite a young man came across and asked if I could retrieve his motor cycle as I had a steel helmet! When I saw where it was, it was not difficult to follow his reasoning. It was leaning against the side wall of the house which showed even greater signs of structural damage than the one I had just left. The roof was gone and the distorted brickwork looked decidedly shaky. Kicking pieces of debris out of the path I advanced upon the motor cycle, brushed away by hand the odd brick and slate resting on it, and gave it a quick pull upright and pushed it towards the road. Thank goodness it was not in gear, or left with brakes on, as no sooner had I taken its weight from the wall, than the wall began to collapse. Despite some nimble footwork, one brick did catch me fair and square on the top of my head. It made a small dent in my helmet, and that was all, but I would hate to have been without it. I passed the motor cycle to its owner and we stood there and watched as the remainder of the house slid, almost in slow motion, to just another heap of rubble.

Whilst these episodes were taking place, Alf had gone ahead further up the road, and he now came running back calling for me to join him. I grabbed my cycle and ran with him to Wharncliffe Road, where he said a street surface shelter had collapsed, as the result of a direct hit on the house on the opposite side of the road. Five years before, when I was a van delivery boy for a bakery business, the bombed house was one of my calls, and I knew the couple and their daughter who lived there. Now it was just another mound of debris.

The problem however, was the collapsed shelter. It appeared that a couple, with their young daughter, were making a Sunday afternoon visit to his widowed mother. They had gone to this brick-walled and concrete-roofed surface shelter almost immediately following the warning sirens, and then the old lady wanted a blanket to keep her warm, and the child had asked for her dolly. Mum went for the dolly, and dad for the blanket, but before they could get back, the bombs were falling and they were forced to lay in the hallway. The shelter, being between them and the house directly hit, no doubt saved them, as the blast caved in the wall of the shelter farthest from them. The six inch thick roof toppled in, and then the vacuum force, following the explosion, did the rest. Before we could achieve anything it was the large heavy pieces of the concrete roof that had somehow to be moved. We had hopes, because we knew that inside the shelter were support walls, and that none of the roof concrete appeared lower than about two feet above the road level.

By this time there were at least half a dozen or so able-bodied men helping, and with the aid of some roof timbers from the destroyed house we levered away a piece of concrete that was leaning against a corner of the brickwork, which, at roughly five feet, was the highest still standing.

With the strength and fury that is born of desperation, we all heaved, pushed, and pulled wherever we could, and then suddenly the concrete piece swung out and on to the road. In the now-exposed corner was a wicker chair and a very dusty old lady sat with her hands up to her face. A little, single, trickle of blood had run down between the middle fingers of her right hand. Someone said, 'OK Ma, you'll be all right now', and hands went out to help her stand, but as they touched her, the hands fell from the face and the body began to fall forwards in the chair. I could not believe what I was seeing as I looked straight into the eyes that would see no more. I had never seen a dead person before, and apart from the trickle of blood that had emanated from her nose, there was not another mark. As the men lifted her out, I knelt down and peered under the next lump of concrete that seemed to be supported by the remains of an inner wall, and rubble from the collapsed brickwork.

Pulling the loose brick and rubble away and throwing it out behind me I penetrated into a cavity and saw the foot and shoe of a little girl. I yelled for help which was readily to hand, and a group of men prised up the piece of concrete roof that had formed a lid over this separate chamber until it was raised high enough for me to lean in and lift the child out. There was not a mark on her, but the whiteness of the skin and the limp limbs, plus the wide open unseeing eyes told me that the struggle had been in vain. I knelt there on one knee, cradling the poor little soul in my arms, and unashamedly letting my own tears run down my cheeks to drop without hindrance on the pale face in my lap.

Someone said, 'Bring her out, son', and as I stood up and turned, there before me stood her father, his face distorted with the sudden double tragedy that had been thrust upon him. He held out his arms, and without a single word I gave his dead child to him. I found out later that he had walked away, three-quarters of a mile, to the nearest casualty station, in Sydney House, bearing his pathetic burden in the hope that she was not dead.

For myself, nothing would ever seem quite the same again. The tears dried themselves, but inside I felt a controlled cold, but terrible calm, and in that moment I knew what was meant by the 'killer instinct'; and even now, over forty years later, although the murderous thoughts that were uppermost at the time have long disappeared, that silent poignant episode that passed between the little girl's father and me remains as vivid in my memory as at the moment it occurred, and tears well up in my eyes as I write.

There are, I suppose, moments in most people's lives when suddenly and unexpectedly they are confronted with tragedy, or some other traumatic event over which they have no experience or control, that causes them to think on the great imponderables in life and death, and leads on to the inevitable questioning of the doctrines we hold. This was mine.

Fortunately, there was no time to dwell on it then. Someone came from further up the road to see if anyone could help a woman whose husband had been killed in the raid on

Cunliffe-Owen's, and was lying in his open coffin in the front-room, smothered with ceiling plaster and broken glass. I did not fancy that job, and a voice calling from the destroyed house gave me another one and banished all other thoughts from my mind. Someone had heard faint sounds of human voices from inside the ruins. Carefully we began to tunnel into the wreckage, stopping now and again to get a bearing on the voice, and calling to whoever it was that help was coming. It seemed slow and hazardous and then someone called out, 'Gas!' By now a 'pukka' air raid warden was on hand. 'Douse all cigarettes, men', he ordered, then crawled forward into the tunnel himself.

I leaned back against my bike and the nearest garden fence; it was dusty and tricky work forming a human chain passing bricks and wood and bits of furniture out as the tunnel progressed. Now there was a spell whilst the warden made his assessment. He did not take long either, and quickly but with quiet authority, he ordered the men to work no more than five minutes at the end of the tunnel, or less if they felt any effect from the gas leak.

He turned to me and said, 'Is that your bike, lad?' I said it was so he said, 'I want a gas party here quickly' and asked would I go to Woolston Police Station, which was the local Incident Control Centre, and tell them his requirements.

There were only two ways I could outflank that burning crater by the railway bridge, and the quickest and shortest way was to use the bridge where 'my' Bofors was located. Pedalling furiously, I barged through the gun site, noticing that, although so near to the action, they seemed intact. I carried my bike down the steps, then set off again. This was the first I had seen of the damage on the other side of the railway line. More shops, adjacent to the steel railway bridge, on both sides of the road, were badly damaged. I proceeded up the hill to the railway station. To my dismay there was a rope across the road and a policeman on guard. As I approached he put up his hand and called out, 'unexploded bomb.'

Once again the black helmet must have helped, as before I reached him I yelled out, 'I want a gas party urgently', and for him to lower the rope. He did, and I whizzed by riding on the footpath, as far away as I could get from a small hole in the road. As soon as I had turned the corner I heard the 'crump' and knew that my luck was holding.

Once in the Police Station a helpful sergeant took my message and telephoned the Corporation yard, and that was that. I sat down, and someone brought me a cup of tea which really tasted good. Suddenly reaction set in and I felt very tired. The sergeant asked me for details of the situation from which I had come. He alerted the ambulance and fire service, and then suggested perhaps I should go home.

Since writing the above, I have had copies of the A.R.P. 'Incident Reports' appertaining to the raid on Sunday, 15th September, 1940 sent to me. They confirm very largely my account and add that '9 died, 19 were seriously wounded, and 23 more casualties received treatment. Thirty-four buildings were completely destroyed, 81 had to be demolished, 351 were damaged but repairable, and 755 suffered minor damage'. Confirmation is also there that, 'the only unexploded bomb was in Garton Road and exploded about 2 hours later after the raid, and that the Authorities had difficulty in obtaining information from the bombed area due to communications disruption'. This no doubt explains why the police sergeant sought to obtain my 'on-site' report.

I went back to my girl's home and told them briefly what was happening, and about an hour later Alf returned with the wonderful news that they had got all three, Mr and Mrs Diaper, and their daughter, Gwen, out of the demolished house, shocked, smothered in dust and dirt, but relatively unhurt. They were huddled together under the staircase. Then I went home; it must have gone 9p.m. I told my mum and dad the brief outline of events, and then went to bed and slept like a log until it was time to go to work the next morning.

Chapter Twelve
The Tuesday Air-raid

Like so many others, I was amazed to find the Woolston works intact when I clocked on at 7.30a.m. the next morning. If memory serves me correctly, only one skylight was broken, and that by a piece of rubble.

With the benefit of hindsight, and some research, there appear to be three reasons for such luck. The first, is that the ground level rose sharply from the works site, which was only two or three feet above the high tide level of the Itchen River, so that 'my' Bofors gun on the railway footbridge was a good fifty feet above that level, and from there one completely overlooked the Woolston works, and the houses in the road between (Laurel Road). Wharncliffe Road was even higher than that, and from Bridge Road to Wharncliffe Road, a distance of no more than 100 yards, the Ordnance Survey maps show a 30 to 40 feet increase in ground height; so add the height of a normal house, and the total must have been approximately 100 feet — a natural screen from aircraft coming in low from the East. Secondly, the anti-aircraft guns really put up a very good and sustained barrage, but the final contributions for the lack of success came from the Luftwaffe itself. Last of all, the attack coming from the eastern direction meant that the factory target was at its narrowest.

The Woolston factory was roughly 600 feet long (that is along the river's edge), and irregular in its width, being approximately 390 feet at the floating bridge end, and 270 feet at its new office block end, so the best line of attack would have been on a north/south axis, and in view of its narrowness, in single file, each bomber acting independently. However, on Sunday, 15th September, we were being attacked by Test Group 210! After Von Rubensdörffer's death on 15th August, the Group's command had been passed to Hauptmann Von Boltenstern, who was shot down and killed on 4th September leading a raid attempting to knock out the radar station at Poling in Kent. Since then, Hauptmann Martin Lutz had been in command, and it was he who led this attack of eighteen ME110s, each with two bombs; some accounts say 15 aircraft and they may be right — I did not stop to count!

The Messerschmitt 110 was originally intended as a twin-engined two-seater fighter to protect German bombers, but in that role had proved unsatisfactory, and had been adapted for this bombing use, as mentioned earlier. The trouble was that there was no proper bomb aiming equipment, and the tactic devised was to keep a tight formation, go into a shallow dive so that the lead pilot could observe the target for as long as possible, then, on his judgement and order over the radio, for all bombs to be released simultaneously. This method has recently been substantially confirmed by Otto Hintze.

By this method, and the other factors mentioned, the Sunday attack was about one hundred yards adrift; to the right and short on his line of flight, with the tragic results described for many homes — but without causing any hindrance to the vital production of Spitfires.

Another item of importance became known as a result of this raid. Up to this date (15th September) TG210 was thought to have been based at Calais-Marck, but on their return flight after the bombing they were intercepted and attacked by fighters of 607 Squadron R.A.F. west of the Needles without incurring any losses. The Squadron's report mentioned that 'TG210 seemed to be heading for the Cherbourg peninsula'.

From this our intelligence people deduced that this crack group had been moved south and, with their known propensity for attacking high priority targets, drew the appropriate conclusions. My own interpretation was that TG210 had been switched from Kesselring's

Air Fleet 2, to Hugo Von Sperrle's Air Fleet 3, and it appeared that each Commander had his own Intelligence Department. This assumption is borne out to some extent by the captured aircrew maps, one showing clearly Thorneycroft's marked as A. V. Roe's Aviation Assembly Works, and another (now displayed in the Southampton Hall of Aviation) equally clearly marks out and identifies the Spitfire works as such. Oblt. Otto Hintze has since informed me, via my author friend, that at the time TG210 was in fact based at Denain, south of Paris, and was using both Cherbourg and Calais-Marck airfields as forward satellite bases for refuelling and rearming purposes. Von Sperrle, the airman who's experience went back to the First World War, as opposed to Kesselring the Army Commander, had told a meeting of the German high-ranking officers which included Kesselring that his tactics of persisting in bombing airfields without eliminating the fighter supply factories would fail.

After Hitler and Goering had decided to bomb London into submission, practically all Kesselring's, and most of Von Sperrle's bombing forces were used to that end from 7th September onwards, day and night, but Von Sperrle had not taken his eye off the ball, and whenever an opportunity arose, whatever bombers he could spare went for the factories.

Subsequent to the Sunday raid there were the odd alarms, both by day and night. Some must have been caused by reconnaissance aircraft photographing what should have been one well-shattered factory, and apart from this, very little happened in our locality for over a week. The weather also deteriorated, particularly on the first Monday and Tuesday, and the next Sunday was foggy during the day, but it cleared for a nasty night raid to be made on London. It was our lull before the storm.

On Tuesday, 24th September 1940, it was a typically bright autumn day. The morning was uneventful and, as usual, I cycled home for lunch. Our cycle racks were on the ground floor of the Mould Loft building, built a couple of years earlier on the opposite side of the road, and 50-60 yards north of the new office block. I mention this for one other item that I think will interest those interested in the career of R. J. Mitchell. The Mould Loft was normally out of bounds to most of us but, during 1938/9, the local evening Technical College ran a course on Lofting, and the instructor was Don Snooks, who was the Chief Loftsman at Supermarine's. I took this course, among others, and got a first class pass. Naturally Don was looking for 'bright boys', and the idea was mooted that I might join his team. I did not do so, but he did show me round, and there at one end was a half scale 'mock-up' of a twin-engined fighter. Most people will have read and seen drawings of R. J.'s four-engined bomber, in fact at Woolston in 'K' shop we built two fuselages, but I wonder if anyone can bring out more information on what must have been, this, his last design? Since this was written, a book entitled *Supermarine Aircraft from 1914* has been published, and shows a photograph of this 'mock-up' as I saw it, although the date attributed of 1936 is incorrect, because neither the building or 'mock-up' were in being then.

At half past one on Tuesday, 24th, we were working to the delayed warning system, the town sirens having sounded some minutes before. Before our works klaxon could sound, the sharp cracks of the big anti-aircraft guns at Netley were heard, and then the familiar bark of the Bofors. My working position was, as I have said, in 'K' shop, and that was at the end adjacent to the floating bridge. The works entrance was the other end, but there was a stores entrance at our end, and the internal door between workshop and store was now permanently opened in daytime as an emergency exit, and it was toward this that I made a rapid retreat.

By the time I had reached the road, the gunfire was terrific, and no sooner had I reached the newsagent's shop on the opposite corner, when I looked up and to my left, there they were, with the bombs already leaving their racks. Screened by the shop, I had no idea if anything else was coming from that direction, so I flattened myself into the gutter — and waited. The exploding bombs made the ground tremble and kick, and for a moment or so, although it seemed longer, there was just nothing one could do. Apart from that momentary glimpse, I did not see the bombers again, and my first indication that the danger was over was the cessation of gunfire.

I got to my feet and looked round, the works seemed all right, so I ran back to get my steel helmet and gas mask. On coming out again I became aware of a lot of activity at the north end of the road, so I ran that way to see what had happened.

Opposite the Woolston works entrance and new office block there had been built a paint and dope shop, and later on behind them, actually tunnelled into the rising ground, a first aid, casualty, and raid control centre.

People were now coming out with bags marked with red crosses, and metal stretchers, all heading for the Itchen works, just a few hundred yards up the road. I joined them, and soon people, running, walking and stumbling, came towards us from the opposite way. Some looked dirty, others limped, and almost all had that strained, shocked, look in their eyes.

Attempting to break through the opposing group, we drew level with the Itchen works. It was all too apparent, the cause of their distress. On my left the factory, untouched except for one tiny piece of corrugated outer cladding, but in front, in the roadway, and into the tunnel under the railway embankment were dozens of people, like a disturbed ant-hill, rushing back and forth, digging, grabbing, and pulling, all with frenzied speed. It took a moment or two to assess the situation, and then I too became one of the ants.

What had happened was the very thing that had been foreseen when I and others had declined to use the shelters. The whole bomb load had dropped short, and straddled the railway embankment (miraculously untouched) but had hit the shelters, the road, and the people who were making for them.

There were only three bombs on the works side of the railway, two whose crater edges literally touched right in the narrowing entrance to the tunnel, and one against the works fence, right alongside an air raid shelter, which had partially collapsed. On the other side of the railway there were many more, but I did not see them until the next day.

Tragic though it was, it was a blessing that the warning period was so short, otherwise, those who normally used these shelters from the Woolston works would have been choking the tunnel entrance, and would have run right into disaster. As it was, it was obvious that there were a lot of casualties; some poor souls had been blown up on to the railway embankment and lay like bundles of old clothing. Others had been blown into the embankment lower down, and were buried, or partly buried, by the earth thrown up from the craters. Here and there a limb protruded, or perhaps just the colour of the overall or jersey could be seen, and it was to these that the survivors who had collected their wits, and we luckier ones from the Woolston factory, turned our attention, tearing away the earth with our hands, lifting them out, trying artificial respiration, calling for stretchers, and of course inevitably having to leave some lying there when we realised they were beyond our aid.

God alone knows how long we struggled there, or how long we laboured on the collapsed shelter, when it was found that people were trapped inside. I can recall the sirens sounding a warning, and remember seeing a German aircraft about a mile away travelling south, obviously a photo-reconnaissance plane, who collected a few bursts from the anti-aircraft guns.

Thinking this was a prelude to another attack some, including me, started to move away, but a chap from the Design Office stood on top of the shelter and called out. 'Never mind them, let's have you all here!' I have always admired that man for that, as panic and flight was stopped dead in its tracks by his solo example of leadership at that moment.

By this time (whatever it was), funny little canvas covered ambulances began to arrive, and I began to help to load the stretchers in. Each ambulance took four of the metal stretchers I had seen earlier. Turning back to the damaged shelter after loading one of the ambulances, I noticed a man walking toward the Sports Club building which was at the far end of the forecourt of the factory. He wobbled a bit as he walked, and then, as he reached the club, he put his left arm out for support, then slowly crumpled to the ground. As I seemed to be the only person to see this, I ran over to help. He was dazed and probably shocked, and he had most likely just come out of the damaged shelter — I will never know — but I helped him to his feet and, with his arm round my shoulders and mine around his back, I began walking him to the road and towards the casualty station. Half-way down the road, one of the ambulances stopped, and I sat him on the floor of the gangway between the two pairs of stretchers, climbed in myself, and off we went.

At the casualty station entrance it was all coming and going. I helped the chap down who I had collected, and a local G.P. arrived on an autocycle just as I was giving a hand unloading the stretcher cases from the ambulance. To my astonishment he said, 'Don't waste time on him — put him over there.' I looked, and then I got the message, as the stretcher case we were so carefully handling was dead.

Once the ambulance was unloaded, it was speedily reloaded, with the stretcher cases from inside the casualty station who required hospital treatment. What I have not mentioned before, was that these canvas-covered ambulances were driven by women — some of them quite young. When this particular ambulance was filled, the lady driver came round to the back and asked if I would go with her on the journey to the hospital, as she said unloading was a bit of a problem at the hospital end. I agreed, and got into the back, and we drove off. Looking at the four men on the stretchers I wondered if there was anything I could do to make them more comfortable. The first thing I noticed, was that only two had pillows, and that one fellow's head was bouncing up and down on the tubular crossbar of the metal stretcher. It was plainly causing him some discomfort, so I supported his head with one hand.

We were heading for the Royal South Hants Hospital in Southampton and, as we reached the main road at the bottom of Athelstan Road, one of the chaps with a pillow made a noise which I can only describe like a punctured tyre. His head flopped to one side and one look told me he had died. With what to me, even today, seems a bit callous, I pulled the pillow from under his head and placed it carefully under the head I had previously supported. There was a reason for this.

During the week after that Sunday raid, I was talking to a St. John Ambulance Brigade instructor, and seeing that I was upset by those events, he gave me a piece of advice which stood me in good stead from then on, and still does — over forty years on; it was this. 'If you are ever faced with an accident, or injury, get in and help, get the blood on your hands and remember one thing — it is not your blood! If you cannot be of assistance, then bugger off and get out of the way.' Over the years I have had good reason to respect that advice, and I suppose the pillow shifting was its first usage.

When we passed over Northam Bridge the warning sirens wailed again, and my lady ambulance driver drew into the curb and stopped. Through the canvas flap I asked what was wrong, and she told me she could not go on as she was afraid. I jumped out of the back, said, 'Move over, love', got into the driving seat and drove on to the hospital. We unloaded our casualties, handed them to the hospital staff, then with a dab at her eyes, and a bright, if forced, smile, my lady driver drove me back to the Woolston works.

If that lady should perchance ever read this, please do not think anything other than what I have always thought, that you were very brave, and that your example helped me, as I hope that for a few moments I may have helped you.

By the time we returned, it seemed that everything had been attended to, so as it had gone 5p.m., I went to the cycle shed and rode slowly home. Our house was a semi-detached of the older variety — no bathroom, an outside loo, etc., with a side path to the back door. Halfway along the side of the house, my father had built a partition with a wooden, half-latticed door in it. As I opened it and pushed my cycle through, a few feet away stood my mother. She had been there a long time, just waiting and fearing for my safety. She was so relieved to see me and put her arm round my shoulder as we went into the house. This simple act — no words were spoken — just suddenly overwhelmed me and I burst into tears, sobbing bitterly, and saying, 'my poor mates', over and over again. Wisely, she let me sob it out and carried on preparing the tea. I had not given a thought throughout the whole of that afternoon that someone might be worrying about me. Its realisation was the straw that broke the camel's back and brought the tears.

Thankfully I had no difficulty in sleeping that night, and the next morning was back at work as were most of the other employees. Gradually we learned of the human cost of the previous day, just over 50 killed and 160 injured. The official Incident Report (No. 45) states that it was impossible to determine an exact number of casualties. Their approximation was 42 dead, 63 severely wounded and 98 with minor injuries. The curious thing was that I never recognised any of the dead or injured that I had seen, yet I must have known most of them, even if only by sight. Not even in retrospect years after could I ever put any recognition to anyone.

Later that Wednesday morning, my foreman, Bill Heaver, came over to me and told me quietly that one girl had been killed yesterday. He knew that a few weeks previously I had had quite a crush on her, and we had gone to the Grand Theatre together. She was a secretary, and known to the lads as 'the girl in green' because of the smart green outfit she wore, with a little fur hat. Her name was Peggy, Peggy Moon from Canada Road, and a lovelier girl one could not wish to know. Now she was dead, and how grateful I am that I was not the one who found her — but what a waste!

Years later, when researching, I found that this latest air raid was also carried out by TG210, and again led by Martin Lutz, this time with plenty of fighter cover including some from ZG76, but both bombers and escorting fighters were all ME110s. This time they did not get off unscathed, as ZG76 lost two aircraft (shot down), and TG210 one.

The Messerschmitt 110 of Balthaser Aretz, damaged by A/A in a raid on Southampton by Erpro: 210.   *J. Vasco*

Chapter Thirteen
The Thursday Air-raid

Martin Lutz was awarded the Knight's Cross for this raid, but three days later, leading 19 ME110 bombers with 30 Heinkel 111 bombers for a follow up wave, in an attack on the Bristol aeroplane factories, they were caught by five squadrons of fighters from Air Marshal Brand's 10 Group, near Yeovil. Lutz himself was shot down by Spitfires and died at his aircraft's controls near Cranborne Chase. The two raids on aircraft in the Bristol area are chronicled in a book *Luftwaffe Encore* by Ken Wakefield.

Wednesday evening, after work, I went up to the Itchen works, the crater holes had been filled, and I climbed to the top of the railway embankment and there saw where some of the other bombs had fallen among the lines of shelters. I took a photograph, strictly against regulations, but it was not very clear when developed.

Thursday 26th September started off as usual, with one notable change in my routine. Having been nearly caught in the factories by the 'delayed warning system' on the Tuesday, that idea was tacitly dropped, but in addition I had decided (amongst others) to leave my cycle against the factory wall outside the store's entrance doors.

At 4.15p.m. that afternoon, the town sirens sounded and the factory klaxons wailed out simultaneously. Once again I moved smartly out through the stores, and on to my cycle, and away up Portsmouth Road. With me was Fred, a young man who had joined our wheeling squad and was already showing some promise. He suggested we go to his home in Sholing, being not so far as my own home, which I agreed was all right with me. It was barely a mile away, and no sooner had we reached there than the guns opened up, and this time I could hear the aircraft. We lost no time in joining his mother and brother in the Anderson shelter in the garden.

The familiar crump of bombs and the full cacophony of anti-aircraft guns, plus the unmistakable sound of aircraft engines, seemed to fill the whole air. Once again as the sounds subsided, we emerged from the shelter and after a couple of minutes decided to return, although the 'all clear' had not sounded. As we were about to mount our cycles, for some unaccountable reason, I had a strong feeling that we should not go. Rather embarrassed, I told Fred that I wanted to stay for a few minutes longer. With his easy going manner he accepted my request, and a few minutes later, just as I was beginning to feel a bit of a chump, the anti-aircraft guns opened up again, and once more we dived into the shelter, as the second wave of bombers swept in. Again, all the similar noises were heard, and once they had ceased we proceeded to cycle back to work.

This time there was a rope stretched across Hazel Road at the floating bridge end, and soldiers with rifles and fixed bayonets were preventing access to all and sundry. Beyond them it was painfully obvious that this time the Luftwaffe had at last scored. Very little of the roof and windows remained. Bent and twisted steel structures protruded uncovered into the sky, and the road was littered with debris. There did not appear to be any fire. Gradually the crowd of returning employees built up, and soon an announcement was made for us to disperse in case of another raid, and return in the morning. I rode home via Peartree Green, and from there I could see that the Itchen works had been hit as well. Ironically, delivered to my home that very day was the aeronautical magazine *Flight*. Its main item that week was headed 'A real thoroughbred' and it was on the Spitfire. I still have it.

The next morning before 7.30a.m. a staff official informed us that we were to report to the local Labour Exchange, from whence we should be instructed what to do. In my case

ITCHEN
ASSEMBLY
UNIT
½ MILE

K SHOP

Top: Supermarine's Woolston factory after the raid of 26th September 1940.

Above: The photograph which I took from the Floating Bridge on 28th September.

Left: Interior view of bomb damage of 'P' shop, balcony in 'K' shop and immediately over my workplace. Note the superficiality of the damage.

they took down my name, address, trade, and 'K' shop number, and said, 'report again tomorrow after 9a.m.'. Much later I found out what had happened regarding the raid.

On the day before, to us the relatively quiet Wednesday, the Luftwaffe had carried out a sharp and effective attack on the Bristol Aircraft Works at Filton, near Bristol. This was in R.A.F. 10 Group's area, and they assumed, from their radar plots, that the main raid was intended for the Westland Aircraft factories at Yeovil.

Diversionary raids were made on Plymouth, Portland, Swanage, and Falmouth, and R.A.F. fighters were sent up to meet these attacks, plus three squadrons positioned to meet the supposed threat to Yeovil. However, behind this screen, fifty-eight Heinkel 111s, accompanied by other bombers from TG210, had made straight for Filton, with TG210 leading the way, until they turned east on a diversionary tactical sweep.

The raid was concentrated and effective. Production was halted and numerous casualties were suffered. The Heinkels were from KG55, and these raids took place between 11.00a.m. and midday, but they were caught on the way back and five of their number were shot down and others damaged. TG210 made another attack on the Plymouth area at 4.30p.m. during that same afternoon (see *Luftwaffe Encore* by Ken Wakefield).

Apparently emboldened by these successes, Von Sperrle decided to repeat the attack on the Woolston Supermarine Works, which must have seemed to him to have borne a charmed life. This time it was at least attacked along the right line; i.e., parallel to the river line, on the north/south axis.

Screened by over 60 ME110 fighters of ZG26 the 60 Heinkels of KG55 attacked in two waves in block formations. It is my view that the block formation, which gave the 'carpet bombing' effect, was a mistake. As each wave of Heinkels totalled 30 or thereabouts, it must have been at least three aircraft across in width, and, I suspect, more likely five.

No-one, so far, has been able to tell me what the formation was, and even today a lot of people do not believe there were two quite separate waves, but this latter point I have been able to confirm, as well as by the curious hesitation of mine which had always established it beyond doubt in my own mind.

The Heinkel 111 bomber had a wing span of 74 feet 1¾ inches, and allowing that they must have had at least half a span between each aircraft when flying in battle formation, means that no more than three aircraft in each block width could have been over the widest end of the Woolston works, and two would amply cover the narrowest end, and that would mean that one of each of their wings would be outside the factory area.

Consequently only a portion of the bombers could hit the target, and because the bomb bay's mechanism and design only allowed bombs to topple out singly, the very length of the factory would most likely cause under, or over, shooting.

According to the best evidence I have been able to obtain, it is generally agreed that the Heinkels dropped seventy tons (in quantity just over 200) of bombs in the two waves, but despite what looked like massive damage, only seven bombs hit Woolston works, and one hit Itchen. Some others hit the Itchen works shelters again, and others fell in local residential areas, some even on the opposite side of the river including the docks and gas works.

The official Southampton casualty figures for this raid was 55 dead and 92 injured; of these, somewhere between 20-30 were killed at the Supermarine Works, and about 35 injured. It has been impossible for me to clarify the figures better than that for this particular raid.

The damage was also, by comparison with effort, minimal. About three Spitfires nearing completion were destroyed and only 20 or so damaged — but over half of these were repairable. Most of this damage was caused by the one bomb on the Itchen works, where it also spelt 'finis' to Mitchell's bomber — the fuselages we had made at Woolston were in

The abandoned and stripped Itchen Works following the raid of September 26th, taken from the riverside by air. Note in the background the fatal railway embankment archway.   *Vickers*

A Naval manned machine gun on a blockhouse on the opposite river bank from the Woolston Works.
                    Southern Newspapers

the Itchen works, and now one was peppered with holes, and the other suffered the indignity of being wrapped round one of the steel girders that supported the roof.

For years I was intrigued to know in which order the factories had been bombed, and then one day I met a colleague who was on duty at the damage and casualty control post, behind the paint and dope shop. He was able to tell me that the first wave went for the Itchen works, but one of their bombs had fallen short and set fire to the paint shop. He, and others, had turned out to deal with that when the second wave arrived, and plastered all round the Woolston works.

The loss to the actual raiding force was quite light; one Heinkel bomber, and two of the ME110s were all shot down by Hurricanes, but in the battle with the higher covering fighter screen of ME109s, the R.A.F. lost two Spitfires and two Hurricanes, with two more Hurricanes damaged. Two of our pilots were killed. One other item worthy of note, is that another ME110 was separated from the attacking force before reaching its intended target by two Spitfires of 92 Squadron R.A.F., and was forced to land intact near Hailsham. The Royal Aircraft Establishment at Farnborough were most pleased to receive such a welcome gift.

The next day I reported to the Labour Exchange and was told to come back on Monday, so I crossed the river on the floating bridge and surveyed the damaged factories from there. The roof's corrugated asbestos sheets had nearly all disappeared, and the glass was almost non-existent, but the main brickwork and vertical girders looked pretty good. The river end of the new office block had sustained some damage to one corner. Apart from the roof, Itchen works showed very little damage from where I was looking. I went along the opposite river road, into the Chapel area and by the gas works. There seemed more damage here than at Woolston, and one thing that I recall, was a small car blown on top of an Army blockhouse, alongside the level crossing at Chapel.

On Saturday, I decided to see if it was possible to obtain my tools from the Woolston works. The rope barrier had been removed, and soldiers were stationed at the office entrance, the main works entrance, and at the Store's doors. The latter was most convenient to me, so I explained what I wanted to one of the soldiers, showed him my Company Identification Card, which bore a photograph and shop number, and with the reminder 'not to hang about' he let me in.

To my surprise, people were working, not at their usual jobs, but packing up parts and tools, and most marvellous of all, uprooting the row of fuselage building jigs. Beyond them I could hear the machine shop with its familiar whine; it was working, and had been since Friday. The damage, thank goodness, was mainly superficial.

I collected my tools and leather apron (only wheelers had leather aprons, and it was almost a badge of office) and carried them out and home. I did not know it then, but that was the very last time I would step into dear old 'K' shop, as such.

Today, the Itchen Bridge sweeps over it, and the first single bridge support, a massive concrete pillar, is as near as I can figure it, right where the last of the Spitfire fuselage jigs was positioned. A few bays of the original wall, separating 'K' shop from the floating bridge dock, are still there.

My Monday visit to the Labour Exchange informed me to report to Hendy's Garage in Southampton at 7.30a.m. the next day — with tools. This was a result of that typically British aptitude for improvisation, although due credit in this instance must be given for its Canadian application.

Beaverbrook had been appointed by Churchill to act on his behalf to increase aircraft production. Some may not have liked his methods, or even his manner, but it will stand the test of time that in this particular activity, his contribution to the salvation of this Country will ensure him his place in history.

F.C.D. 585

VICKERS-ARMSTRONGS, LIMITED.
SUPERMARINE WORKS.

FACTORY CIVIL DEFENCE

This is to certify that the bearer:

Mr. ....C.R. RUSSELL...............

Clock No....WX 56.............is a member

of the....RESCUE SERVICE...........

....

Bearer's Sig....C. R. Russell......

Controller....Du Darling....

VICKERS-ARMSTRONGS, LIMITED, SUPERMARINE WORKS.

EMPLOYEES PASS No. 2251.

NAME   Cyril R. Russell.

NATIONAL IDENTITY No. ECCE/188/3.

SIGNATURE
OF HOLDER   C. R. Russell.

James Bird.
GENERAL MANAGER.

2251

DATE 16.1.43.

All I knew of him up to then was that he was a newspaper proprietor who, after his appointment by Churchill in May 1940, had first gathered a small team of expert advisors, one of whom was Trevor Westbrook, one time Works General Manager of Supermarine's.

He soon sorted out his priorities, and those which affected us at Woolston were to stop the bomber development immediately, cease production on the Walrus amphibian, and pass all tools, drawings, materials, etc. to Saunders-Roe at Cowes for them to continue. Again I believe I can dispose of two more minor myths. Beaverbrook made these decisions certainly no later than very early in June 1940 — not after we were bombed — and, as I was involved in making Walrus keel plates and wheeling float panels, which came to an abrupt end in my work's notebook in the middle of June, this substantiates the fact.

I have also seen a story published that when Saunders-Roe took this Walrus manufacture over, they had to design and fit a wooden hull. This is doubtful, as jigs, part-finished hulls, and full back-up was given — most of the jigs, etc., being towed down Southampton Water to Cowes on a pontoon that Supermarine's owned, and was in fact the salvaged floating bridge hull that had sunk in an accident before the war.

The Saunders-Roe company were experienced flying boat constructors — quite equal to Supermarine's — the Saro Cloud being just one example. The only reason I can think why they may have switched to a wooden hull would be to conserve the more strategic duralumin metal, but such a move would have necessitated some redesign and tooling with its consequent delays.

Personally, I have never seen a wooden-hulled Walrus, but a Royal Navy contact has said he knew of two being made, but that they were too heavy, so the project was abandoned. I would still like to establish it positively one way or the other.

However, at that time, June 1940, Lord Beaverbrook had other far more important issues to tackle and, having ensured that the parent Supermarine's effort was concentrated on the production of the soon to be vital Spitfires, tackle them he did, especially in respect of the 'shadow' factory at Castle Bromwich, Birmingham, where the problem echoed back into the pre-war days.

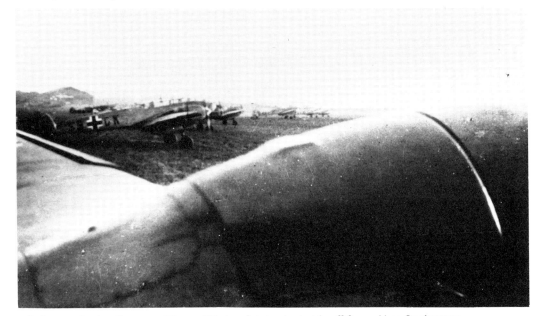

A photograph taken from one of Erpro: 210 aircraft just prior to take-off for a raid on Southampton.

J. Vasco

Above: The Air Minister, with Test Pilots Jeffrey Quill and George Pickering.

Left: Sir Kingsley Wood, Air Minister, on a visit to the Supermarine Works before the War.

Chapter Fourteen
Castle Bromwich

The story of Castle Bromwich to the middle of 1940 is a sickening tale of Ministerial ineptitude, Bureaucratic incompetence, Managerial weakness and ignorance, and an overdose of 'Worker Bloodymindedness'. Strong words, but borne out last year when their Chief Test Pilot, Alex Henshaw, admitted in a magazine article that, 'Castle Bromwich was the sick joke in Aviation circles'. It was a pity he glossed over the truth to the detriment of his own autobiography.

The idea of 'shadow' factories originated in the mind of one of the British motor car construction 'Lords' who suggested it to the then Air Minister after the rearmament decisions of 1935. From what can be gathered from some pre-war aviation magazines, the idea was first rebuffed by the Minister who, no doubt guided and advised by his Civil Service advisors, insisted on all sorts of 'ifs' and 'buts' as part of any official contracts, which they must have known were unacceptable commercial risks.

The matter was reopened again when the next Air Minister, Lord Swinton, took office, and after the all too common bureaucratic paper-chasing, it was agreed that the Nuffield organisation would 'shadow' the Spitfire production, and the Austin Group the Fairey Battle light bomber. I mention these two as each is reasonably comparable in construction methods, size, and building time, and both were to be built within Birmingham City area, and would have broadly similar skills and labour resources to draw on.

From the start, Fairey's were involved with Austin's and gave them all the technical help they could on the Belgian, M. Lobelle's, sleek design, which had its first flight five days after the Spitfire's, although an order for 155 was placed in 1935 giving Fairey's a headstart. However, various modifications tended to offset this lead, and the contract cover for the Austin Motors 'Battles' was issued on 17th August 1936. That the aircraft was a miserable failure in its wartime duties is accepted, but considered irrelevant to the construction comparison I am making.

In both cases, new, purpose-built, factories were erected with all speed, and in Castle Bromwich's instance they had tooling — rubber presses, brake presses and the like — which the Woolston Supermarine factory had never known. The first rubber press for Supermarine's was installed at a Newbury dispersal unit in 1941.

For some reason, that has never been clear to me, the Vickers Aviation Chief, Sir Robert McLean, who was also chairman of Supermarine's (as the company had been wholly taken over by Vickers in 1928) arranged with Nuffield's that the liaison would be via Vickers at Weybridge. This may have worked had Trevor Westbrook been available, but he left Vickers after a Board disagreement in which the workpeople threatened to strike if he went — a most unusual occurrence!

Although the vital jig and tooling information, a complete supply of the relevant drawings applicable to construction, plus sample components, as examples to view were sent from Woolston, the liaison was conducted with Weybridge being an unnecessary intermediate postman both ways. Even late in 1938, Supermarine's began to see this was not working as it should, and eventually a number of Supermarine technicians were sent to help out. Despite an initial massive order for 1,000 Spitfires to start off with, and the consequent almost 'open cheque' to purchase materials, etc., word soon passed back from our chaps there that the project was 'bugged' with industrial action (or inaction) which, so far as I know, fell short of a complete factory shutdown, but was fragmented into areas where the

The Fairey 'Battle' light bomber.

An Armstrong-Whitworth 'Whitley' bomber.

cumulative result ensured no Spitfires reached the flight testing stage. Even before War was declared, this state of affairs was known to Cabinet Ministers and the companies involved, with the additional emphasis being made by Fairey Battle's emerging and delivered from Austin's to the R.A.F.

The Air Minister during this crucial stage was Sir Kingsley Wood, but he seemed more concerned with his political image, making well-photographed and reported visits to aircraft factories (including Supermarine's) instead of tackling this problem right under his nose.

No Spitfires had emerged from Castle Bromwich when War began, and when Churchill became Prime Minister in May 1940, that was still the position. Despite the wishes of the King, Churchill insisted and got, four days later, Lord Beaverbrook as his Minister for Aircraft Production. It proved to be an inspired piece of 'casting'.

When Beaverbrook saw that not one Spitfire had yet come from the enormous and expensive investment at Castle Bromwich, he sailed into battle in typical Beaverbrook style. He sent Sir Richard Fairey to assess the situation and report back to him personally. With the experience of setting up a similar plant only a few miles across Birmingham, Sir Richard's report did not take very long, and it confirmed all Beaverbrook's worst fears.

Very few people would say that Beaverbrook was a popular man; in fact the pugnacious and opinionated way he ran his newspaper left little room for friends and made him many enemies. Never one to suffer fools gladly or afraid of stepping on a few toes, he sailed into all and sundry, whether they be civil servants, managers, or men whom he considered at fault. Via the telephone mainly, his rough, rasping voice, devoid of any of the pleasantries, became the scourge that demanded action. He accepted no excuses from anyone, and if necessary made staff changes to get his way. There were dozens of stories about those telephone calls; a number of them with little doubt apocryphal — but it worked. The triangular line of communication between Nuffield and Supermarine's people was quickly established as a straight line, and senior, knowledgeable men from Woolston moved into positions where they could use their influence. Most of the detrimental hold-ups from the workers' side had been made to appear as disagreements over the bonus incentive prices, although in every case all the times or prices had been based on those already well-proven at Southampton for two years.

To be fair to the employees at Castle Bromwich, it now seems, with the benefit of hindsight, that the delaying tactics were part of a politically-motivated activity — and we now know that something similar was happening in Coventry, where Whitley bomber production suffered in much the same way.

The impact of the fall of France and the Dunkirk evacuation only made a swift and speedy resolution to these problems more urgent. What was said to workers, who stopped work for financial greed at a time such as this, has never yet been revealed — but something must have transpired, and it would not have come from the Management whom the employees had been defying in dribs and drabs since the factory had opened. The peculiar thing is that even now, 45 years later, not one word of how this change in attitude was achieved has leaked out. I suspect that this is due to those workers concerned being too ashamed — and with good cause.

My own suspicions are that certain people were told that either they started working or they would be 'called up'. That would be in keeping with Beaverbrook's normal way of handling staff problems, except that in his newspaper empire 'the sack' would be used instead of 'call-up', and his well-known characteristic of not mincing words. Such was the intensity and ferocity of Beaverbrook's unflagging verbal tirades that a subterfuge was arranged to reduce the pressure on the Castle Bromwich Management.

Ten complete Spitfires in component form were taken by road from Southampton, reassembled, and test-flown by Alex Henshaw and his test pilots, then proudly signalled to

Beaverbrook's Ministry of Aircraft Production as what became known as 'the ten in June'. This was hailed as a triumph and somewhat cynically celebrated by presentation cigarette lighters — suitably inscribed — to those concerned in this charade by their Managing Director.

Whether this caper was used again in subsequent months I do not know, but suffice it to say that gradually the log jam was broken and Castle Bromwich began to perform the function for which it was intended, and by the following February they had delivered over 400, which gives some idea how large the delayed production must have been. The famous (or infamous) 'ten in June' were dispatched to the R.A.F. Maintenance Units, and my information is that their first issue to an operational squadron was made in late August/September 1940, so it follows that the true Castle Bromwich contribution to the vital 'Battle of Britain' must have been exceedingly small.

However, then and later, Lord Beaverbrook's achievements and drive during his period as Minister of Aviation Production stands head and shoulders above any Minister whose responsibility this was, before him, and since. When one considers the situation our troops and airmen were faced with from 10th May 1940 onwards, it is pure speculation to wonder how much difference 500 more Spitfires might have made on events had they been available then — as they should have been — but one is entitled to wonder; and even if Air Marshal Dowding had been spared his dilemma and stubborn refusal to let Spitfires go to France, and more Spitfires could have supported the Dunkirk evacuation and bloodied the Luftwaffe's nose, who can tell what the course of events might have been.

When the German bombers commenced roaming over our island, and Castle Bromwich, Birmingham and Coventry felt the terror that came in the night, one can only hope that those foolish and misguided people, who had allowed political manipulators to sabotage their productive efforts, saw or learned the error of their ways — although the recent years in the motor industry inclines one's thoughts to the contrary.

Not that these two instances in aircraft works were alone in 'downing tools' whilst the country was in peril. There were many others, as diverse as miners to public transport drivers — but very few accounts were published in the press which, as part of the national propaganda machine, was endeavouring mainly to sustain morale. Certainly I take pride in the fact that at no time, or in any of the Supermarine units I worked, was there a single stoppage except by enemy action — never for personal greed or any other selfish motive.

Chapter Fifteen
Dispersal

Beaverbrook came to Southampton as soon as he was made aware of the bombing of the Woolston and Itchen works on the afternoon of 26th September 1940, and inspected the damage for himself. Although from outside and more especially from photographs taken from the air, this damage looked far more serious than it was; practically all the jigs, tools, finished parts and materials escaped damage at Woolston, and the one bomb that landed in the Itchen works had ruined Mitchell's bomber fuselages stored there. In Spitfire terms, some 20 or so fuselages were holed from flying bomb fragments, but most were capable of being repaired as well as a Sea Otter and a Stranraer and, as already mentioned, only three or four were complete write-offs. There was dust, pieces of glass and the debris from the roofing everywhere, but the skeletal ironwork was only slightly damaged.

Beaverbrook, after no doubt having had the lucky escape of the major tooling, etc. drawn to his attention, made the decision to disperse. Personally, I have always thought that his decision may have been influenced by that fact that Luftwaffe reconnaissance photographs would show a completely wrecked pair of works and shrewdly decided to abandon them, so by this means allow the Germans to think that Spitfire production had been stopped. Whether this view of mine is correct I cannot say, and I put it forward purely speculatively as a possibility.

For whatever reason the order to disperse was given, and with it the requisitioning authority to take over whatever buildings were considered suitable, the action that followed by day and night was little short of miraculous. It is not my desire to denigrate other accounts of the dispersal of Supermarine's, but there has been published one account that is so ridiculous that if only in the interests of those of us who participated, I must place on record this personal experience.

I have mentioned that most of us had to report to Woolston Labour Exchange on the day after the bombing, and how I went back into the works to collect my own tools, etc. on the Saturday, and saw for myself that men were busily uprooting the vital jigs, whilst the almost undamaged Machine Shop was actually working under the missing roof. On the following Monday I was informed by the Labour Exchange to report to Hendy's Garage just off Southampton High Street, and upon arrival, there were fuselage jigs that had been uprooted from Woolston, and reset in what had been, on the previous Thursday, one of Southamptons' largest garage and car showrooms. So in five days after what had looked a disaster, I was back building Spitfire fuselages; and I was by no means the only one, or this the only working unit. This, to the best of my recollection, notes and diary, is what happened.

Firstly, Beaverbrook made his dispersal decision then got down to the detailed requirements. He either sent for, or had brought with him, one of the aides he had recruited from industry, and this gentleman, who I remember as a big, bluff, dark-haired Canadian, somehow in the chaotic situation at Woolston, came into contact with Leonard Gooch, my erstwhile tutor in mathematics.

His Works Engineer's office would be the place where all the plant layout drawings were kept, and these drawings would show the dimensional sizes and scales essential to the resiting of everything to be dispersed. Although I have to return to Len Gooch later (after the war) and give my opinions of other matters that do not reflect to his credit, it would be a very mean person who did not render to him the credit (and my respect and admiration) for being the driving force behind the success of the Spitfire dispersal. Whilst his seniors

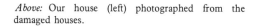

Above: Our house (left) photographed from the damaged houses.

Right: Brother George returning to his Regiment, October 1940. Note the houses in the background.

After the first 'Blitz', November 1940. The same houses after a direct hit on a dividing wall.

appeared bemused or temporarily stunned, Len grasped the problem, and with Beaverbrook, who had a knack of picking the right men for certain jobs, plus the weight of the Government Requisitioning Officer's backing, he literally took off.

The first moves were to get the Design Office staff and their precious drawings to a Southampton University building, whilst simultaneously the administrative and management functions were accommodated in the whole fourth floor of Southampton's Polygon Hotel, with the Salary, Wages and Cashier's departments moving into 'Deepdene', a large private house in the Midanbury area to the north-east side of the town. Gooch was not involved in those moves other than the Works Engineer's Office being one of the offices moved to the Polygon Hotel. He was busy with locating and approving the sites for relocating the production shops. It was quickly realised that premises with good concrete floors and large uncluttered areas free from stanchions and pillar supports for reasonably higher than average ceiling clearance, plus fair size access doors, were required and, in this category, immediately obvious and available, were car showrooms and garages. One marked advantage in favour of their requisitioning was that the vehicles within could be pushed out into the roadway, and the area required cleared in a matter of minutes.

Hendy's went first, then as this simple solution caught on, down went Carey and Lambert's, Wadham's, Lowther's and Seward's. Practically opposite Seward's Motors in Winchester Road, the Sunlight Laundry and, at Weston, a part of the 1914-18 War Rolling Mills building were annexed for the Tanks and Coppersmiths. Then like the spreading fingers of a hand, the search for places out of Southampton and its dangers went fanwise north to Reading, Winchester, Chandler's Ford and Newbury, and westwards to Hursley, Salisbury and Trowbridge. The efford was remarkable and the major credit for this belongs rightly to Len Gooch, and this was recognised when things had settled down, by his appointment as Works Manager in 1941.

Although some accounts, including a speech of his own in 1976, say he was appointed Works Engineer in December 1939, I can only say that it is not as I understood the situation, for reasons which I shall elaborate further later. Opportunity had knocked on Len Gooch's door and he seized it, as he was entitled to do; no one else appears to have grasped the moment, and in the dislocation and confusion of war no one can reasonably begrudge him his due.

The speed of events are reflected in my own moves. Tuesday and Wednesday I worked on fuselages in Hendy's Garage, and on Thursday I was sent to Seward's Motors which, apart from being used as a dumping and sorting ground, provided just enough room in the front part of its upper floor for the wheeling squad to be reconstituted after we had sorted out our wheeling machines, jigs and materials. It was all rather like Fred Karno's Army as some jigs were still missing, as well as certain material gauges being unavailable.

The fact that I and my wheeling colleagues were at Seward's, as described, illustrates one of my criticisms of the particular account I referred to earlier, as that publication has a photograph of a fuselage out-of-jig assembly line on that same Seward's floor, instancing it as part of a 'pre-bombing dispersal plan' and dating it as 1939. The author has since conceded that my assertion that the photograph could not have been taken until at least mid-1941 is correct.

We moved from Seward's to the Agricultural Showroom of Hendy's at Chandler's Ford on 22nd October 1940. As our wheeling machines, benches, and other equipment were all relatively small and easily moved, it was only natural that we would be pushed around until things settled. It was also necessary that our supply of shaped fuselage panels be maintained, as at that time we were Supermarine's only source of supply. At first, the five of us were located at one end of the building; the major portion of it being fitted with racks and gradually filled with the salvaged finished parts from Woolston and Itchen. We travelled

Top: Hendy's Agricultural Equipment showrooms at Chandler's Ford at the time of its requisitioning in 1940.

Centre left: Hilton Duxbury and C.R.R. on the ejected farm equipment on the forecourt of Hendy's.

Left: The Hut Hotel at Chandler's Ford which helped out with the feeding problem during our settling in period.

Above: The Conservative Club, at Chandler's Ford, and my first digs.

Hilton Duxbury, 'Mac' Mutten, Ron Gerrey, Jack Rolf and Charlie Chapman at Chandler's Ford, 1941. Note the wing in the background salvaged from Woolston.

Panelbeaters at Chandler's Ford, 1941. From left to right: 'Mac' Mutten, C.R.R., Hilton Duxbury, Ron Hill (Inspector), Charlie Chapman and Jack Rolf.

to and from our homes in Rolfy's car, and even arranged with the landlord of the adjacent 'Hut Inn' to lay on a cooked meal for us at lunch times. However, as the winter crept in and the night raids commenced, this travelling became an increasing hazard. Fred Waygood, who was not a 'wheeler', did not join us after the bombing and regrettably I never saw him again — something that one had to get used to more often as time passed. Hilton made the first sensible move. He packed his home and family off to his north country origins, and found himself some lodgings in Chandler's Ford. Once the window black-outs were fitted to the showroom he was able to continue working after dark, while the rest of us had to make the evening dusk scramble for home before the sirens interfered with our journey, or left our families wondering. Hilton suggested I should follow his example, and after that awful weekend's bombing at the end of November/beginning of December, my parents urged me to do so. My mother found some digs for me, through one of my aunts, in the Conservative Club at Chandler's Ford. This move, whilst well-intended, was a mistake, as my working hours clashed inconveniently with the King family's commitments of running the club. However, fate took a hand, and the husband of Hilton's landlady was called up and I was offered the chance to go there, which I gladly accepted.

During the period from October, Hursley Park, the home of Lady Cooper, was requisitioned, and the Design Office moved in to be followed by the admin. people from the Polygon's fourth floor. Outbuildings on the Estate were used or new ones erected to accommodate the Garage and Transport Department, the Mould Loft, Arthur Black's Test House and, in the fullness of time, a large experimental hangar run by Frank Perry.

The requisitioning of premises were not all smooth actions — some of the occupants objected furiously. Two instances that I can vouch for were the Agricultural Showrooms at Chandler's Ford and the Barnes Steamroller factory at Southwick, on the Wilts/Somerset border.

At Chandler's Ford, the Requisitioning Officer had to bring in his own labour gang and police attendance while the machinery was removed from the building and left on the grass forecourt (see photograph of Hilton and I sitting on one piece). At Southwick the owner of the premises took the wheels off his heavy lumbering giants and yelled blue murder to his M.P. In the end he had to give way, although he was allowed to keep one part for himself. Southwick was vital as this was where most of the leading edge jigs were hidden from enemy eyes.

There is one Beaverbrook story that Gooch told me personally. Discussing the dispersal with the 'Beaver' in a front-facing room of the Polygon Hotel, the Minister's eyes alighted on Southampton's Civic Centre complex, and upon being informed that one large portion of it was the Guildhall suggested it should be commandeered to erect some of the jigs in. I understand that it took quite an effort to persuade the Minister that 'sprung' dance floors were not stable enough for the purpose.

Gradually order was made from the original upset from the bombing. The toolroom went to Lowther's Garage in Southampton and wing and fuselage jigs and their out-of-jig assembly stages were established in Carey and Lambert's, Wadham's, Hants & Dorset Garages and the original Hendy's, but with the onset of the night area bombings which drastically cut into the hours men could reasonably work without unnecessary risks, greater emphasis was placed on having alternative supply sources in the towns away from Southampton.

Newbury took most of the Machine Shop and, in due time, a purpose-built factory was erected at Shaw where, among other new equipment, they installed Supermarine's first Rubber Press, an innovation that I had to wait until 1947 before seeing and using in another company.

Trowbridge had the wing leading edges at Southwick, as mentioned before, plus Fore Street Garage in the Trowbridge town centre, which became virtually 'F' shop, with Vernon Hall having his Area Manager's Office there, and Rutland Garage next to the Army Barracks' wall in Bradley Road as another Coppersmiths' Department.

Salisbury had fuselages in Wessex Motors, wings and a fuselage out-of-jig assembly line in the garage of the Wilts & Dorset Motor Company, sub-assemblies of various kinds in Anna Valley Motors, and three miles north, on the Amesbury Road, they took over the flying field and small hangar belonging to High Post Flying Club. Here the aircraft were assembled and test flown as they were shortly earlier, at Chattis Hill, near Stockbridge.

In a relatively short time, each of the 'Areas' became almost complete Spitfire Production Units, independent of each other with their Area Managers responsible to Len Gooch as Works Manager. These were Reading under Ken Scales, Newbury under Tom Barby, Salisbury under Bill Heaver, Trowbridge under Vernon Hall and the largest, Southampton, which included Chandler's Ford and Winchester, under Arthur Nelson. That comprised the basic post-bombing dispersals, and as time went on each was added to, with the object of making them all self-contained.

The airfield at Aldermaston was used by Reading and, when air raids got quite warm, the development aircraft, with the test pilots, wisely moved to Worthy Down, although Eastleigh still maintained its output as the Southampton area airfield undisturbed throughout the war — a bonus not really expected.

Keevil Airfield was built during 1942 on the lush farmlands surrounding the picturesque village of Steeple Ashton, roughly 7 miles from Trowbridge for use by R.A.F. and U.S. units. By requisitioning a piece of the farmland just outside the airfield's perimeter hedge, a purpose-built hangar gave Trowbridge its own airfield, a portion of the boundary hedge being removed to give access to the runways and airfield proper.

I believe that by the end of 1944 there were some 60 odd units in the organisation, 46 of them production units and the others stores and other supporting functions. The labour force swelled in relationship to the overall increase of floor area. The original 'few' of 600 or so in 1936, which had doubled by the 1940 bombing, was now nearer a total of 10,000, of which nearly half were women or girls. As it was essential to the dispersal plan to have a nucleus of the 'few' spread over these units to pass on their knowledge and indeed train this vast influx of people who mostly had no experience of aircraft or even factory life, so it will be understood when, in June 1941, the wheeling squad split up and moved on. So at the end of this chapter on 'Dispersal', I can conclude with this, and relate the subsequent moves mainly as they affected me and those with whom I had the closest contact.

Although it had been an advantageous move for me to go into lodgings at Chandler's Ford with Hilton, during those winter months from December 1940 to March 1941 our Agricultural Showroom unit was as cold as ice, especially after dark when we two would work on until 8.00p.m. We had a few scares from the German raiders when bombs were dropped in the general area by accident or design, and one night, a night fighter caught a bomber less than a mile east of us, and it exploded in the air. It was such an explosive force that we wondered how any night fighter could escape the blast. One stick of bombs dropped across the north of the village, hitting one house in particular, totally destroying it and its inhabitants, including a young child, whose body was found next day in the front garden fish pond. The blitz on Southampton is adequately covered by others, but on the weekends, when I could get time off, I always returned to either my parents, or my girl friend's parents' home, but these visits almost always entailed long hours in the Anderson shelters, with the dreadful noise of unsynchronised engines, as the Luftwaffe stooged around in ones and twos, loosing off either high explosive bombs, incendiary canisters, and the occasional parachute mine.

Like most people, we had our close shaves, but the overall effect of the carnage in September and this nightly helplessness had begun to affect me, so that from January onwards, whenever the warning sirens sounded, I just could not stop my legs from uncontrollable shaking. This was cured in a quick and tragic way.

In May 1941, our squad was informed that we were to be dispersed. Rolfy, Charlie, Fred and myself to Trowbridge, Mac Mutten to Southampton, and Hilton to Newbury. The move was scheduled to take place in the week following the Whitsun break. This was not good news to our landlady, as with three children to keep, our contributions to the family budget were a useful supplement to her husband's Army pay. She took it bravely, and we arranged things so that she could spend the Whit weekend with her children at her parent's home in Salisbury. With Hilton having additional leave to visit his family up north, I said I would see to myself for the Monday to enable Mrs Newman to have extra time with her folk.

When I returned to the bungalow on the Monday night, I was surprised to find her husband, Jim, there. He told me he had obtained leave and asked where his family were. I told him, and he said he would go to Salisbury to meet them in the morning. We chatted for a while then I went to bed. In the morning he brought me a cup of tea, then I left for work with the promise that he would leave me a midday meal on the gas stove. Upon my return at lunch time I found that, like a fool, I had forgotten to transfer my keys to my working clothes. Hearing the hissing gas under my lunch, and cursing my own stupidity, I sought a means of entry. I did not really expect to find one, but I was lucky, my own bedroom transom was open, and by leaning in through it I managed to open the larger window below it. The inside kitchen door appeared stuck as I went to open it, and it took some forceful shoving before I could get it open sufficiently to get my head around to find what the obstruction was. There on the floor staring up at me were the wide eyes and bloated dark red face of Jim. He had gassed himself.

For one terrible moment I wanted to turn and run as far as I could and put this latest horror behind me, but, thank goodness, some semblance of self control remained, and caused me to think that I might be able to save him. That next five minutes were the most frantic in my life. Forcing the door very hard against the towels he had stuffed along its bottom, I got into the gas-filled kitchen. I turned the gas tap off to stop that fearful hissing which had a purpose so different from what my thoughts had been, and then tore away all the clothes and towels he had used to block the outside door. With them away I unlocked it and flung it wide open, pausing for a moment in the sweet fresh air to relieve the effect from the gas I had already swallowed and inhaled — then back in, threw off his Army great-coat which he had used to cover himself and the open oven door and which, when he had lost conciousness and fallen back, had half wrapped itself around his body, then, by his feet, dragged him outside on to the path.

There wasn't a soul about to help, so as he was still quite warm I tried to force the gas out of his lungs. His stomach was as hard as a football and distended and when my arms failed to move it, I knelt on him and jumped up and down with my knees, but it would not budge. Dismayed with the failure I left him there, found a small boy in the road and asked him to stand by the front gate until I returned, and not to let anyone go in. Then I ran across a piece of waste land and two hundred yards up the road to the doctor's surgery. Luckily I caught the doctor just as he was returning from his visits for lunch and, after a few brief words of explanation, we returned to my lodgings in his car. The little lad was still standing faithfully at the gate. It only took the doctor a few moments to determine that Jim had been dead for some little time, and that my efforts to revive him were well over an hour too late. We carried him into the front bedroom and the doctor informed the police.

After giving my story to the constable I went into my room, packed my clothes, etc., and left.

I couldn't have stayed on to see Mrs. Newman's shock and grief, so that evening after work I went back to my parents' home and spent those last few days travelling back and forth with Rolfy and company. The day they moved to Trowbridge I spent at the inquest, with a final sad farewell to Jim's widow. Apparently he could not settle to Army life and was absent without leave, then feeling cornered by his act and fearful of the consequences, he had taken his own life. Another little tragedy amidst so many at that time. Only one good thing came from it. My nerve returned and I never shook ever again.

Some thirty years after the War, Southampton people were astonished, and justifiably angry, to learn of a report from an organisation named 'Mass Observation' containing adverse reports on the morale of its citizens under the German air bombardment at night. Fortunately a few of the principal civic officials of that period were still alive, and soon forcefully refuted this unwarranted slur, to such an effective extent that an official Government rider was added to the report disclaiming its validity. Herbert Morrison, the wartime Home Secretary, believed these types of reports on other towns also, even to declining to acknowledge their contribution to the War and withholding their advance to City status. Coventry was another.

Leonard Gooch, Joint Production Manager. *Vickers*

Chapter Sixteen
Production Facts and Figures

Before I continue with narrative relevant to my own move to Trowbridge, it might be convenient to pause and examine some aspects of Spitfire production, quantities and supply, up to this point.

Over the years since 1940 some confusion seems to arise when the 'Order of Battle' figures for Hurricanes and Spitfires are given as 19 Spitfire Squadrons and 29 Hurricane Squadrons at 1st July 1940. My information relates solely to Spitfires, although similar principles will apply to the other fighters.

A 1940 squadron of Spitfires comprised 16 aircraft, usually made up as three flight sections of four, normally identified by colours, and four reserve aircraft. Therefore on this basis there were 304 Spitfires in the 19 front line squadron's operational service.

In the years before the war, the Air Ministry, via the policy-making Air Council, had decreed that the operational squadrons should be backed up by a reserve of 2¼ times their number of aircraft against losses that might arise from accident and enemy action. This formula would mean that in July 1940 there should have been 684 Spitfires in addition to the 304 in squadron use, making a total of 988. Although no Spitfire had been sent to France, for which due credit must be given to Air Marshal Dowding, we had suffered some losses during the Dunkirk evacuation, and in flying accidents prior to that over the period since the first squadron was formed, No. 19 at Duxford in 1938. Did we have this number, which must be nearly 1,000, produced all told? The answer is, thankfully, very nearly! My figure is 834.

As I have already mentioned, I still have in my possession the notebooks I used to keep for a record of jobs and bonus payments, and as a prime source of reference are probably quite unique. It will be recalled that I left the Spitfire fuselage production line in January 1939, my last job there being top, bottom and side plating of production No. 217. My notebook shows that I went to Eastleigh to repair two completed aircraft fuselages with production numbers 692 and 694 on 7th June 1940.

Company and Ministry records show 308 delivered by the outbreak of war, and the original 310 contract completed a few days later, on 7th September 1939. The second contract for 200 was completed by 20th January 1940, with three component sets being sent to Castle Bromwich on 24th January as guidance samples for familiarisation. The third contract, again for 200, continued the run, but of these, 17 were cancelled from the contract on 9th June 1940, which neatly lines up with the Castle Bromwich infamous 'ten in June', and most likely seven for their July quota.

Jeffrey Quill's autobiography gives the following deliveries of Spitfires, but it should be remembered that the fuselage jigs at Woolston dictated the numbers that could be produced once the wing problem had been solved:

1939 September 33, October 48, November 50, December 40.
1940 January 37, February 45, March 42, April 60, May 77, and then June 94, July 140, August 190, September 148 and October 128.

but I feel that the latter five months may include the Castle Bromwich output, although the fuselage build-up at Itchen, due to the earlier wing shortage, may account for an above average production rate.

Some indication of the attrition rate may be judged by the total loss of Spitfires, during the 'Battle' period, of 474 which, by the end of November 1940, had increased to 567. How many were damaged and repairable I can only leave one to judge by the R.A.F. Maintenance Units returns on 'Spitfire aircraft available for issue', which in July stood at 156, but four months later had dropped to 115. It was a close run thing'!

As the years since that unforgettable 'High Summer' have passed, new documentary evidence has gradually been released to show, albeit with hindsight, just how important the 'Battle of Britain' was to the eventual outcome of the War. My submission is that it was the very 'turning point'; the moment when, for the first time, the might of Nazi Germany suffered its initial major defeat. Its effect so influenced Nazi thinking that at first they almost appeared to brush it aside as a momentary aberration of fickle fate, and turned away in disgust to tackle the 'Russian Bear', and when those plans went awry, the earlier latent and suppressed fear of defeat arose again like a creeping growing miasma to infiltrate, and finally overcome them. Had the R.A.F.'s 'thin blue line' failed to hold, and turn back the Luftwaffe, that failure to maintain the essential air superiority would have inevitably led to an attempted invasion — that is certain. Whether this would have succeeded or not is a speculation I am not competent to advance further. All I do know is that my 'gut reaction' then, and now, is that we would have been hard put to defeat any such attempt.

What was the vital 'key' to that R.A.F. successs? Without deprecating any of the great achievements by the only other effective fighter aircraft, the Hawker Hurricane, one is bound to ask, 'could we have survived without that 'edge' of extra speed and manoeuvre-ability that Mitchell's superb creation, the Spitfire, supplied?' I suggest not! Putting aside all the well-worn statistics in the perennial Hurricane versus Spitfire arguments, the basic fact is that the Spitfire allowed the Hurricane to operate by mainly taking on the Messerschmitt 109. It was the old 'horses for courses' theory again. As I've mentioned, it was a close run thing — far closer than we knew at the time — and almost certainly closer than we can ever hope to survive again!

However it is only fair to report that Castle Bromwich at long last made a contribution, after being kicked into life by Beaverbrook and, eventually, by the end of 1942 reached a monthly output of 320. Nevertheless, had the Luftwaffe attacked Supermarine's in June 1940, and made a proper job of it, and also hit the right hangars at Eastleigh, one hardly dares to contemplate what might have been. However, they failed to do so in a mixture of muddled strategies and unbelievably poor 'Intelligence' which, not forgetting our brave pilots, gave us just the amount of time we badly needed — all too often at a tremendous personal sacrifice by them.

Bringing the production output down to personal terms, the following is a condensation from my notebook.

From February 1938 to January 1939, with Arthur Newland, we completed the fuselage top, bottom and side plating of 63 Spitfires. From January 1939, in Jack Rolf's section, my tally was 218 Walrus Keel Plates (approx. 40 A/C sets), 20 Walrus Bow Plates (10 A/C sets), 308 Spitfire Flare Containers (154 A/C sets), and 140 Spitfire Cockpit Coaming Channel Stiffeners (70 A/C sets) up to the declaration of war. From then on until the bombing it reads 220 Walrus Keel Plates, 110 Walrus Bow Plates, 654 Walrus Float Panels, (approx. 40 A/C sets), 940 Spitfire Fillet Panels (various approx. 100 A/C sets), 130 Spitfire Flare Containers, 424 Spitfire Cockpit Coaming Channel Stiffeners, and 1,200 Spitfire Access Door Frames shaped (approx. 600 A/C sets).

During the latter period I also worked with Jack Rolf doing the modifications required on the Walrus development prototype, later named the Sea Otter, making and fitting the bow panels, then shortly afterwards changing the Nacelle shape to eliminate tail unit buffeting that arose from its original circular cone shape.

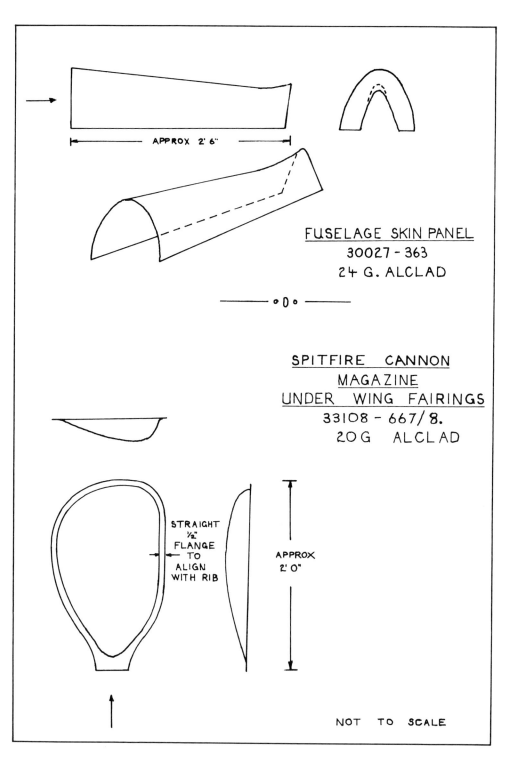

APPROX 2' 6"

FUSELAGE SKIN PANEL
30027 - 363
24 G. ALCLAD

∘ 0 ∘

SPITFIRE   CANNON
MAGAZINE
UNDER   WING   FAIRINGS
33108 - 667/8.
20 G   ALCLAD

STRAIGHT
½"
FLANGE
TO
ALIGN
WITH RIB

APPROX
2' 0"

NOT   TO   SCALE

After the bombing, and during my brief spells at Hendy's Garage, Seward's Motors and the Agricultural Showroom at Chandler's Ford, the tally continues; 1,042 Spitfire Fillet Panels, 110 Spitfire Fuselage Panels 30027-363 (the little beast?), 280 Spitfire Cannon Wing Fairings, and 2 off each of 5 Spitfire Griffon Engine Cowling Panels.

The cannon fairings arose in a peculiar manner. The car belonging to Mr Butler, the Production Engineer, had its bonnet and one wing damaged in the Woolston bombing, and he couldn't spare it to be repaired as his Production Engineer's duties were intimately involved in the Dispersals, so one morning, when he was at a meeting, one of his Planning Engineers drove it from Hursley Park to our section at Chandler's Ford with authority to get it repaired. Rolfy gave the job to me and once the dents, etc., were planished out, away it went. When the original cannon installation in the Spitfire proved a failure, a redesign was done by Hursley. Needing to prove the design of the underwing fairing, and not having an experimental workshop at that time, the young Planning Engineer remembered my work on Butler's car and, on his own initiative, brought the drawing down to me. From the contour lines on the drawing, I made a series of templates and then blocked out on a sandbag the main shape, wheeled it smooth and more accurate, formed the peripheral attachment flange, then telephoned my planner friend, Tim, who came and collected the panels, and me, to try them against the trial installation on a pair of wings at the Sunlight Laundry unit. With a few minor adjustments to ensure the fairing did not foul the cannon feed mechanism, a pleased planner took my originals to Newbury where a drop hammer forming tool was made from each. During the time before the drop hammer was successfully producing, I kept the line going with, all told, 172 aircraft sets. It was during our sojourn at Chandler's Ford that I became, officially, a 'skilled' man.

Chapter Seventeen
Trowbridge and Air Ducts

The day following the inquest, the train bore me westwards to Trowbridge, near the Wiltshire/Somerset border. It was my first real experience of leaving home, as from Chandler's Ford, contact had been easy to maintain. I had an address to go to where I would be sharing 'digs' with Fred Veal at the Brown's house in Bradley Road. Having met Mrs Brown I dumped my case in the bedroom I was to share with Fred, and had a wander round the small country town, which appeared to be mainly sustained by Ushers Brewery, various cotton mills, the Wiltshire County Offices in an impressive building, and as a dormitory town for Western Railway employees attached to the Westbury railway staff. My new landlord, Clarence Brown, was a driver for the railway, and there was an Army Barracks right opposite the house.

The next morning I went with Fred to our new location, a corrugated-iron shed which had been part of Barnes Steamroller Factory at Southwick, some two miles closer to the Somerset border. Our wheeling section was confined to one corner of the iron shed, the remainder being occupied by sub-assembly work from Bill Mills' balcony, the main building being used to assemble and complete the wing leading edge assemblies under Bob Randall, now the Unit Foreman, with Bill Mills as his deputy. As a consequence, apart from using the time office and inspection departments and the usual communal offices, we operated as an autonomous unit.

The remainder of the Trowbridge area at that period was just Rutland Garage in Bradley Road housing the Coppersmiths, and the mid-town Fore Street Garage, where Vernon Hall had his Area Manager's office, and housed a strong contingent of 'F' shop, from whence he came. We had delivered to us our own stock of sheet materials, and a number of job cards, so settling in was comparatively easy.

Most noticeable was the lack of concern over the war; the necessity to sleep with one ear cocked for the warning air raid sirens was soon forgotten, although it was soon reinstated on our occasional visits home. For what little free time we had, there were 52 pubs and 3 cinemas, and if we managed a Saturday afternoon and evening free, we soon found Bath with its theatres, Joe Loss and band with dancing in the Park Pavilion, as well as the more cultural interests, the Abbey, Roman Baths, and the wonderful sweep of Royal Crescent.

Fred and I had settled down nicely with the Brown family and, having similar tastes, shared practically all our free time in each other's company. It was too good to last, and the first intimation of change we had came after five or six weeks when Jack Rolf told us he was going back to Southampton. Having left a wife and house there, it was to be expected. This then precipitated another crisis in our small section. We assumed Charlie would take over charge of us, but he told Rolfy that he did not want the responsibility and turned it down flat. Finally they agreed that if I would accept the job, Charlie would be quite happy to work for me. Flattered by their confidence and Charlie's assurances regarding my responsibilities I accepted, and Rolfy went home, and through his other moves that followed, we did not meet again until 1946. As my new function only involved me in issuing out successive job cards and engaging a young lad as our labourer to move and cut metal to the templates and generally keep the equipment and floor clean, my duties were scarcely onerous until a check revealed that we only had three weeks work and material left.

I mentioned this to Bob Randall, who undertook to inform Mr Hall so that it could be raised at the fortnightly Area Manager's meeting with Len Gooch. Nothing happened until we were only a few days away from the work drying up. Fortunately, Gooch himself came

Above: The Brown family at Trowbridge, 1941.

Right: Fred Veal and C.R.R. at the Brown's front doorway, 1941.

Below: The Barnes Steamroller factory requisitioned at Southwick, near Trowbridge, Wiltshire, in 1941.

Vickers

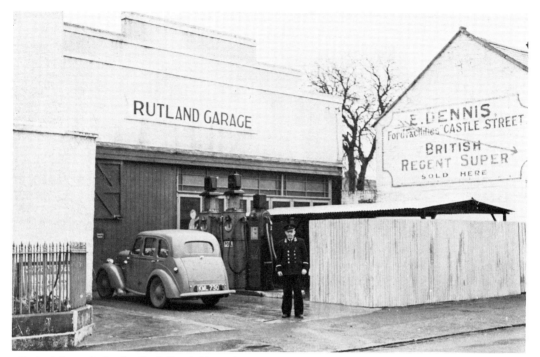

Rutland Garage in Bradley Road, Trowbridge and requisitioned for the Coppersmiths. *Vickers*

Fore Street Garage, a requisitioned building in the centre of Trowbridge. *Vickers*

to visit the Trowbridge area, escorted by Mr Hall (who did not know me from Adam) and, seeing me in our corner, came over to enquire how we had settled in. This enabled me to raise the situation with him directly. Vernon Hall's eyes blinked behind his pebble glasses as our cause was expounded to the Works Manager, with a familiarity and temerity he himself would not have used. He was even more impressed when, two days later, a large van arrived bringing some two tons of various gauge duralumin sheet metal, and a tea chest filled with order job cards. There would be no need to worry about future work for six months at least. The next piece of good luck came by pure chance.

After the Area Manager's meeting in the first week of September 1941, among the new work or modifications Gooch farmed out to the various areas was the drawing for an air duct, to be installed in the aircraft of the Photographic Development Unit of the R.A.F., to bleed hot air from the engine via ducting to the cameras which had icing problems. This collector duct at the engine had been entrusted to Mr Hall, for his Trowbridge area to make.

I heard later that he had hawked this drawing around, only to be told by his foremen and chargehands it could not be made within the Trowbridge facilities. On this visit to Southwick he was escorted round by Bill Mills, as Bob Randall was away for the day, and as they were leaving to go to Mr Hall's car, he happened to mention his disappointment at having to return the drawing to Gooch with an admission of failure. I'm sure Bill Mills' request to see the offending drawing was little more than a polite gesture of shared concern more than anything else, but the result was quite beyond either of their expectations. All that Bill Mills knew of me was that at Woolston his balcony had overlooked our wheeling squad workplace, and he may have noticed when I was bashing out Walrus bow panels and the like, and my name, because I had taken Jack Rolf's place when he had left Southwick.

Whatever inspired him to say, 'Have you shown this to young Russell?', to Mr Hall, he couldn't even explain to me afterwards, but Vernon Hall grasping at any straw asked 'Who?' Explanations followed and the first I knew about it was when both men came up to me and asked if I would look at the drawing. I did, and the problem was explained.

There was something about Vernon Hall's dread of Len Gooch that came through as he spoke, and although I could not give a simple 'yes' or 'no' answer, I asked if he would leave me the drawing to study for 24 hours. I believe he was glad to get rid of it. I've no desire to labour this anecdote unnecessarily, but it does illustrate how fate, 'Lady Luck', or whatever it is, works, and also shows how one can get 'lost' in a problem.

The drawing (30064-675) showed three views and dimensions of a collector duct, with a rectangular open forward end stiffened and lagged where it fitted to the engine. Moving aft it first stepped up about an inch and a half (obviously to miss some other piece of equipment) at the bottom, then continued for a further nine inches which went through a 180 degrees half circle section, and back to the rectangular front.

Looking down on its plan form, it narrowed slightly from the front and curved inside the half round ends so that these two sides became three inch round tubular ends. Off centre, and protruding from this tube-shaped aft end, was another three inch tube, tilted up a few degrees and fitted into the main body pointing aft. Reduced to simplest terms it was an irregular box about ten inches long and wide, with a rectangle opening at its front end, and three circular outlets at the back (see drawing).

Apart from the full scale views, the drawing only specified the material (aluminium), the details of the strip of lagging, and the bifurcated copper rivets to hold it, and one other ambiguously worded remark — 'Weld where required' — which proved to be the key.

As I looked at the drawing I became sucked into the challenge it presented, and vague ideas began to form in my head. I sat at the bench drawing possible weld lines and trying to work out how the complicated shape could be made, and what tooling I might need. My fellow squad members came and looked and with that happy rapport we had, shrugged their

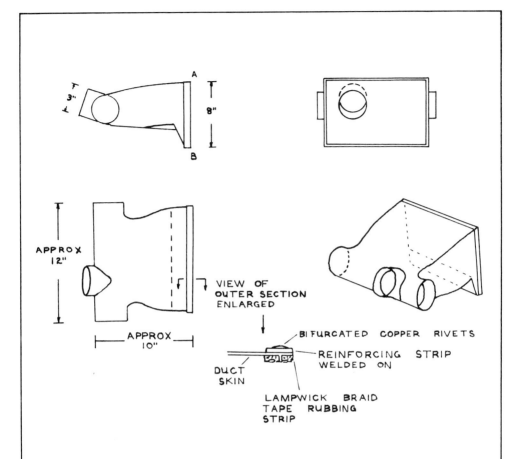

AIRDUCT FOR HOT AIR SUPPLY TO
P.R.U. SPITFIRE CAMERAS

ORIGINALLY PART NUMBER 30064—675
THEN PRODUCTIONISED TO 35364—29. 20G ALUMINIUM

WHEN PRODUCTIONISED THE MAIN BODY WAS A ONE PIECE WRAP-ROUND FROM 'A'
TO 'B' IN TOP LEFT VIEW. TWO SEPARATE SIDE PIECES AND THE OFF-SET FRONT TUBE
FORMED THE REST OF THE MAIN BODY. ALTHOUGH NOT SHOWN, THE SIDE'S TOP AND
BOTTOM JOINTS HAVE ½" RADII.

NOT TO SCALE

shoulders and said, 'It's all yours, chum.' I became so engrossed in the problems, that evening came, the lights went on, the shift finished and went home, and the next thing I knew was Bob Randall enquiring, 'What's going on?'

Apparently the shed I was in had no nightshift, and the night warden on his rounds had come across what should have been a deserted unlit shop, now one with a solitary person poring over a drawing and making notes. Not knowing who I was, not having been told anything, he assumed the worst and with commendable discretion quietly retreated to his gate house and telephoned Bob Randall at home in Trowbridge. He, being equally unaware of the day's events, was sufficiently alarmed to come out by car to find out. It was a quarter to midnight, but once explained, all was well. Despite the late hour I expressed my views on how I thought the duct could me made. To his credit Bob grasped the essentials and said he thought it worth a try.

Taking me back to my digs in his car he said he would talk to Mr Hall in the morning. The next morning at nine he came over to my bench to say Mr Hall wanted us in his office at Fore Street. To cut a long story short it transpired that my ideas were successful, and with the help of a Greek cabinet maker named Christoludes, who made the forming blocks as I required, and an excellent aluminium welder whose name eludes me, but whose 'Friar Tuck' nickname described his tonsured head and rotund body very aptly, Mr Hall was able to take the finished article back to Hursley for design approval, plus a couple of suggestions to improve its manufacture.

Two weeks later I was seconded to Fore Street, given a squad of fitters and welders and began production of 205 ducts to their new part number 35364-29, which we completed between 14th October 1941 and January 1942.

During this high spot in my working life, Charlie Chapman was moved to Reading, and a new factory unit was opened at Hilperton, just north of Trowbridge, under Tommy Welch, to which Fred and I transferred.

In the December I made the mistake of getting married. With the benefit of hindsight it was doomed from the start; we were a pair of incompatibles in almost every way, yet it went on in fits and starts for five miserable years, tearing the emotional guts out of our lives. It is best forgotten, and has no place in this story, save as a backdrop to those five years and its precipitation of my move to Salisbury, and elsewhere.

In January, whilst still at Fore Street, I asked Mr Hall if he could get my wife and I transferred back to Southampton. He was sympathetic to the domestic reasons, and asked on my behalf on his next trip to Hursley. Con Mann even created an inspection job for her. The person Hall asked refused, and as he was one of those new parasitic growths that appeared to infest industry at that period — the Personnel Officer — I decided to go and beard this newcomer in his den.

My first meeting with him was strangely similar to every future meeting with his type — a complete and utter washout. He had said 'No' and that was all there was to it! I left his office and angrily walked the few steps to Len Gooch's office. He saw me and listened to my tale of woe and said he'd see what he could do. On 23rd March 1942 Fred Veal and I reported for duty at High Post Airfield. My wife went back to her mother.

Inside the little hangar at High Post airfield, between Salisbury and Amesbury. *Vickers*

High Post. The hangar photographed in 1985.

Chapter Eighteen
Salisbury — High Post Airfield and Wessex Motors

The tiny hangar where Spitfires were assembled, and the airfield from which they flew and were tested, has to be seen to be believed. Originally intended for use in maintaining the types of aircraft that were used by pre-war flying clubs, the hangar was just large enough to take three Spitfires, providing the first two had their tail ends pushed into the opposite rear corners so that the third could get its tail and fuselage between them, its wings then blocking the other two in. If either of the side ones had to come out first, the front one had to be pushed out on to the tarmac apron to give enough manoeuvring space. The push-open sliding doors were just high enough to permit the propellers to clear at the top, as long as the three blades were in the 'Y' position. One side of this little hangar had a brick built lean-to addition, which housed the armoury and toilets.

For canteen facilities we had to trek over half a mile across the airfield, or along the roadway that ran beyond its boundary hedge, nearly to the Wessex Pyrotechnics factory, where the flying club's little wooden club house was situated. Later on in the war — after I had left in the autumn of 1943 — a large new hangar was built across the road, and became Jeffrey Quill's Test Flight Headquarters. Today it is still there, plain to see, almost opposite where the golf course commences. Just a few yards away is a clutter of small buildings behind some petrol pumps, and it is difficult to segregate the one I am referring to as it has been so built around with other typical wartime small buildings, that even my attempts to photograph it were frustrated. However, it is still there, behind the petrol pumps and a few yards from the High Post Hotel. I saw it whilst writing this story, and I am still amazed how we achieved so much in such cramped and primitive conditions.

The general pattern of work was all completely new to Fred and myself. The plan was for fuselages built at the Wessex Motors unit to go to the Wilts & Dorset Motor Services garage in Castle Street, where they would be fitted out to the same standard as used to apply at Itchen works. Alongside them in the same building, the wings were built in jigs, and completed out-of-jig to their final standard, including the undercarriage legs and wheels.

Anna Valley Garages, nearly opposite, in Castle Street made various sub-assemblies to support the main components and provided Bill Heaver, my old Foreman, with his base as Area Manager. These completed main components would be transported by low loader 'Queen Mary' type vehicles to High Post. Each wing would arrive leading edge down in a castoring wheel purpose-built transport trolley. The fuselage, not being so heavy, usually came on a stand that picked up with the two lifting jack points under Frame 5, and a cradle under Frame 19, which invariably had an additional sling to keep the two together. Muscle power and a couple of 'skates' moved the fuselage inside, and the same manpower pushed the wing trolleys in. Then came the tricky bit.

'All under the wings' would go up the cry, and all the men left whatever job they were doing so that a wing could be pushed over, freed from its trolley to be supported on the 12 to 15 men's backs. Once there, in accordance with the instructions by Jack Draper the foreman, it would be shuffled into position until the front and rear root fittings were in correct alignment with their fuselage attachments, and the fixing bolts driven home. This procedure would be repeated for the opposite side wing. Once this was done, the hydraulic piping would be joined and the undercarriage tested for functioning with a hydraulic jig. As soon as the Inspector signalled that this was satisfactory it was 'All under the wings' again and the same brute force was used to lift the whole aircraft clear of the trestle support at Frame 5, and the undercarriage lowered and locked allowing it to take the aircraft's weight on its wheels — much to our relief! The tail end cradle and sling was easily removed, and once down on its tailwheel our small staff would pounce on it to complete and test all systems, fit the wing to fuselage fillets, the camera gun mounting in the port nose fillet, cut and fit all the engine cowlings, fit the propeller, the guns, both cannon and machine guns, the propeller spinner, then a touch of paint to the unpainted parts we had fitted, and another Spitfire was ready for its push outside for engine running and eventual test flight.

It used to take roughly 2½ days, of day and night shifts, to achieve this result and with three on the go together, the overall effect used to be six aircraft per week produced. Despite the dangerous manhandling of the wings we never had an accident which, in the circumstances, was quite remarkable.

During flight testing, it was usual for one or two of us to be in attendance in case a cowling panel required removing for minor adjustments, or to lay over the tailplanes to keep the rear end down when the pilot revved up to check on the engine's functioning, and to dress the trailing edges of an aileron, if the pilot found it flying one wing low. Jeffrey Quill was very particular about the inherent stability of the aircraft he tested — and rightly so. To be at this, 'the sharp end' of Spitfire production was of great interest to me, and once I became 'au fait' with the work which was quite new to me, I thoroughly enjoyed it.

In the little armoury the new weapons arrived in heavily-greased condition, and were all stripped down and cleaned before being installed in the wings. One little anecdote of this particular aspect came whilst I was there. The armoury employees were on the same bonus incentive scheme as the rest of us (something I shall have to explain more comprehensively later), and one day there was quite a rumpus. Somehow it came to light that the aircraft they were booked on had been shot down a month or more earlier, and they were working a 'fiddle' from the accumulated time they had in hand.

Prior to Fred and me arriving, the front wing fillets and engine cowling had been done by Claude Harris and Bill Shadick. We were paired with one each of them and began the day and night shift. After the first month learning the ropes, Fred and I paired up as the night shift team, and soon our competence was equal to Claude and Bill's. It was as well it was, for we had to make special efforts to get Spitfires to Malta and meet a deadline for the new aircraft to go on board an aircraft carrier. As a result, to reach the target, the whole High Post team worked straight through with minimal meal breaks for 48 hours. Gosh we were tired — but triumphant — our target met, a matter acknowledged by Bill Richardson, the Deputy Area Manager, who brought us a crate of beer on our next nightshift. Shortly afterwards we had a rush to fit tropicalised air intakes, incorporated into a new deeper-bellied bottom cowling panels, which were urgently required for North Africa.

I haven't specified the different 'Marks' of Spitfires we worked on, as anyone who has delved into this minutae will know how confusing it can get, but at High Post it was from Mk. 5 upwards.

Working on an airfield is vastly different from the confines of a factory workshop. The close contact with the completed product, and the knowledge that what one did, if not done properly, might risk the life of any of the pilots we got to know, induced a form of self-discipline, and of course always, whilst on dayshift, there was the flying to watch. Many of our Spitfires were test flown by service pilots who were 'resting' between operational tours of duties.

One I remember very vividly — was a Belgian — and as mad as a March Hare. I was in attendance on him one day, and while chatting during a minor engine adjustment by our Rolls-Royce representative, he bet me that even if I stood on the battery trolley-acc, he could still come upon me by surprise and force me to jump down. He did too — after throwing the 'Spit' all over the sky he went low below the hump in the middle of our airfield and I expected him to come powering in from the Pyrotechnics works direction but, cunningly,

Wilts and Dorset Omnibus Garage, Salisbury, where Spitfire wings were built.   *Vickers*

Anna Valley Motors in Castle Street Salisbury, and the area head office of Bill Heaver.   *Vickers*

he went further towards Salisbury along the Woodford Valley, then turned in over Old Sarum and hedge-hopped to finally hurtle in over small woods on my left, and so low that had I not jumped, I'm sure the whizzing prop would have decapitated me. When he landed I had to concede that he was the victor, but the final laugh was on him. He reported to the Inspector, of vibration in the port wing, and at the Inspector's request I removed the port nose fillet panel to allow him to look inside. As I drew it away I noticed a square inch of metal just beyond the first wing nose rib. Lifting it out I was amazed to find it was eighteen inches long — obviously a riveter's bar and weighing all of two or three pounds.

Poor old 'Belgie', he had been throwing the 'Spit' about with this great lump of metal clattering about loose in the wing. The inspector, quite rightly, had all the access covers and wing doors removed, but despite a rigorous search with torchlight, and mirrors on sticks, no damage was found. I hope 'Belgie's' luck held for the remainder of his wartime flying. The 'dolly bar' was never claimed by any riveter.

In addition to our use of the airfield, R.A.F. Training Command used it to practice 'circuits and bumps', and landings and take-offs by Airspeed Oxford twin-engined trainers. Sometimes these embryo bomber pilots would perform flying feats not included in any flying manuals. On one instance a heavy one-sided landing bump caused the port undercarriage to collapse, and then it careered on, until he throttled back and the aircraft slithered to an eventual halt on its starboard wheel and port wing without casualties. Another Oxford was not so fortunate. Two miles away, and lower than High Post was, and still is, the experimental aerodrome of Boscombe Down. It often provided us with fleeting glimpses of new aircraft on test and still secret. I saw the Fairey Barracuda, Blackburn Botha, Avro Lancaster and an eight-cannon Hurricane at various times, among quite a few others.

The take-off flight paths from Boscombe Down, which had a long runway, ran usually north to south, or vice versa, depending on the wind. High Post, all grass and quite lumpy, was conditioned generally by the wind sock, but very often the pilots would practice crosswind landings and take-offs. On this particular day a Lancaster coming up from Boscombe Down was struck from underneath by an Oxford up from High Post. There was one almighty bang, and when we ran to see, all that was left was a pile of wreckage spread over the field only half a mile from us on the edge of the Amesbury Road. Everyone in both aircraft was killed.

One of the events that left an idelible impression on me was in 1943, when we all became aware of an unusually heavy growl of approaching aircraft. Rushing on to the tarmac apron we saw, in formation and flying low, something like 250 American Flying Fortresses. The ground trembled as they passed over us — a majestic and awesome sight as we watched them fly away south, just to the east of Salisbury.

Two hours later the same growl arose from the south and again we watched the formation return. Still flying low, and still attempting to keep to the formation which now had great gaps in it, with aircraft showing all manner of battle damage — pieces missing from wings, rudders and tailplanes, engines stopped with feathered props, and one which had one engine actually hanging down — they sailed just as majestically by for their home bases, probably in Oxfordshire, this time urged on by the silent prayers of those who had witnessed their magnificent and brave daylight flight out to the Continent, where 'our lads' had found it better to go mainly by night, and their battle torn, but proud return.

Another facet of High Post briefly mentioned earlier was the location of the canteen. This never worried most of us on day shift, but on nights, especially the winter ones, we were glad of the blazing fire in the clubhouse hearth, and a warm meal. Our little hangar's heating system just could not cope with the bitter winter winds, perched as we were on one of the highest points around, and roughly equivalent to the tip of Salisbury Cathedral's spire which, at 404ft., is the tallest in England. These walks, always in groups and by the roadway, generally became sing songs on their return journeys. We would sing all manner of songs, from the latest record hits to musicals, and even light opera. Goodness knows what anyone at about at 1.00a.m. thought, if they heard 'Shine Through My Dreams', or the latest Sinatra or Crosby offering, apparently emanating from the ground of that dark hill top.

With the Germans engaging in their 'Baedeker' raids, and Salisbury a likely target, the blackout was carefully observed. Suddenly, in July 1942, I was told to report to the Wessex Motors unit, only a hundred yards from the cathedral itself. So, not without some trepidation, I left the happy, if spartan, life I had grown used to on an airfield. It allowed a sense of cameraderie, due to the few working there and its isolation, that appealed to me. Its Foreman, Jack Draper, looked as though he would be more at home on a farm, yet had that happy knack of getting things done in a manner that was unofficious. It also meant I would leave behind Fred Veal, who had shared much of the past three years, as well as my newer-found colleagues, like Claude Harris, Bill Shadick, the other two 'tinbashers', Nobby Clarke the painter, Vic Woodgate of hydraulics, Pat Gregory the nightshift chargehand on the night that 'Enoch' had a totally unexpected epileptic fit to cause us two no end of bother one winter's night, and the two girls whom I'm sure will be pleased to be identified as, the 'Compass Swinger' and 'Armourer'.

These sudden moves to wherever our superiors thought we were needed became a routine occurrence as the war moved on, and the Spitfire was adapted to meet the necessary changing roles. In their way they made me feel that I was accepting some of the disciplines imposed on the Services, and therefore, to a lesser degree, more a part of a nation at war.

The Wessex unit in New Street was another requisitioned garage engaged in manufacturing fuselages, much the same as we had in the old 'K' shop. In fact, it had more ex-'K' shop colleagues than I ever found anywhere else, so my adjustment to the new shop was correspondingly easier. Its Foreman was Charlie Whettleton, who had been the riveting chargehand in 'K' shop and who, with the aid of the ex-fuselage lads to support him, found little difficulty in coping with his slightly more onerous responsibilities. 'Bill' Heaver, the Area Manager, was responsible for pulling me out of High Post, as he had the responsibility of building the new Seafire fuselages. I describe it that way because a large number of completed Spitfires were converted into 'Seafires' by the fitting of arrestor hooks and some additional stiffening. The 'pure' Seafire, however, had to have the catapult launching fittings as well as arrestor hooks, and it was these catapult fittings that were the problem. They were fitted mostly in the stage between structure completion and before the shell plating of the area below the cockpit. It was hardly a sheet metal worker's job, filing duralumin blocks to fits obtained by 'blueing in', followed by drilling and tapping for bolts, the whole assembly having to be impervious to the pushing of a 1½ thousandth of an inch feeler gauge, and a jig pin that had to move freely in its attachment fitting. It was more of a fitter's job, but they were in short supply in Salisbury and Supermarine's generally. It is also quite difficult to describe, but I will endeavour to do so.

The two bottom longerons from Frame 5 aft to the rear of the cockpit were unlike any others in the Spitfire fuselage, being each two flanged plates of 16g. (.064in.) riveted at right-angles to each other, so that the top one lay horizontally and its external flange provided a side skin plating location and fixing, whilst the vertical web did the same at the bottom. It was like an inverted 'L' shape, with a substantial flange at each open end, so that prior to shell plating this left a four inch right-angled cavity, and it was into this space that the catapult fittings were positioned, just forward of the rear wing spar attachment fitting at Frame 8.

First came a quadrant-shaped dural block of approximately 3in. wide. This had to be blued fit against the two faces of the longeron, and filed so that its curved face lined up

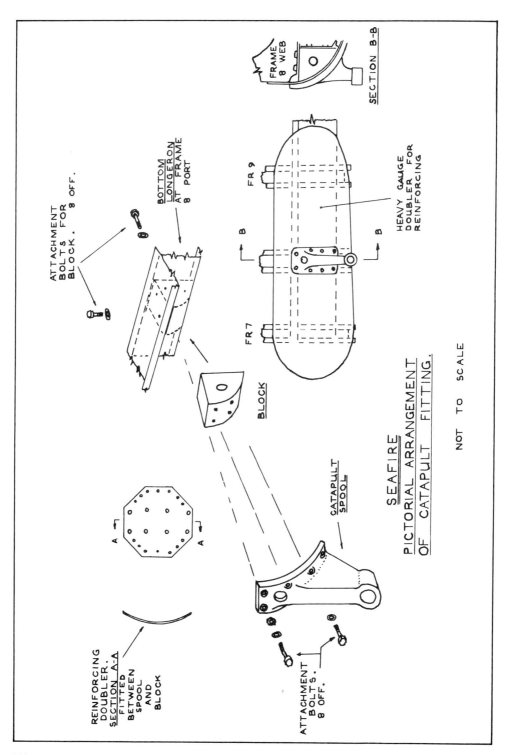

SEAFIRE
PICTORIAL ARRANGEMENT
OF CATAPULT FITTING.

NOT TO SCALE

cleanly with the two skin flanges. Once this had been achieved, the block and longeron faces were drilled, tapped and bolted with ¼in. steel bolts (see drawing).

Over this assembly was positioned and fitted a suitably shaped 18g. reinforcing panel, snugly fitted to the curved block face and extending roughly 4in. over the surrounding structure all around the block, to transfer some of the stress loads that would occur on cata-pulting. Having got this far and cleared Inspection, one then had to fit the catapult spool fitting. This was a forged duralumin fitting, its upper part a ¾in. thick curved platform that had to fit accurately over the curved block just fitted, and pick up both the top and bottom flanges of the longerons.

From its curved platform dropped, pendant like, an integral arm, roughly 9in. long, and having at its bottom end a circular 'bole' with a machined hole through it of some 1in. diameter. This hole had to be located to the jig point that was affixed to the cement floor, with a sliding arm that would be held by a jig pin when in its correct position. So the oper-ation for fitting the 'spool' was to file, scrape, and check, so that the jig pin through the 'bole' remained reasonably free, whilst an overall bearing surface was created against the doubler and blocks previously fitted. Due to the high loads transmitted during the actual catapult action, Inspection were very careful to ensure that the connecting faces had to have a satisfactory blued contact all over, and even edge gaps, especially in the region of the eight retaining bolts, were not accepted if a 1½ thousandths of an inch feeler gauge could be pushed in (.0015in. is approximately the thickness of a human hair). The eight attachment holes all had to meet 'B' fit requirements, so had to be reamed and, due to the curving shape of the base platform, counterbored to ensure that the bolts and their washers laid with all loads equally distributed.

Having successfully negotiated all these hurdles, the final operation for those of us on the catapult spool fitting was to affix a 2ft. x 1ft. elliptically-shaped 14g. or 12g. reinforcing doubling panel, longways around the assembly, by cutting a close-fitting hole to suit the platform foot of the spool, and making it a good fit to the surrounding basic structure, thus spreading its strength over a greater area.

I think, on reflection, that this job was perhaps the most difficult and demanding I ever did whilst on my tools, and as it was quite impossible to do in a single shift, we were paired off with a day or night shift partner. It speaks well of these pairings that despite the many pitfalls along the way, especially when an error at the latter end of the job could have rendered all the previous work useless, I cannot recall any of the pairings failing or falling out. I must admit that the occasional break from the job came as a welcome relief and allowed me to do other jobs for a change.

Most of my spell at Wessex was on night shift, and during my infrequent periods on days, the Luftwaffe showed itself again. On one occasion two fighter bombers dropped their couple of bombs near the railway station, and then a Heinkel bomber made a low run, just north of the cathedral, dropping a few bombs on the eastern side of the city, while its rear upper gunner sprayed machine gun bullets in our direction without much effect.

During one day shift spell I had a young lad, fresh from school, brought over to me by Charlie Whettleton 'to look after'. He was a polite, nice lad and I showed him as much as I could on the various jobs I had (not the catapult spool). Whether I fired his enthusiasm or, as he still says, 'worked him to death', I'm glad to say Eric Ranwell stuck to the task, climbing eventually to the Design Office, then to Liaison Designer at Eastleigh and Chilbolton after the war, and for the past twenty odd years has done pretty well at Boeing-Vertols in the United States. We have maintained contact ever since that first Wessex meeting which created a lifelong friendship.

Another chance meeting at Wessex very nearly set me off on an entirely different career after the war. Like all of our units, the hardcore 'Supermariners' were now outnumbered

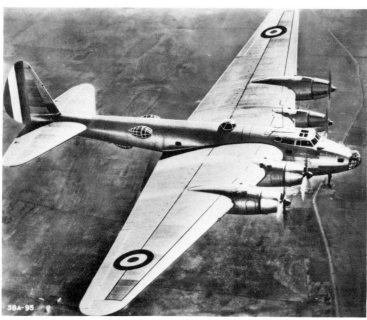

Above: An Airspeed 'Oxford' RAF training aircraft, after a single wheel landing at High Post, 1942.

Left: An American 'Flying Fortress' bomber.

by the many of both sexes who, by virtue of the Essential Works Order, had to leave their pre-war occupations if they were not considered as contributing to the war-effort, and were directed to us and other armaments works of a similar nature. They came from all walks of life —milkmen to musicians, waitresses to models, prima donnas to prostitutes — and it is only fair to add that so far as I saw, they all did a very good job. Many and most had been uprooted from their homes and familiar districts and sent to parts of the country absolutely unfamiliar to them, and to live either in lodgings or hostels. With husbands called up into one or other of the Services, young married women, childless and not expecting, formed a good part of these 'directed persons' and in the topsy turvy state of the world at that time, and the feelings one always had that tomorrow might not be for us, the barriers of pre-war conventions waned, and many 'liaisons of convenience' were formed. During my time at Salisbury, my 'holier than thou' upbringing was still dominant and thus I was not involved, although aware of some of these happenings.

Among these directed employees at Wessex was one 'Benny' Goodman, whose nickname was as a result of his previous employment as a clarinetist in a nationally-famous London dance band. Earlier, I have mentioned my penchant for imitating Bing Crosby, and one night, when I was inside a Spitfire fuselage before its tail unit was fitted, and assembling a pair of tail parachute doors, I was belting out 'Mexicali Rose' under the impression that amidst the shop noise I would not be overheard. Benny had been passing and stopped to listen, completely unbeknown to me as I lay on my back working above me, and at the end of my rendition surprised me by sticking his head inside the tail end frame aperture to enquire if I had been in the business before the war. I did not have a clue what he was on about. We met during the midnight meal break and he explained that 'the business' meant 'show business', and that to keep his professional occupation up to standard he, and a couple of others, had formed a small group and provided the Saturday afternoon Tea Dance music in the local Cadena Restaurant.

To cut a long story short, he persuaded me to sing with his little band and from that contact was born the Supermarine Salisbury Area Concert Party, a venture that provided me with a new interest out of working hours (which was badly needed at the time), and hours of fun as well as amusement and entertainment, not only to our own workmates, but to quite a lot of others as well, with shows and dances at the Assembly Rooms over W. H. Smith's bookshop in Salisbury. At one stage we were auditioned for a possible 'Works Wonders' broadcast, but not, at that time, considered as quite up to the B.B.C.'s standard.

I have a lovely memory from those days which surfaced just eighteen months ago when I was a patient in Salisbury Infirmary with lung congestion. The ward maid of some sixty summers asked one of the nurses to enquire of me 'if I used to sing at the dances during the war?' We enjoyed quite a chat once the contact was effected, wallowing in the nostalgia of days long gone. It is amazing how she could recognise me after forty years, but she said I was only fatter and had lost my wavy hair; but back to work.

After eight months, I was transferred back to High Post Airfield on 21st March 1943. My notebook shows that my last jobs at Wessex were to fit those reinforcing doublers to Seafire fuselages numbered 213 to 219 (shop numbers). Upon my return, I persuaded our Compass 'swinger' to join our Concert Party — she had a good soprano voice as I knew from those late night sing songs coming back from the canteen.

One other event had occurred during my absence, Fred Veal had been called up by the Royal Air Force in the December. As this had a depressing effect, due to the circumstances I have briefly mentioned before and have no desire to air here, and despite the new interests which I maintained, overall the prospect of another bleak winter was weighing heavily on my mind, and I suppose it showed. However, aid was at hand.

Keevil Hangar built for Spitfires at Steeple Ashton seven miles from Trowbridge, in 1943.   *Vickers*

The Keevil staff in 1945. Archie Preskett is seated directly under the Spitfire's spinner.

Chapter Nineteen
Return to Trowbridge

Bill Heaver, for all his apparent appearance of aloofness, cared for his workpeople, especially those whose antecedents went back to Woolston and his own 'K' shop. Four months after I had left Wessex he came on one of his rare visits to High Post and, during it, he enquired if I would care to go to a new airfield unit recently opened at Steeple Ashton, near Trowbridge.

I grasped the opportunity to get away from the personal domestic situation which had deteriorated and was, had we been wise enough to acknowledge it, beyond redemption. The flat we had in the High Post Hotel was vacated, the furnishings stored by an obliging uncle of mine in Southampton, and I went to Trowbridge, whilst my wife went back to her mother again. So in August 1943 I returned to the Brown family home in Bradley Road, and caught the next morning's lorry transport to Keevil Airfield.

Keevil Airfield was like so many during the war, created from suitably located and flat farmland which, in this instance, lay adjacent to the pretty little Wiltshire village of Steeple Ashton, notable for its wonderfully executed many spired church which still looks, even today, as if someone wanted to try out in model scale the architecture for a cathedral, and on its small village green the old 'lock-up' and a sundial clock-tower.

The new hangar built for Supermarine's and Spitfire test flying was erected just outside the airfield proper and its hedged boundary, on land closer to the church. Our entrance was by way of a narrow lane through farm gates, and via a rough track that twisted and turned perhaps 300 yards. At the gate in the surrounding security fence was a small brick gate-warden's building, and then a few yards on, the (to us) large camouflaged hangar, and beside it the canteen building and boiler house. Compared to the High Post facilities it was a palace. Purpose-built and planned, it had large sliding doors opening on to the concrete roadway that not only led to the gap cut in the airfield boundary hedge for our access to the runways, but incorporated along it a properly marked-out compass swinging pad away from the metal mass of the hangar which could affect the compasses.

The large doors and the ample unobstructed concrete floor within, allowed a 'Coles' crane to eliminate the backbreak of physically humping the wings and fuselages etc. There was ample space for six Spitfires down each side, and sufficient room between the two lines to manoeuvre any of the twelve without detriment to the others. Down the side nearest the airfield were built, on to the outside wall, the various offices, etc; the Armoury, a First Aid Room with resident nurse, the Foreman's Office, Time Office, and smaller ones for the A.I.D., Inspection, and Rolls Royce rep. An exit through the middle of these offices led on to a small roadway across which were the canteen and kitchens, and also provided access to the toilet facilities. At the end opposite to the main door were wire fenced-off compounds, holding finished parts, A.G.S., and Embodiment Loan items, with their own smaller sliding door for the use of delivery vans and lorries. With its good lighting and heating, it was a marvellous place in which to work. The foreman was Archie Preskett, who I had never met before, but who quickly won the respect of all for his quiet, firm, and gentlemanly authoritarianism.

I had not come to Keevil alone. With me were transferred 'Nobby' Clarke the painter, Vic Woodgate the hydraulics man, and Hilda Henry, the fillet fitter and compass swinger, and our Concert Party soprano. The 'hardcore' from High Post had been supplemented by others with experience from other areas including one other 'K' shop man, Jack Lansom. Around this larger core of experienced people were over a hundred 'directed' workers from

Trowbridge and the surrounding area, with some from much further away, such as Bristol, Weston-super-Mare, Wales, Oxford and London. All told, there were at least 150 persons employed.

At this time the course of the war had shifted significantly in favour of the Allies. North Africa had been cleared, and Sicily invaded successfully.

On the airfield proper, we could watch, during our meal breaks, the giant Stirling bombers, the smaller Albermarles and the United States Thunderbolt fighter squadrons that were based there, and went raiding over France at times. Brest Harbour in daylight was one Stirling raid, not particularly accompanied by success, as the big four-engined heavy bombers had an altitude capability that left a lot to be desired, and they were badly mauled.

Nevertheless, our particular product was still in great demand — it was, as is well-known, the only Allied fighter that maintained its front line operational rating for the whole of the war. This involved many modifications and changes to keep to the ever-changing demands of wartime requirements, and although at Keevil we were not bothered with Seafires or the tropicalised Spitfires, quite often we would have at least three different Mark Nos. among our twelve, from the 8s and 14s with either Merlin or Griffon engines and their differing engine mountings and cowlings. It was amazing how quickly we all settled into an efficient routine, and seeing so many Spitfires going out, and with the operational activities very apparent on the airfield, I'm sure most of us felt closer to the war itself since those days and nights of 1940.

We operated the basic two shift, month about, day and night shift, on roughly a one third total staff on each, the other one third being those whose duties were exclusively for daytime. The six 'tinbashers' formed three teams for the nose fillets and cowling routine, similar to that at High Post, and we became more proficient with the repetition. Jack Lansom and I formed one squad, and in conjunction with our other colleagues, and Archie Preskett's benign agreement, we worked our shift rota so that one squad did the nights and two always were on days, where we were more in demand for attendance on test flights. This of course gave each squad two months on dayshift and one on nights.

Jack and I had little difficulty in meeting the demands required of us and, quite frequently, we would have time to spare. Rather than waste it — and after a brief spell of making cigarette lighters — I preferred to find myself other things to do. I helped in fitting and testing the hydraulic system, poked around in the Armoury where the cannons fascinated me and, whilst on dayshift, even got our soprano to show me how the compass swing was done and the deviation cards were compiled. On another occasion I made a knee pad clip-board for a young R.A.F. pilot doing a 'rest' period from operations. His name was Banner, and he was later to die testing a Spitfire at High Post. This far in the war the ugly hand of the grim reaper had passed me and my family, but within six weeks of moving to Keevil it struck. It was presaged by a curious incident. I was on nightshift and under a 'Spit', cutting and fitting its front bottom fillet panel on the starboard side. Just before midnight I felt, as I thought, unwell, but the feeling was as if I had suddenly been enveloped in a thick black depressive cloud. How long this lasted I have no idea but, as it gradually lifted, I felt all the strength drain from me. It was something I have never experienced before or since, and I went out into the night and wandered around until I was myself again.

Six days later, after wisely letting me finish my meal, Mrs Brown broke the news to me that my brother had been 'killed in action'. The last I had heard from him he was in North Africa. I asked for leave of absence and went home, but both my parents were so shocked and distraught that I thought my presence constituted an embarrassing reminder of their loss so, after a twenty-four hour stay, I pleaded urgency of work and returned to Trowbridge.

Apart from the routine work carried out at Keevil Airfield, which was substantially the same as that described for High Post, there were other happenings that may properly be recorded here.

One concerns another 'resting' pilot; this time from the Royal Navy, Lt. Peter Hill. I came to know him through being 'in attendance' on a few of his test flights, and during adjustments between flights Peter would generally park himself where he was always assured of a cup of tea from the ex-ballet dancer nurse, who despite her years fluttered her eyelashes at Peter's roguish and deliberate playing up to her. She often became the butt of his outrageous sense of humour, and her peals of laughter were heard all over the hangar on these occasions. However, it was for a different reason that I remember him. On the airfield proper, there was one squadron of American Thunderbolts; great, hefty single seat fighters, with large radial engines that snarled very noisily.

For some reason, on this particular occasion, they were practising flying a diamond outline formation very low down and, using the runway as their guideline, roared backwards and forwards. Their great Pratt and Whitney engines made a hell of a din at each pass and this racket got under Peter's skin.

I was attending his test flight, and as he settled into the Spitfire cockpit for the second flight, I checked that his restraining safety straps were alright, and he shouted in my ear above the running engine noise, 'Watch this — I'll shut those buggers up.'

No doubt his subsequent actions were reckless and dangerous but, in wartime, different standards applied, and I have never seen the like of it since. Taxi-ing out to the end of the runway I watched as he received his green clearance light from the control tower, but he delayed and appeared to me to be checking his engine revs. What he was really doing was watching in his rear view mirror for the return of the diamond formation of Thunderbolts. Timing his run exactly, he belted down the runway, then, with great precision, pulled the Spitfire's nose up into a near vertical climb and, to my open-mouthed astonishment, barrel-rolled his aircraft right through the middle of the diamond.

Those 'Yanks' must have had the fright of their lives as they broke their immaculate formation outwards away from this unexpected intrusion in their midst. Peter Hill carried on flying upwards until he reached the altitude required for whatever check he was making, whilst the Thunderbolts formed a large circle round the airfield and began to land. Before half of them were down Peter returned and joined their landing circuit.

When he eventually landed and taxied back to where I was, he switched his engine off, climbed out on to the wing, and passed his parachute down to me before jumping to the ground. He gave me a big wink and tapped the side of his nose with one finger, indicating that he did not want me to say anything. I told him I had never seen anything like it and I remember his reply to this day, exactly as he said it, 'Neither have those Yanks. I flew alongside one in the circuit and his eyes were stuck out like dogs' balls.'

A complaint was made to our Foreman immediately by telephone, by the U.S. airmen, and the Control Tower, but Peter explained over the telephone that it was quite accidental as he was having trouble with his engine revs and had no idea of the approach of the Americans from behind him. He apologised and got away with it. I suppose he had a valid point that he had been given the green by the Control Tower who should have 'red-flared' either him or the Thunderbolts off.

I asked Jeffrey Quill recently if he, as the Company's Chief Test Pilot, had received any notice of the incident, but he could not recall ever hearing of it. Sadly, Peter Hill survived the war only to die from tuberculosis afterwards. In a letter to me, Mr. Quill described Peter as a 'gutsy chap', which sums up the man I remember very aptly. Another 'gutsy' performance occurred one lunchtime when I had taken my sandwich meal out on to the airfield to eat whilst watching the flying activity.

Most people are aware of the Air Transport Auxiliary Service, which was mainly composed of women pilots whose wartime job was to collect and ferry aircraft to their various destinations. Some of these pilots were mere slips of girls, but they flew practically every type of aircraft, and their courage is legendary. It was one such slip of a girl who arrived at Keevil on this particular day to take away one of our finished Spitfires. She taxied it down to the runway start, did her checks, and received her 'green' for take-off. I watched as the usual Spitfire 'wiggle' was countered by her rudder control and she set off with ever increasing speed down the runway. She gently lifted the aircraft off the ground, then a crosswind caught it and it drifted to her left.

Alongside the runway at approximately two hundred yard intervals were heaps of granite rock, for emergency filling of bomb craters in runways in the event of bombing, and just as she selected undercarriage up, so the drift caused her port wheel to strike the top of one of these heaps. The whole undercarriage leg snapped off at the wing pintle on which it hinged, and fell to the ground.

The Control Tower klaxon blared out its warning alert to the standby ambulance and fire tenders, who moved along the other side of the runway to where they considered she might eventually come to rest, but the Spitfire flew on, gained a little more height, and then turned to fly alongside the Control Tower with its one remaining leg still down.

I suppose the pilot was given some indication of her predicament from the Control Tower; anyway she flew on a mile or so, then turned, and with no fuss or bother made an approach to land on the grass within yards of where I was. I could see her clearly as she went by me with the hood opened, and she made the best single wheel landing I've ever seen, cutting her throttle at just the right moment as the Spitfire held for a moment on its one wheel then the port wing went slowly down, until its tip took some of the strain, and the whole aircraft slewed to a halt.

I like to think my sprint was worthy of the occasion, but when I reached the aircraft everything was switched off and a young unflurried woman was busy shaking out her hair, having just removed her helmet and goggles. Calm and brave, she remains in my memory as epitomizing Britain's women at war.

Without any doubt the high spot of my time at Keevil came on the night of 5th/6th June 1944. I had been home to Southampton for the weekend, prior to returning to a new stint of nightshift. Southampton and its surrounding districts were choc-a-block with troops and their equipment. Down on the Weston shore and in the docks were hundreds of various types of landing craft and ships. Early on the Saturday night an enemy reconnaissance aircraft had caused the air raid sirens to sound, but as it was obviously only one aircraft, and attracted just token anti-aircraft gunfire, we watched as it dropped a line of flares. I have little doubt that its photography was rendered useless by the smoke screen issuing from containers placed all around the town, whose contents stank to high heaven.

Listening, last year, to the television coverage to celebrate the fortieth anniversary of 'D' Day, I noticed that most of them stressed how a ten mile band of coastline from the Wash to Plymouth had been 'sealed off' and I'm left wondering how I got in on the Friday night and came out on the Monday afternoon without being checked. Was it that trains just passed in and out without a check? It was obvious that the Invasion was about to take place, but the only check I received was as we arrived at Keevil on the Monday night, just before 8p.m.

An Army squad stopped us on the farm path to our hangar. During the identity check I looked under the canvas cover of our lorry, to see we were being carefully covered by a Bren gun, set up a few yards further on. In the few moments of change-over, the dayshift people indicated that the airfield might stand looking at. It did, but our gap in the hedge was guarded by armed soldiers. Beyond them, however, it was plain to see the rows of aircraft and gliders bearing their 'D' Day identification broad black and white stripes painted on wings and fuselages.

As nothing appeared to be moving, we returned to our work until, at midnight, a distinct, but loud, rumbling sound gradually increased to the roar of many aircraft nearly overhead. Rushing outside, there was a sight previously unseen in the war, of a large formation of aircraft with their navigation lights on, and towing gliders. It was very impressive, and as one wave passed from our sight and sound, another hove into view, and we guessed their purpose.

Somewhere, about 3a.m., the aircraft on our 'drome started up, and we stole out again to see this operation in progress and this time, despite the calls from our chargehand for his missing flock to return, half of us stayed hidden within the hedge to watch something, we guessed then, we'd never see again. Stirlings and Albermarles, towing Horsa or American Waco gliders, went rumbling down the runway, their exhaust pipes stabbing the night with flame, as they strained for maximum power to get themselves and their trailing charges off the ground. On and on they went, with little space between them, all of them aware that this 30 second run was all that lay between a successful take-off or possible oblivion.

Some literally staggered into the air at the last moment, just clearing the boundary hedge at the end of the airfield, and one, an Albermarle I believe, towing a Waco glider-load of troops, failed to gain enough height to clear the low Wiltshire hills three miles away, smashing into them with a blinding flash that told its own story, but still the others sped down the runway, assisted, I trust, by the silent prayers of their hidden observers.

As dawn broke we crept back to our proper places, trying our best to look as though we had been there all along, but within the hangar little groups were huddled in conversation with a larger group endeavouring to find out something from a radio, all hoping to have confirmed that which we had seen was the opening gambit in the long awaited Invasion to free Europe.

We were back in our homes or lodgings when Eisenhower's clipped manner of speaking told us over the radio that 'D' Day had arrived, and landings were in progress.

During my dayshift spell, prior to this memorable night, I had been asked by Archie Preskett if I would represent the Keevil unit at the Area's Joint Consultation meeting at Bradley Road, as our union convenor, who usually went, was away temporarily. This was one of the so-called democratising schemes instigated by the Socialist members of the National Government Cabinet, and a foretaste of things to come. I was a member of the Sheetmetal and Braziers Union, and had been since I was eighteen. Our hangar convenor belonged to one of the non-craft unions, who during the war flourished and grew by representing semi-skilled or unskilled personnel, and consequently, from these early beginnings, by virtue of their larger numbers, have since come to have a disproportionate weight in industry, without the moderating balance that the craftsmen can provide. It was the custom of our convenor to go around the hangar seeking matters that he could raise at these meetings in the two days immediately preceding them. I always considered that the correct way to air a grievance was for the individual to take it up directly with the Foreman, therefore I went to the meeting without anything to report, but with an open mind and willingness to report back if required. I think now that Archie Preskett had summed me up by then, and my choice as 'rep' was not exactly a fluke — in which case I must applaud his astuteness.

We met in the Conference Room at Bradley Road works (now Hattersley-Hewletts) and with Mr. Hall in the chair, and flanked by Leslie Brown his deputy, and Audrey his secretary, we all sat around the long conference-type table and, quite by accident, I ended up in the seat at the far end, facing Mr. Hall. The events of that day have carried over the years, as, whenever possible, that is the seat I take in meetings, looking directly at the Chairman and able to see all the others along each side.

I sat and listened, expecting to hear either justifiable grievances, or proposals from the shop floor that would aid or increase production; the matters I understood to be the reason for these meetings. To my surprise, and I may add my growing annoyance, all that came forth were piddling little complaints about the shortage of 'loo' rolls here and no soap there, cold meals in canteens, bad lodgings, underpayment of bonus, and a whole host of trivial matters, all of which should have been, and could have been, dealt with by the Foreman, Personnel Department, or the Unit's Time Clerk. This went on for an hour and a quarter, Mr. Hall pleasantly and politely answering where he could, and asking Audrey to make a note where he couldn't.

Nearing the end of the meeting's scheduled time, and as I had not said a word, Vernon Hall looked up at me, welcomed me to the meeting as Keevil's temporary representative, and enquired if there were any matters I wished to raise? That did it!

In my iciest voice, and restraining the factory language that was in my mind to use, I told my so-called representative colleagues just what I thought of their whingeing and whining 'complaints', explained what I thought the meeting was for, and finally apologised to Mr Hall for his having to sit through such drivel. When I finished there was a stunned silence. I saw a little smile flicker across Vernon Hall's face, and his eyes lit up behind his pebble glasses, but he did not say anything as the meeting broke up in unaccustomed disorder, and I hastily left to travel back to Keevil with Tommy Durham in the Area's car. Tommy was big, bluff and Irish, and had known my father in the years before the war in Southampton. He shared a common interest in singing with me, and that day we gave full vent to the Neopolitan song 'Cateri Cateri' all the way back to the airfield. It got the grouse off my chest — but I was never invited to another Consultation meeting. I never mentioned it to Archie Preskett and he never asked, but there was a sequel!

After 'D' Day, and during that hard slog to capture Caen, Mr Hall sent for me to go to Bradley Road, sending the same Tommy Durham and car to collect me. Archie Preskett did not know why, and I couldn't think of any reason either, as my unexpected contribution to the consultation meeting was too distant in the past for any disciplinary action, and even our night watching the gliders go to war had appeared irrelevant in the general euphoria that the event had created worldwide. So much for a guilty conscience! The reality was completely unexpected.

Before supplying the explanation for the summons, and lest it slips my mind, it would be unfair not to say a word or two about all those people who, in many instances, were obliged to take us 'War-Workers' into their homes under the billeting regulations then in force. I can only speak with any certainty on those with whom I came into contact, although there were one or two quite extraordinary stories that I'm sure were true but, as they are not mine, must remain unquoted without better verification.

I have already mentioned some of my 'digs'; the Kings at the Chandler's Ford Conservative Club, and the tragic end to my stay with Mrs Newman. After my first stay with the Browns in Trowbridge I had rooms, then quickly lodgings again, with the Brookman family in Trowbridge, before having to retreat to Salisbury where a milkman's wife proved to be a little too over zealous for my partner's taste, so she found me safer lodgings with Mary Burch. Mary proved a godsend to me during this particularly tricky domestic period. Both her sons were away in the Services, being but a year either side of my age, and her husband, who had been the Foreman at the Wilts & Dorset garage, now commandeered, was an R.A.F. reservist, and he too was away in that Service. More modern in her outlook on life than my own parents, she provided me with good advice and help, quite over and above the board and lodgings which was the basic requirement. Once she learned of my penchant for Bing Crosby, she used to get up especially early, so that I could listen to the early morning quarter hour programme of the 'Old Groaner' broadcast on the American Forces Network each Tuesday, and it was Mary who urged me to take up Benny Goodman's offer to sing with his group, by saying she had heard me singing in the bath and thought I should.

Those days in her 'semi' at 78 Castle Road, Salisbury, have fond memories for me, and I'm glad we were able to meet in happier circumstances long after the war. After a spell in one of the flats of the converted High Post Hotel, I returned to the Brown's at Trowbridge and the disconcerting news of my younger, and only, brother's death. In the intervening time between, when Fred Veal and I shared a bedroom, the Brown's two sons had grown to 12 and 10, and prior to my return had a bedroom each. A friend of Mrs Brown, who lived with her husband in more modern premises nearby, suggested that I come and stay with her. As it seemed beneficial to all concerned I agreed and moved, only to return post-haste one week later. My new landlady had soon made it clear when her husband was at work that I was expected to supply a physical need that he was not performing to her satisfaction. Still, at that time, retaining my last remnants of early training and 'honourable' behaviour, I left hastily.

Clarence Brown, the engine driver, laughed when I told him privately of my reason for this rapid return, intimating that he understood that was the reason for the arrangement. I wish he had told me earlier! However I had imposed on the Brown's enough and, 'aided' by the Billeting Officer, moved a week later to another digs which were by far the worst I have ever had. The first night in an attic, shared with a beery Irishman, found me a mass of flea bites in the morning, and the following evening, whilst we were all seated around the dining table, I'm damned if the Paddy did not take his shoes and socks off and cut his toe nails. I went into work so steamed up over this that I seriously considered whether the amorous landlady might not have been the better bet after all, but I was saved 'from a fate worse than death' by Vic Woodgate who arranged for me to share his digs with a Miss Moody in Gloucester Road.

Vic was a lovable man, always cheerful, always kind. A milkman in Salisbury before he was first directed to High Post and then with the others to Keevil, he had one glass eye but never let that worry him. May Moody was an unmarried lady who later told me that her boyfriend, whom she had expected to marry, had been killed in the Great War. She was one of those who only loved once, and as far as she was concerned that was the end of the matter. Fiercely patriotic, worshipping Winston Churchill, she was almost the last of a breed of women who now seem to have virtually disappeared — proud, independent, loyal — it was an honour to be known as one of 'her gentlemen guests', and in her care I found my final home whilst I was in Trowbridge.

I still ponder over how three so diverse characters coalesced and found a recipe for satisfactory living. May Moody was a bundling, rotund, spinster, very 'proper' in her outlook on life, careful with her meagre funds, but a good cook, a clean tidy housekeeper, and concerned for her only brother who was, she believed, a prisoner of war in Japanese hands.

Vic, married, with his wife and children in Salisbury, was one of nature's gentlemen and in my book that is one of the highest compliments I can pay. And me?! Probably too earnest, constrained by the environment in which I had grown up for so many years, and just on the brink of breaking out from them, whilst at the same time the overall strain of various personal worries, irregular sleeping and working times and earlier, sometimes unsatisfactory food, which was about to put me into hospital and an operation.

The strange thing was that it worked like a charm. While May fussed around with her duties, always thinking of the needs of her 'gentlemen', we supported her by doing those little jobs for which a man is best about the house. I got Vic involved in the War Workers Recreational Centre (of more later) activities — on coach trips he was the life and soul of

Trowbridge War Workers' Recreational Centre outing to Clifton and Wells in 1944. C.R.R. centre back row.

A group from the Trowbridge area's concert party. Most of them featured in the BBC's 'Works Wonders' broadcast. Excluding the mouth organists they are, from left to right: back row, Vic Cannings, Don Weller, and C.R.R. Front row, Daisy Silcocks, Chrissie Way, Joan Mathews, Joyce Hunt and Stella Mathews. Picture taken during a Concert in Trowbridge Town Hall.

the party — and he counselled and often covered for me when I finally relinquished my celibacy and 'honour' and found an honest, if illicit, intimate relationship with a member of the opposite sex. I kept in touch with May until her death, sometimes going to visit her, and she came to my home when I finally stopped roaming and settled down. She never changed really, just grew older. Her brother survived the war and came home, terribly emaciated by beri-beri and the usual treatment common to Japanese prisoners of war, but, in time, recovered.

After the war, when Vic and I had gone, May continued to take in 'gentlemen guests' to supplement her income, and I still feel it a privilege to have been one of them. At one time I had to do a job that required me to go to Rutland Garage, where the Coppersmiths were located, and, whilst there, during spells of unavoidable waiting, I made a small kettle — a miniature in brass, only about 2½in. high. The main object of the exercise was to shape and make a spout — always considered a tricky metalwork job, as it narrowed from the base to the spout end and was the old 'S' shape. I was quite proud of it and made a good job of its tiny lid and handle, so when it was finished and polished I gave it to May, who was so pleased that she put in on her mantlepiece, where it remained until she passed away.

By and large — and I know a number of my contemporaries agreed — I think the people who took us 'strangers' into their homes treated us very well, and we owe them our thanks and gratitude. Personally, I am sure it was an experience that completely reshaped my thoughts and ways — not always necessarily for the better — in some respects, but provided an experience on which my future was to be based.

Among the employees at Keevil, our nurse was an ex-ballet dancer, and another older gent had at one time been 'on the boards' as a comedian. These two, plus our soprano and myself, cast around and began to create a new concert party. We even began rehearsals for 'blackout' sketches during our lunch hours in the little church hall down the lane which we hired, then word of our little operation — which originally was intended solely for the Keevil employees — filtered back to the new Area Headquarters and factory at Bradley Road, and we were invited to use their far superior facilities in the upstairs canteen, provided we incorporated their own talented people into an Area Concert Party. This we did, and one of those born organiser types, that spring up at times, appeared on the scene. Cyril Barnes had no special talent for parading in public, but in marshalling, arranging, and generally organising everything from props to engagements, he was just the job.

Among the new performers we found were a mouth organ and accordion band, Don Weller, a sweet tenor, the Matthews Sisters, Vic Canning, who was to prove very good competition for me, Dickie Hughes, the patter comedian whose signature tune was 'I'm not all there', and two excellent pianists, Bill Dark and Joe Till, whose performances together on one piano were only equalled by their very careful individual accompaniment for solo singers. There were others whose names time has sadly erased from my memory.

Our initial concerts quickly established the confidence and discipline required, and soon we were going round the local halls. One Sunday afternoon we did a Charity Show in Bradford-on-Avon Cinema which was a complete sell-out. This was no doubt a direct result of our being broadcast only a couple of weeks earlier. Yes, we had actually made a 'Works Wonder' programme at last! The producer, Hamilton Kennedy, whose father was the famous songwriter Jimmy Kennedy, auditioned us in turn, and then selected his half-hour content for broadcasting. We actually performed the show to the night shift in Bradley Road canteen at midnight on a Thursday, and it was recorded, via the G.P.O. lines, at the B.B.C.'s Bristol Studios, and then broadcast on the following Saturday lunch time.

After that the Ministry of Labour's local office picked us up, and provided coach transport so that we could cover a far wider area and many more different types of war workers, from the Irish labourers, digging out underground caverns for machine shops at Corsham, to, of all places, two separate shows at Salisbury for the 'Spitfire' workers there! The afternoon show was in a familiar venue to me — the Assembly Rooms — and in the evening at the canteen of Style and Gerrish's departmental store (now Debenhams). One thing that particularly pleased me was that Bill Heaver and his wife came to both shows.

Leaping ahead a few years to explain a remark I made earlier about 'nearly changing my whole career', I had better explain that after the war, in 1947, I spent a solo two weeks holiday at Butlin's Camp at Clacton. Egged on by a female aquaintance, I entered the 'Sing with the Squadronaires' contest, not only winning it but also receiving an offer from Jimmy Miller to become his band's male vocalist. His pianist, Ronnie Aldrich, who still plays on the radio, was instrumental in the offer being made, as his delicately beautiful accompaniment for my rendering of 'Tumbling Tumbleweeds' undoubtedly brought the best out of me. However, at the time, I had just had news of a new job that I badly wanted, so — for better or for worse — I turned the singing opportunity down. I still wonder what might have been.

It can be deduced that the persons mentioned above, each in their own way, contributed to the moulding and shaping of the person I became. Without them, and the circumstances the war imposed, I doubt if the years ahead, either in or out of the industry I loved, would have been so rewarding. In retrospect, it is apparent that the naive youth who commenced this journey had begun to flex the wings of ambition to achieve the desires which it entailed. In its way, the summons to the Bradley Road Works, which we left to pay a deserved tribute, was the beginning or awakening that other options existed which had not been considered.

The Ministry of Labour had designated certain areas — mainly where war work and war workers had been dispersed, and where the normal recreational facilities and other things were not usually available — as places where they would set up War Worker Recreational Centres. The Ministry undertook to erect the building, equip it, and pay its rates, etc., and provide a full-time paid warden. The local war works and other agencies were instructed to form a Management Committee to run the centre. Vickers, as the company was now generally known, were allocated one representative place on the Managing Committee, and it was this post which Vernon Hall was offering me. I was not only surprised, but quite flattered, and with a few detailed enquiries settled, I accepted. It was an own-time commitment — unpaid of course — but nevertheless, in my view, a worthwhile cause.

It was a decision I have never regretted, and at the inaugural committee meeting we settled the various responsibilities, electing, as Chairman, the Manager of the town's largest store, a Treasurer and a Secretary — this latter post falling to me. Other committee members included the local Catholic Canon, the District Billeting Official, and the local newspaper's Editor, plus two other companies' nominees, and the warden as an ex-officio member.

The building, at the end of Innox Road, had a nice size main hall at the rear, a small reading room and, across the front to the right of the main entrance, a comfortable lounge with fireside-style armchairs, circular tables and chairs scattered over its centre space, except in the way of the bar type counter where tea, coffee, soft drinks and various eats could be purchased. Left of the main entrance a corridor separated the committee room and the warden's office from the toilet facitilies and three bathrooms. I mention the bathrooms as they were an inestimable blessing as the majority of Trowbridge houses, at that time, did not have such a facility, making the weekly bath often embarrassing and inconvenient for both lodgers and landladies alike.

The venture was a success from the start, with volunteers taking on the sub-committees we created for Entertainments, Catering and Outside Activities. Each Saturday evening we held a dance to gramophone recordings, and through the summer months arranged coach trips to Bristol, Bath, Cheddar, Wells Cathedral and the like. We established a small library from gift books and, over one weekend, we held a musical competition, open to all-comers, which was extremely well supported, and provided quite a high standard of entry. Our Works Concert Party contributed the soprano who sang 'The Pipes of Pan', and Don Weller, our tenor, sang 'An English Rose'. My favourite memory is of a young girl in a blue dress and shoulder length black hair who played Debussy's 'Clair de Lune' at the piano, with a touch as delicate as the moonbeams themselves. As we had advertised this event publicly, a number of members of the public subsequently came forward to help in our other activities. This was doubly welcome, as not only did we receive their help, but it enabled us to integrate more and more with the Trowbridge residents, who earlier in the war had, with some justification, attributed the influx of strangers, whom they were obliged to take into their homes, as our fault, and worse, considered our presence as making their town an enemy target. Fortunately, this latter feeling was largely dispersed when a low-flying German aircraft either lost, or fleeing from the well-defended Bristol area, let go a couple of bombs within the Trowbridge town boundary. This occurred whilst I was in Salisbury, and it was noticeable, on my return, that Trowbridge now considered itself 'bombed', and equal in status to the Southampton people and, in the final reckoning, I for one was glad that these false and unavoidable barriers were eliminated, and would wish to express my appreciation to the people in Trowbridge who mostly did their best to make such 'unwelcome guests' as comfortable as they could.

There was also a spin-off for me which, at the time, I did not foresee. The experience of the joint consultation meeting had opened my eyes a little, but participating in the decision processes of the little club, and having to learn the rudiments of the ways which committees work and run, even to the extent of acting as Chairman on odd occasions, were all 'grist to the mill' of experience, that in the years to come was to prove invaluable. Just as doing those odd jobs at work, not within my own trade, enabled me to understand and appreciate the wider aspects of aircraft production so, in due time, these many facets of occupation and administration eventually came together and 'gelled' to my advantage.

If there is one thing that I would sincerely hope may come from my story, it is that the young men of today — particularly the school-leavers and those so desperately seeking work — who, perhaps like myself, do not have the twin benefits of a good education or wealthy start in life, will take heart and even inspiration from my experiences and, rather than take or seek the higher paid jobs with little or zero future prospects, will go for those jobs where a trade training in basic skills are comprehensively and clearly offered, and not the most money.

Any Engineering Manager or Executive will soon tell you that skilled men — in all categories of manufacturing — are in short supply today, even though the unemployment figure of 3 million is just as high now, per capita of the population, as it was when I took the lowly grade of 'handy lad'. To my mind, the present attitude of young people, to sacrificing the money-grabbing syndrome so prevalent, is very largely due to two main factors —neither of them the fault of the young people themselves — the poor general standard of post-war education which, despite its obviousness, my generation did little enough to check, and the unwarranted, and plainly stupid, actions of some Government and Union policies which compel employers to pay wages that are ridiculously disproportionate to the investment he makes in the training of an unskilled, and often immature, young person. Believe me, in all modesty, I have very good reasons to know.

By 1944 the Spitfire had really reached the end of its development, and the Design Team, under Joe Smith, which had maintained it thus far, felt obliged, at least, to create a newer aircraft which incorporated all the lessons learned, and improvements that were now to

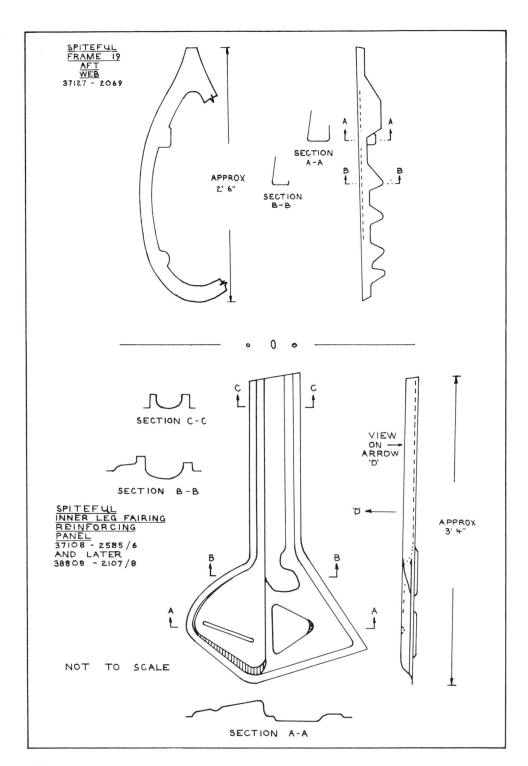

SPITEFUL
FRAME 19
AFT
WEB
37127 - 2069

APPROX
2' 6"

SECTION
A-A

SECTION
B-B

A A

B B

SECTION C-C

SECTION B-B

SPITEFUL
INNER LEG FAIRING
REINFORCING
PANEL
37108 - 2585/6
AND LATER
38808 - 2107/8

NOT TO SCALE

C C

B B

A A

VIEW
ON
ARROW
'D'

'D'

APPROX
3' 4"

SECTION A-A

hand. This aircraft was named Spiteful, and its new type number was 371. Distribution of the manufacturing content was parcelled out to the areas at Gooch's Area Manager's meeting, and the Trowbridge area was charged with making the empennage end of the fuselage, which incorporated the built-in fin.

This unit was similar in general outline to the Spitfire, but larger, and had a fixed fairing below the rudder. To get production under way before the major machine and press tools were available, the early quantity of parts were to be made by hand with mainly 'Jabroc' tools. It was this decision that caused my transfer from Keevil Airfield to Bradley Road in January 1945.

There is little doubt that my move was inspired by Mr. Hall's recollections of the air duct, four years earlier. My new task was to make the frames, including the fin spar frames, the fairings under the rudder, and various details for the rudders, tailplanes, elevators and associated structures.

As part of this new design, as distinct from the Spitfire, Bradley Road had been chosen to pioneer the new 'Robinson' process; a full scale layout idea similar to, but much more advanced than, the old mould lofting scrieve boards, and now drawn on to photographic film and subsequently printed (as many copies as required) on to light alloy sheets (mostly material scrapped due to blemishes and scratches and unfit for use on aircraft), having one side prepared to receive the photo print on a matt finish, produced by the sheet being subjected to agitation roughening by glass marbles on a special table with a 6in. rotary mechanical action. From these printed plates, with their mass of extra detail — position of holes, extrapolation of flange depths, etc. — it was possible to make tooling templates for cutting blank sizes, and to check that the finished article met the peripheral shapes and limits required, as well as set the position of tooling holes. It was a vast improvement or extension of the old Mould Loft principle, and soon became standard practice in most aircraft factories.

The Spiteful frame 19 was the joint frame between the fuselage and tail unit, as on the Spitfire, so consequently was really two frames that abutted back to back. With the larger fin, etc., the aft portion necessitated extensions to its aft facing flanges to pick up more of the tail units stringer and longerons and, to achieve these extensions, the flanges had to be 'drawn' by hand forming over a 'Jabroc' block for three inches in those local areas. As the tail unit continued to reduce in its oval fuselage size until it reached the front of the fin, this inevitably meant that all the rear frame 19 flanges had acute angles (less than 90 degrees), from minus 3 degrees at the sides, to an awful minus 13 degrees at the bottom and its smallest radius curve. It was quite a job (see drawing).

Apart from this frame, it became apparent that my responsibilities included all the other difficult parts, leaving the reasonably straight-forward stringers, brackets, longerons, etc. to other Bradley Road staff; this also included my completing any sub-assembly involved to keep the jig assembly team going. Therefore I made three of each part initially as a batch quantity, only to find that as the first structure was completed, it fell to me to shape its skins. All in all it was quite a lot to do but, on my own, encouraged by Vernon Hall and Les Brown rather than chased, it was something I could throw all my energies into, and see and feel well-pleased with the results. Conrad Mann who had been 'K' shop's Inspector prior to the 1940 bombing had, on dispersal, become the Senior Inspector to the Trowbridge Area and, as with the air ducts, ever ready with a quiet word if I needed a point of guidance within his field, or a quick inspection to prevent delays. 'Con' was a big man, in every sense of the word, always calm and approachable, and someone to whom one gave respect out of sheer admiration for his whole attitude. I saw and spoke to him last about two years ago, when Mitchell's memorial stone was unveiled, and in the intervening years he has since passed on.

From January to 1st May 1945, I worked hard and happily, and then my 'tummy', which had been troubling me for some time, laid me low in Trowbridge's Cottage Hospital, and it was a half-dozen semi-inebriated nurses who, with kisses and bottles of beer, came and told us of the German surrender on 8th May 1945. My brother would have been celebrating his twenty-fourth birthday had he survived. Six days later I came out of hospital, having had an operation before V.E. day and, after a two week period of convalescence, I returned to work.

I am not sure whether Bradley Road had also been charged with making the Spiteful wing — I should have known, as there were definitely some wing jigs just inside the main entrance on the left, and I recall them being in the capable hands of Bob Randall of Southwick memory — but I am not positive. I am inclined to believe they were, because, apart from the fact that the main design change in the Spiteful was the introduction of the 'laminar flow' wing, the undercarriage legs were lengthened, and I was presented with the knotty problem of making, by hand, the leg fairing's inside stiffening skins. This was another beast of a job — in fact I find it impossible to describe it in words — but I have drawn it. For those who like the minutae, the part numbers were 37108-2585 and 2586. It became, like some of the other jobs, a mixture of challenge, worry and, finally, triumph.

Whilst I was taking a week's holiday in Cornwall, the Japanese surrendered and at last the war was over. There was an understandable urge by those who had been displaced by the war to return home and begin their own lives again.

In Vickers the contraction began as soon as was possible, the requisitoned buildings being closed, cleared, and returned to their owners. In Trowbridge, Fore Street Garage, Rutland Garage and the Southwick Steam Roller Factory went first, then the Keevil hangar was handed back and went to the farmer. The operational airfield was never finally vacated and the runway is still used today, mainly for testing 'drop-loads' from aircraft. A few of its old R.A.F. type hangars remain, but show signs of wear and the ravages of time. Strangely enough our old hangar is still there and used by a transport business.

Recently I went back to see it and, once inside, if one ignored the various crates littering the place, it was so easy to slip back in time and visualise it as it was, and curiously imagine hearing the old familiar noises. The canteen building is in a bad state but, in the main hangar, even the original black-out blinds across the rooflights have never been removed, and flap down in varied size pieces where wind and time have split them.

The Hilperton works were emptied and in time demolished for a housing project, but Bradley Road was retained by Vickers for a number of years after the war. Today it has a new style porch entrance, and its front facing wall is almost completely covered with ivy, whilst the land between the road and the front wall is covered with small trees, like an orchard. Fore Street Garage has disappeared and Rutland Garage is now a modern petrol forecourt. Even the barrack wall and the barrack buildings have gone, and out at Southwick I found no sign of the steamroller factory that I recognised.

The first rumours about jet aircraft began to circulate and, as if to confirm them, this led to the cancellation of the Spiteful project and, as sure as night follows day, yet another move for me.

Chapter Twenty
Post-war Changes

Originally it was intended for me to be posted to the Experimental Hangar at Hursley, and all my working gear was taken by the firm's transport to that unit on the midday lorry. However, later that same day, as I was making my farewell tour of Bradley Road, word came through requesting me to report instead to Eastleigh. Whatever caused the change still remains one of those little mysteries of life, and now, in the light of what was to follow, I consider it overall to eventually have been to my advantage. It was in this unexpected way that, on 7th January 1946, I rejoined Jack Rolf and the wheeling squad. Only Hilton and Freddie Waygood were missing, and I never saw either of them again — Fred Veal was still in the Air Force, and in India.

The work was mainly making spares, cowling panels and fillets, for the large refurbishment and resale of Spitfires that was in hand with various foreign governments. Only one new job was present, the Vickers Viking passenger aircraft's tailplanes and fins for their British European Airways order on Weybridge. A few of the skin-plating panels required a little shaping, but generally the work was mundane and, after what I had grown accustomed to, lacking in that essential challenge that had served me so well.

This situation changed when, at Vernon Hall's request, I was 'loaned' back to Trowbridge. The first time occurred in July 1946 for two weeks (the limited period due to my holiday booking), and then five weeks in the following October; both occasions enabling me to stay once again with May Moody. The reason was that a development of the Spiteful in a Naval form, named Seafang, plus a few Spitefuls, were to be completed to fully assess the 'laminar' wing. For me, they came at a most fortuitous time, as after one last attempt to resurrect an already dead marriage which failed miserably, a legal separation was obtained which, after the then three years statutory period of 'desertion' entitled us to a divorce.

There was something about those two return trips to Trowbridge in the changed national and personal circumstances that provided an opportunity to reappraise my own future. Confidence in my abilities in my chosen trade was high and to my mind acknowledged by others with the two recalls; my personal life no longer clouded by the feelings that an unsatisfactory marriage had overshadowed for so long, and there grew a 'get up and go' desire to reach out beyond the limitations of being just a good 'tinbasher'.

My youthful shyness and naive understanding of life had long since gone, aided immensely, as I realised later, by the rougher side of factory life. The shocks of war, the unavoidable deceit (in those days) of illicit affairs with the opposite sex, living in other people's homes, accepting responsibilities at work and at play, all helped to make me feel I was ready for a new challenge. As if on cue, a few months later, in 1947, there appeared on the works' notice board a posted notice inviting applications from suitable works' personnel to apply for staff jobs in all skills as Planners, Ratefixers, or Estimators.

The thought of being able to rise up the ladder in the company which I had virtually grown up with appealed to me instantly, so with due care and attention I composed and submitted my application. Three weeks later I received a letter from the personnel manager to inform me that after due consideration they declined to take my application further. Not even an interview — my hopes and, as I saw it, justifiable expectations — hit an almighty low.

A week later, Len Gooch, on one of his visits, made a point of coming over to where I was working and 'explained' why my application had been turned down. In his own words it was, 'You are too damn useful where you are.' Instead of placating me, as I am sure he intended, it had exactly the opposite effect. The sheer injustice of it hit me — and hard. For over eleven years I proved myself in every duty that the company had required of me, given unstintingly of my time and services, both inside and outside the normal calls of duty, and had always kept to the forefront of my work the company's good name and interests. To be refused the opportunity to advance myself, for what was a blatantly selfish reason, fired my blood with a burning desire to try elsewhere in a manner I had never experienced before. I felt so sick over it that I determined that I just had to get out.

Two things occurred almost simultaneously. Bob Pearce, who had been a fellow tinbasher and friend, especially following my separation reaction period, suggested that I join him at Cunliffe-Owen's, a mere 400 yards away from my present job, and a national aeronautical magazine that I subscribed to published an advertisement for Planners and/or time served tradesmen to apply for a 'new and exciting' project connected with aviation. I took the first and wrote for the second.

Once my notice was handed in, the reaction was almost immediate, but despite the requests to reconsider, and the reversal of the earlier decision, my mind was made up and, not without some deep feelings of regret, I packed up my things, gathered my cards and final pay packet on 8th July 1947, left the Eastleigh hangar from which the prototype Spitfire had emerged on her maiden flight, and severed my long link with Supermarine's.

It could have been an unmitigated disaster, and only confirms that it is generally undesirable to know what the future holds for us as, unknown to anyone at Cunliffe-Owen's, the failure to sell any of their Concordia passenger aircraft — and it was the prototype on which we were working — was already causing grave concern to Sir Hugo Cunliffe-Owen, who was financing it.

What guardian angel was responsible for the welfare of yours truly at that period and inspired me to put two irons in the fire at the same time I'll never know, for having commenced my new job, I had an interview for the second in less than a fortnight. After that, I had the last week in July and the first in August holidaying at Butlin's. Shortly after my return a wheelchair-bound Sir Hugo came through our shop with none other than Trevor Westbrook in tow as advisor. The very next day the entire workforce on the left of the workshop's centre gangway were given their termination notices. Fortunately I worked in the other half, but I doubt that any of us had any illusions regarding our future prospects.

The job for which I had been interviewed was to select a small team to introduce into British European Airways' Northolt maintenance base workshops and hangars, 'some of the disciplines of the aircraft industry', which up to then were operating more on the lines of R.A.F. Transport Command, with a large complement of its ex-staff running it, but without the necessary control the R.A.F. enjoyed by virtue of its Service nature.

The idea appealed to my tastes very much, but it was my first (and last) experience of the convoluted ways in which nationalised industries were run, and although in these early days it only involved me in two more 'Selection Boards', both having any number between six and ten members on them, and asking their own various questions without the interviewee having the slightest idea what their particular position or function was, my application received their approval and, just before the final axe fell at Cunliffe's, I was able to start my new post on 29th September 1947.

It was then I found that the 'small team' was very small indeed, a total of seven, including myself, with all but one other, either Planners or Ratefixers from De Havilland's or Vickers at Weybridge. It also necessitated my going back into lodgings again, but this time I was lucky enough to find myself with the Jacob family in South Ruislip.

As this story is intended to cover my time and experience with Supermarine's, I shall not detail the next 2¾ years, except to say that they were absorbing, instructive, and successful, and that in that same period I was divorced, married someone else and, as a consequence due to the first signs of my forthcoming son and heir, the accommodation conditions that applied where we lived, and the post-war price and shortage of alternative housing, it became imperative to make yet another move.

It was the same accommodating 'Aeroplane' magazine that provided the opening I sought, with an advertisement under a box number for a ratefixing post in the South of England. To my surprise the response to my letter came from Vickers South Marston address, but the location of the vacancy was stated as at Hursley Park Experimental Unit.

After an interview at Hursley with the Chief Ratefixer, who was completely new to me and, as such, an unknown quantity, I was offered the position, which I accepted, and after giving the customary notice to B.E.A., returned with my wife to live temporarily in my parents' home once more in Southampton — and Supermarine's. Within a couple of months we obtained a house of our own in Woolston, and in October our first son was born. He weighed in at 10¾lb. — quite a whopper!

It was in this return to Southampton that I met with a comrade-in-arms of my brother's and heard from him of the bitter struggle the invading force endured at the Salerno landings. Apparently the Hampshire Regiments, engaged in the initial phase, ran into unexpectedly strong enemy resistance, and in the bloody fighting to retain a toehold, my brother's platoon — in which he was a lance-corporal bren gunner — were trapped in a narrow lane by a German tank. The lane is now renamed 'Hampshire Lane'. At long last my mind was set at rest about that.

My new job as Ratefixer in the Experimental Unit was nicely positioned to observe all that went on to change a Designer's dreams into reality. To be involved at such an early stage had a thrill all of its own and something that for me never lost its magic. To see the drawings as they were issued, handle the planning sheets detailing the methods and tools to be used, then to be intimately concerned with the men and machines to transform sheet and bar metal stocks into sleek aerodynamic forms to carry men into uncharted skies at ever increasing speeds, is an experience that still holds its fascination for me to this day.

For those readers who have travelled this far along my 'odyssey', it is only fair to explain a little of this ratefixing business, with which I was to be so involved for the remainder of my stay with the Supermarine organisation within Vickers-Armstrongs, or Vickers Ltd. I have mentioned it briefly in respect of the wartime troubles that beset Castle Bromwich, in that they would not accept some of the conversion times from our premium bonus scheme to their piece-work prices. Even today, incentive schemes are used, and mis-used, to either improve individual production effort or, regrettably, as a silly means of increasing basic pay rates, without the production improvement content.

Right from my start with Supermarine's in 1936, I had grown up with the premium bonus scheme based on what is known as the 'Halsey-Rowan' system; there are others of various permutations, the despised 'Bedeaux' scheme being just one, but I have operated both 'premium' and 'straight' schemes, and have no hesitation in stating my preference for the 'premium' type. To apply this (and any other scheme) it is an essential prerequisite that the Ratefixers, at whatever rank, have a sound working knowledge of the practicalities of the work which they are rating, and are individuals who are 'firm but fair', and that basic integrity should work upwards into their management dealings, as well as to each individual worker. If ever there is a Ratefixer's coat of arms, its motto must surely be 'To Thine Own Self be True'.

Jobs are normally broken down into operations, each operation havings its own 'bonus time'. The size and format of these operations depend on various factors; whether they are single-handed, done by pairs of skilled men, a skilled man and a semi-skilled man, a man and a boy, and all the other groupings that can arise.

It is essential that the grouping is shown on the 'breakdown', so that everyone knows on what labour-loading basis it is compiled. This 'breakdown' is the guts of ratefixing, and only where it can be safely supplanted by 'synthetics' based on years of accepted knowledge, or the known and accepted operating speeds of machines for example, should it be discarded. On assembly and sub-assembly work, particularly in the aircraft world, it is a must for production and cost control.

I have deliberately stressed the integrity of the Ratefixer and the necessity for properly compiled 'breakdowns' of operations, as twice, in my own experience, I have been called in to remedy the evils that arise when they were not applied. In the first instance it was too late, and the firm had to be bought out by its major shareholder to save it, and, in the second, I was compelled to make massive staff changes in that department until it was right. It is not the happiest or easiest of jobs, as the Ratefixer is the meat in the sandwich of labour and management. Yet, strangely, if done correctly, in the knowledge that one's actions can determine a man's wages, or undermine the financial viability of a company, it brings its own satisfactions, and perhaps, best of all, the trust of the workpeople. Any company that fails to recognise the validity of both these factors as they intertwine is heading for trouble.

The 'breakdown', say for instance, for a small single-handed sub-assembly operation, is in line entries of the sequence in which the job as envisaged by the Ratefixer is best done, having due regard to the tooling available, the standard of finish of the detail parts being assembled, and the category of the labour involved.

Generally, each operational breakdown begins with its first line entry as 'Preparation'. This entry will have a variable time, to allow for the man to book on at his Time Office, gather up the parts he has to assemble, fetch the drawings applicable, and perhaps go to the stores for either finished parts, materials, A.G.S. or embodiment loan items, or even to get to some awkward place to work.

After preparation, the line entries state the building sequence, each line bearing the Ratefixer's assessment of the actual estimated time to be taken by the average skilled or semi-skilled man or woman, using average effort. This is so that those who prefer to exert more effort, or are better skilled, will obtain the additional recompense and reward for using them.

These line entries, known better as 'elements', when concluded, are all added together and a contingency percentage allowance of the total (usually 10 per cent) is added, and this total final figure becomes the 'actual'. With premium bonus this 'actual' is now usually doubled, the new figure becoming the 'time allowed'. This doubling is a safety factor for both management and man as, whatever time is saved, it is then shared equally between the man and the company. Thus a 99 hour time-allowed job, done in 49½ hours, yields 24¾ hours pay to the man at the bonus rate, on top of the 49½ hours pay of his normal flat-working rate.

In all the companies in which I worked, the bonus rate was usually twopence an hour or so below the basic hourly rate. It is not essential that it should be, but that's how it was. Our hypothetical man would, in the example given, have earned what is generally known as 'time and a half'. Had he only taken 33 hours, he would have received 33 hours bonus payment — or 'double time' — plus his 33 hours at basic rate.

Some companies prefer to wait until the actual job is in progress and have an observer with a stop-watch, to time how long each element takes, and then make adjustments, based on their observer's assessment on whether, in his view, the operator was working above or below an average person's speed. I must admit that I would prefer not to use a stop-watch. My preference has always been to rate a job wherever possible from the drawing, planning sheet, and the listed tools. This pre-rating has one undeniable advantage, as the Ratefixer can check the Planning Engineer's method, and in the event of him discovering a better method, can get it altered and often save on tooling before it is made, and even on occasions suggest a design change that will reduce manufacturing time and costs.

In pre-war days, it was an intrepid Production Engineer who would request design changes, as designers, beset with their own intricate problems, were loath to go back over work they had already cleared but, after the war, a much closer liaison was established, even to the extent that senior production engineers were often party to design problems at a very early design stage, especially when the suggestions made might save pounds in weight (the designer's hope), as well as pounds in money.

It always was, and still is, only natural for people being what they are, to try to squeeze more time from the Ratefixer, but these matters are generally settled most often by Ratefixers going through their breakdown with the operator.

Sometimes this shows that the Ratefixer may have underestimated an element and, if he has any sense, he will amend it there and then. This is another plus for the 'breakdown'. On one occasion, I pre-rated the assembly of a wing spar, and the operator, who was a sensible type, told me he thought I had not estimated it correctly. When we went through the 'breakdown' together, we found I had omitted a row of holes that required not only drilling, but reaming. That involved a considerable addition of time, but it was done right there and then whilst he watched, and we not only were able to agree the new time, but the story spread around the shop how it was done, and proved much to my subsequent advantage.

Castle Bromwich, and most of the car firms, worked on a 'piece price' or 'piece work' principle, where all the time saved went to the employee. All that was required to convert the Woolston Spitfire times to the style they were used to was to use the actual time instead of, as in those days, adding half to it, but apparently that was not enough — they wanted our 'premium' bonus times as their 'piece work' rate, which would have given them the best of all worlds, and which, in many instances, they achieved at the Country's expense, thus getting themselves paid more than we at Supermarine's for identical work (pre-war, we were rated at 'time and a quarter' — hence the half added).

In the post-war era, especially during the period of the Labour Governments, Managements, beset by intractible and politically power-hungry unions, attempted to stem the flood of dispute and unofficial strikes by 'tweaking' their incentive schemes, as a way of meeting the incessant demands for more money. This insidious and ill-conceived idea has to bear a large responsibility for the subsequent spiralling costs and overmanning, making our commodities too dear to sell in overseas markets. The consequences from this are all too plain to see today (in 1985) and its three million unemployed. Once the credibility of incentive schemes were undermined in this way, new ones introduced were mainly cosmetic, and produced none of the proper benefits that should have accrued. There is, today, a need to step back and take a look at the past to see where, and how, it went so terribly wrong.

This perhaps is a suitable point to mention that perennial and hoary subject of the wartime £5,000 price tag per Spitfire, and from my own records, those 'fabulous' wages earned by munition and armament workers. The £5,000 Spitfire price was not far out, if it is taken as the return to Vickers Supermarine for their part only. It must be remembered that the Rolls-Royce engines, the De Havilland propellers and spinners, as well as all the other 'Embodiment Loan' items — radio, instruments, etc. — were purchased separately by the Ministry and provided to the industry.

Of the original 310 order, the first batch of 49 were settled at a price of £8,783 each, the next batch of 26 at £5,782 each, then 31 at £5,768 each, and the balance at £5,696 each. After that, subsequent small price adjustments were made, dependent on the 'Mark' or modifications incorporated. Unfortunately, figures for the Castle Bromwich production are not, as yet, available.

A rare picture of the author at work, making the Cunliffe-Owen 'Concordia' throttles console cover, 1947.

Joseph Smith — Chief Designer, with Chief Test Pilot Mike Lithgow.
Vickers

Stanley Woodley — Superintendent of the Supermarine Organisation, and Special Director of Vickers.
Vickers

Regarding wages, I can only quote from my notebooks of my personal remuneration. I will use the pay applicable to a 'skilled tradesman's' rate, leaving out the period whilst I was still paid at either apprentice or journeyman's rates. Unlike the present way the unions beguile the readers or listeners regarding 'take home pay', which is one of the ridiculous confidence tricks currently perpetrated on the general public, I propose quoting the gross figures — without stoppages!

In December 1941, my rate was increased to one shilling and ten pence per hour (nine pence at 1984 figures). This was one penny per hour extra awarded for the air duct job.

Thus a 47 hour basic week	= £ 4 6s. 2d. on dayshift
6 hours weekday overtime	= 13s. 9d. (3 evenings of 2 hours at time and a quarter)
4½ hours Saturday overtime	= 12s. 4½d. at time and one half
8 hours Sunday overtime	= £ 1 9s. 4d. at double time
Therefore for a fairly normal 65½ hour week	= £ 7 1s. 7½d.
Plus bonus averaging time and ¾	= £ 4 4s. 6d. at the bonus rate of ⅛ per hour

Total = **£11 6s. 1½d.** without deductions,(income tax etc.)

So for a normal week on dayshift, and the 65½ hours worked were fairly normal at that time, an earned amount of £11 6s. 1½d. would be subjected to deductions of approximately £2 4s. 4d. for income tax, 3s. 8d. for National Health and Employment Stamp, and 2d. or 3d. for Sports Fund and the like. I must add however that, in those days, with 'nine quid' in my pocket I felt far more prosperous than 'ninety pounds' would have me feel today.

Nightshift premium pay of one third to basic rate improved this income by two pounds approximately per week, although the week was reduced to 63 hours. Over the whole war period my highest week's pay was £18 17s. 0d. at the end of 1944, but this was due to accumulated bonus payments being cleared, and it attracted £6 2s. 0d. in income tax. My average for the war period was £8 6s. 0d. gross per week. These figures at least will provide some form of yardstick for comparison with any quoted elsewhere by others.

My return to Hursley and Supermarine's was not the simple re-engagement I had at first thought. It took a little time before the reason for my presence was finally spelt out to me. In the time I was away, there had been changes. The organisation had been rearranged. The big South Marston plant near Swindon, which had been a dispersal satellite for Castle Bromwich, had now been passed to Vickers-Armstrong, possibly as replacement compensation for the bombed Woolston works, and this big factory, complete with its own airfield, coupled with the Trowbridge Bradley Road Works, became the Northern Area. The Southern Area was more fragmented. Hursley Park was retained as Head Office and Design Office, with the Experimental Hangar for building new prototypes. Jeffrey Quill and his new test flight team had vacated their large new hangar at High Post, which was built after I had left Salisbury in 1943, and were now installed at Chilbolton Airfield, near Stockbridge. Chilbolton was another airfield hacked out from farmland during the war, and was more convenient to the Design Office, as well as having a long hard runway for use by jets.

Mr. Quill's long and distinguished test flying career was coming to an end and the major testing of jet aircraft had passed into the capable hands of Mike Lithgow.

At Eastleigh, the old wooden hangars and a new flight shed, beside the old crematorium, were still in work, as was the rebuilt Itchen works that had been resurrected to all its former glory with additional balcony areas.

Sqdr. Commander Sir James Bird had vacated his position to enjoy a retired life, sadly to be shortened by a shooting accident. The top position, now termed Superintendent, was in the hands of the long-serving Wilfred Elliot, with Stanley Woodley sitting in the wings at South Marston after distinguishing himself at Castle Bromwich once Beaverbrook had kicked it into shape, and already in line to succeed Elliot.

Apart from the two areas, the situation was also different as each had its Joint Production Manager. In the Southern Area, this was Leonard Gooch and in the Northern Area, Stuart Lefevre — and therein lay one of the seeds of future destruction. To anyone who knew both these men it will be accepted as an understatement if I say they disliked each other.

However, when I joined the small ratefixing team in the Experimental Hangar I was unaware of all the undercurrents that were already running. What I did find was that although Gooch was responsible for the production units in the Southern Area, he did not control the ratefixing or estimating departments, and these functions for the whole Supermarine organisation lay with the Joint Production Manager of the Northern Area. The first intimation I received that all was not sweetness and light came when Gilbert Taylor, on one of his weekly visits as Chief Ratefixer, asked me quietly to see if I could encourage my colleagues to compile 'breakdowns' to formulate their times, rather than putting down a good guess and 'plussing up' after the job was completed. This 'plussing up' was an anachronism remaining in experimental departments since the old Ministry 'cost-plus' days. Now it had come home to roost.

The Ministry had 'requested' that the company apply an efficient method of 'payment by results' to the Experimental Hangar. What had happened, I found later, was that a contract for three jets (which later became the Attacker) for an overall figure of £150,000, had ended up, as near as makes no difference, at £500,000. In the ensuing inquiry into this cost overrun, the ineffective methods for cost control at Hursley Park Experimental Hangar were exposed, so that when the production order for the Attacker was placed, the whole of its productionising, tooling and manufacture was given to the Northern Area.

Faced with this 'slap in the face', Gooch set about consolidating his own position by aligning himself with Joe Smith, the Chief Designer, so that at least he would retain the manufacturing responsibility for future prototypes. This had a sympathetic reciprocity from Joe Smith, as at this time he was a Special Director of Vickers, and must have been aware that the ultimate aim of the main Vickers Board was to effect a transfer of Head Office and design departments to South Marston — a move regarded unfavourably by most of the staffs concerned, who did not view the environs of Swindon as a reasonable exchange for the delights, and their own roots, in Hampshire.

With Joe Smith in a powerful position to influence matters, and supported by most of the design team, as well as Gooch and other senior production staff, for a while it appeared that the Board's intention might be revised. A hopeful sign in this direction had been the repairing and reoccupation of the Itchen works. So for a few years after the war, this waiting game was played without anyone's feathers being ruffled. In that period the design team made their first excursions into the jet age which, apart from developing aircraft whose main principles all derived from R. J. Mitchell's basic design, were the first major designs from the Joe Smith stable.

The first jet, Type 392, was basically a new tube-type fuselage to contain the jet engine and provide the intake ducting, with the 'laminar flow' Spiteful wing attached. Although this is an over simplification, in the broadest terms, that is all it was. Eventually, because the R.A.F. turned it down, it was adapted and 'navalised' as the Attacker, and for a few years met the post-war Naval requirements, but it lacked that creative spark of genius that Mitchell's designs had. It must also be remembered that in taking over a 'going concern', Joe Smith had benefited from Mitchell's team choice but, after the war, a number of the old team sought new futures for themselves elsewhere.

With the loss of the 'spark of genius' in the design office, came a similar loss of 'calibre' people in Gooch's production team. Practically all of the senior Production Engineers had

A Spitfire fuselage modified to accept the Rolls-Royce 'Griffon' engine and the new 'laminar flow' wing that led on to the Spiteful. *Vickers*

Supermarine 'Spiteful' frame 5 bulkhead with datum longeron, showing the stainless steel stiffening channel riveted inside. Note the piano wire central datum passing fore and aft through the cut-out in the frame. Hursley Experimental Hangar. *Vickers* 141

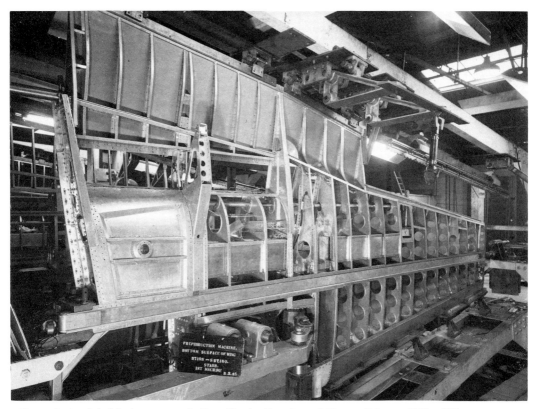

Pre-production Spiteful wing structure in jig at Hursley Experimental Hangar, February 1945. *Vickers*

Another view of bulkhead frame 5 of the Spiteful. Note the Oil Tank and below the adjustable trestle support. *Vickers*

The longer undercarriage leg for the laminar flow wing aircraft. *Vickers*

gone — some because, frankly, they did not like working with him — and to prop him up in those technical and administrative areas where he had no real experience, and which in wartime had not really mattered, a Production Engineer was engaged from outside the aircraft industry; a fault that soon became apparent and resulted in the gentleman concerned being later 'promoted sideways'.

The first major 'crunch' from all this hidden background hit me when we began to build the Type 541 — the prototype which eventually became the Swift. Gilbert Taylor asked me to take care of the wings. Having a major component more or less to myself suited me fine. The two Planning Engineers concerned were Bob Dutch and Cecil Phillips, both contemporaries of my own age group, and the Shop Foreman, Bert Diaper, whom I had known years before, so, with their co-operation, I was able to rate the operations as I wished, with a view to getting a quick output and a balanced labour loading. I made 'breakdowns' as I have mentioned earlier (in fact it was on this aircraft we found the spar drilling omission) and it went along swimmingly.

The Chief Ratefixer, Gilbert Taylor, came in once a week and never failed to obtain a progress report from me, and murmur encouragements which continued until we reached an advanced stage of the wing skinning. With the port and starboard wing jigs side by side, the space between them boarded-over as a working platform, it was, consequently, very simple for the operators doing identical, but handed, jobs to check with their opposite numbers how long they were taking, and how much bonus they made; in fact it provided a competitive edge.

One of the 'planks' of plating midway towards the top end was cleared satisfactorily on the starboard side, and I noted it in the record which I was keeping, but was appalled a couple of days later when the man doing the opposite hand came and asked me, 'to make up the card'. After assuring myself that there had been no extenuating circumstances, I had to refuse him. Although the man concerned was an ex 'K' shop man, and had been with me at Trowbridge, I could not accede to his request, as it would have been a breach of trust to the first man to allow more time for an identical job just because another man had taken considerably more time, or that I knew him personally.

I knew that this type of situation could arise at any time, hence the 'breakdowns' and the 'recording'; in fact I was surprised it had not come earlier, but I think the way the spar-drilling episode had been handled had brought in its wake a feeling of fairness and justice. It was unfortunate that the 'aggrieved' man sought out the Senior Ratefixer when I was away, who promptly did as he always did — bought his peace and quiet life by 'plussing' it up. It was equally unfortunate for him that the girl clerk in our office always passed cleared wing cards to me for my records before despatching them for payment. This led to a furious row between the Ratefixer concerned and myself, as he hoped his action would not have been spotted, because he knew he was in the wrong. When Gilbert Taylor came on his Thursday visit I explained what had occurred and asked him to speak to the Senior about it. He soothed my ruffled feelings in his quiet manner and made it clear to the other chap that it must not occur again. Gilbert had a phrase he used on such occasions. Instead of threatening dire penalties he would just say, 'or else we shall have to part company'! It was a phrase I copied and used later when similar situations arose that required gentle, but firm, handling.

The matter could, and should, have ended there but it did not. The story leaked out, and I was first taken to task for involving Gilbert Taylor who was responsible to Lefevre, and therefore considered by some people who should have known better, as an agent of the 'enemy camp' (Northern Area). The Experimental Manager frostily told me he would not like to work for me. Then Len Gooch got hold of it and ordered more men on the wings, swamping them with labour and nearly wrecking all I had worked to achieve. Realising I would get no help from anyone in the Southern Area, I rang Gilbert at South Marston. Whatever took place, and at what level, I never found out, and was never told, but the following day the surplus labour was withdrawn and the wings were completed as planned.

The efficiency of this plan can best be gauged by the fact that it took five sets of production Swift wings to get down to the time achieved by that prototype set. Despite this, the waters of Hursley had been muddied for me personally, and, shortly after, I was glad to accept a Chief Ratefixer's position that was on offer for me from another company. It would be dishonest not to say that my curtailed return to Vickers was not a personal disappointment after barely a year, but as so often in life 'the mills of the Gods grind slowly, yet they grind exceeding small'.

Even in that short spell, little niggling doubts about the design and production future were creeping into a receptive, if still not fully-comprehending, mind. It was not the Types 510, 535, or 541 that gave rise to these feelings, but the Type 508 which, with its size, two engines, and finless butterfly tail unit, that worried me. It seemed an awful lot of aeroplane for just a single seater fighter aircraft. Even when they eventually dropped the finless arrangement, and reverted to the more orthodox design, it still seemed too big, especially when it became apparent that only the Royal Navy were supporting its advancement, and therefore it had to incorporate Carrier-operation facilities.

However, whatever thoughts were germinating in my mind then were banished by the new challenge of becoming Airspeed's Chief Ratefixer.

It becomes necessary at this juncture to relate events that led up to this move to Airspeed's, and the strange way that seemingly disconnected events were interwoven. I have mentioned earlier that I first met Gooch during my 1938/9 evening technical classes, when during the daytime he was employed in Jack Knowles' Works Engineers' Office. At that time he was teaching mathematics to improve his finances, having married some time earlier.

One night, during the class, when we were all working on a set exercise, he came and sat beside me at the school's desk I was using. We both knew each other as coming from Supermarine's, and little more, but this evening was to change all that. I am sure at this time it is not breaking a confidence to say that Len Gooch was a very troubled and worried man that night — for reasons that were personal and domestic on which I do not propose to enlarge — and for reasons best known to himself he came and poured them on to my youthful shoulders. There was little I had to offer except a sympathetic ear, and, at the time, I believe that was all he needed. Although neither of us ever referred to the matter again, that half-hour created a more than casual acquaintanceship, and his subsequent offer to put me forward to Jack Knowles as a possible member of the Works Engineer's department, and again in 1942 to intercede and arrange my transfer to Salisbury when I had my own domestic problems, showed that he felt the same way.

It was this 'special relationship' that enabled me to speak out so forthrightly, when the work was running out, on his visit to Southwick. It was also this same relationship or understanding that made his rather narrow view of my having a staff job so hard to take, and caused my leaving. Even so, my return to Hursley held no bitterness. In fact, whilst at B.E.A., I had written to Len for some information regarding the card packs that were directly associated with Supermarine's Bonus Scheme, when Reg Burden and myself were engaged in a battle to get a Vickers-type scheme into B.E.A., rather than the unwieldy scheme our boss, Charlie Burgess, wanted to introduce, which was a perversion of a De Havilland scheme.

Suffice it to say here that, after an extensive wrangle, the proposals by Reg Burden and I were considered more practical by the B.E.A. Chief Maintenance Engineer, with the result that C. Burgess was promoted to a higher administrative grade, so leaving the main detailed application of the new schemes at Northolt to Reg, who took over Charlie's position, and myself, in a newly-created post, in charge of the planning and ratefixing of all Northolt's mechanical workshops.

When I left Northolt to rejoin Supermarine's I was leaving a far more senior position than the one I was applying for — entirely due to the anticipated arrival of number one son, and our inability to find suitable accommodation for his advent.

After the 541 wing contretemps, and the realisation that I was now in Len's black books, I began to seek another post which brought about a completely unexpected meeting. After answering an advertisement for a Production Engineer with an Australian aircraft concern, I was invited to meet their Australian representative in the Polygon Hotel — so was Len Gooch, and we came face to face at the bar, in an obviously embarrassing moment for both of us! However, at his request, we agreed not to know each other when the 'Aussie' arrived. As events turned out, the interviewer took me first, and the interview took place in his car down at Southampton's Town Quay where he drove me. Afterwards, he insisted on driving me home and then went back to interview Len who had been waiting in the bar for well over an hour.

To his credit, or maybe because of his embarrassment, Len Gooch never mentioned his long wait, or the fact that we had both been interviewed for the same job — and both failed to get it! The Australian position was eventually filled by a Mr. Erlam, the then Chief Production Engineer of the Airspeed Company. His vacated position was advertised and finally filled by my erstwhile colleague and friend from B.E.A., Reg Burden.

Within his first two weeks, faced with an increasingly appalling financial situation on the production side, especially at the large Christchurch unit where the major components for the Elizabethan aircraft for B.E.A. (Ambassador to Airspeeds) were being built, and the forecast delays on delivery dates, he was placed under heavy pressure by the Managing Director to take 'any steps necessary' to redress the position.

One of these 'steps' caused him to arrive at my home in Woolston and ask if I would ease his load by 'straightening out the ratefixing'. In the light of my unsatisfactory situation at Hursley, I was very glad to accept. It proved to be quite a challenge and an invaluable experience — but we were too late. Two years earlier I am pretty sure we would have succeeded. However, on one fateful morning, four months later, we executives were gathered together and informed by Mr. Nixon that De Havilland's had taken full control of the company. Despite the fact that, in subsequent meetings with the man who De Havilland's put in as their General Manager, both Reg and I were welcome to remain, we both felt that we ought to go.

He went first to a very good job in Scotland and then Charlie Burgess came to visit me, to ask if I would head a team of my own selection, to put into the B.E.A.'s Glasgow (Renfrew) airbase, the same schemes that had proved so successful at Northolt (the account of the Northolt success was recorded in 'Aircraft Production' during 1950 or 1951). I gave him the answer he sought, but then it transpired that, because it was a nationalised industry, the post had to be advertised internally, and a charade of Interviewing Boards attended. I went to Renfrew for the first one — a long, uncomfortable, overnight train journey which no doubt dampened my ardour — and when eventually I did get the official offer and had a chat with James Liddell, who was the Managing Director at Airspeed's, even though it had changed hands, he said, 'if you don't want to go to Scotland, stay here and we'll match their salary offer.' For the first and only time in my life I accepted that kind of offer. When I telephoned Charlie Burgess he was justifiably very annoyed, and it was only years later, when we were both holding similar positions in different companies, and my company was doing some specialised processing for his, that he finally forgave me.

In due time, De Havilland's decided to split Airspeed's into two divisions, Portsmouth and Christchurch. This necessitated me accepting the Chief Ratefixer's job in either one or the other. I chose Portsmouth as the train services and journey times were more favourable to me.

Although it was now fifteen months since I had left Hursley, within the scaled down post-war aircraft industry, news of such events and changes were fairly common knowledge. Nevertheless, I experienced a surprise telephone call at Airspeed's one afternoon from Gilbert Taylor. After one or two polite enquiries about my welfare (aimed mostly at ensuring the telephone switchboard girls would not consider it worth listening to) he asked if I would be interested in becoming his Deputy to take charge of the Southern Area. We agreed to meet on the following Saturday morning to discuss it. We went over the obvious difficulties that would (and did) arise, but I was assured that, although I would be expected to co-operate with Len Gooch, this was not to be to the detriment of my departmental responsibilities which were, via Gilbert, direct to Lefevre. In his usual, careful, but frank manner he left me in little doubt regarding the mess I would be accepting, particularly at Itchen, where the Swift fuselages were just going into production. He admitted that his one day a week visit to the area was nowhere near sufficient to deal with the problems, and that the idea of the new appointment appealed to him, and became an even more pleasant possibility when he found that Lefevre agreed that he could approach me — an unusual departure from the normal etiquette that Vickers maintained.

I accepted, and even Jimmy Liddell wished me luck when I went to tell him. Also one of the shop stewards — their Works Convenor, in fact — not wishing to be seen doing so, came to my outside window to say his own goodbye and best wishes, which, considering some of the battles (including two small strikes) we had had, I thought a remarkable tribute to the way in which a mutual respect had grown out of conflict. So on 16th June 1952, I returned to Vickers Supermarine's for what was to prove to be my final spell, and the last leg of the 'odyssey'.

Chief Ratefixer at Airspeeds, 1951.

Chapter Twenty-one
Decline and Fall

The interest in Supermarine's and the Spitfire still remains quite strong today. Only last year (1984) the Spitfire Society was successfully launched, with Jeffrey Quill as its President. Very little is public knowledge of the post-war activities that went on behind the scenes which eventually brought about its demise, almost in disgrace — a sad ending to a proud and noble name. The only account I have read of it dismisses it in one line as 'political' the inference being that the Government was to blame. In my opinion this was not the reason at all. The truth was much closer to home, and due to certain flaws in management, production and design — the latter most certainly applying the coup-de-grace. This is how I saw and/or understood it.

When I finally rejoined the company, I had to spend my first week at South Marston for a general briefing, and meet some of the new people who were now in undoubted positions of control. This briefing left me with no illusions regarding the task ahead. Wilfred Elliot had retired, and his position as Superintendent had been taken by Stanley Woodley as had been expected. Just as Joe Smith, he had been made a Special Director. Stan Woodley, by virtue of his own services at Woolston before he was seconded to Castle Bromwich, had few illusions about Len Gooch's experience and capabilities.

It would be churlish to deny that, in that fateful autumn of 1940, the success of the dispersal scheme had revolved around the effort and drive that Len Gooch applied to it. His experience then, gained from a railway works apprenticeship and his knowledge of buildings, plant, equipment and their power systems, obtained from the Works Engineer's Office, were exactly those required in the dire situation in which we found ourselves. It is also to his credit that he was able to build on this success and, by delegating through his Area Managers, sustained throughout the length of the war reasonable success as the Works Manager, and it is only fair that proper acknowledgement is made of those achievements.

The trouble came after the war, when the chill winds of commercial competition began to blow. These soon exposed his lack of aircraft production experience, and just how little Gooch understood about the management controls and functions essential to a new aircraft project. It was somewhat similar to the way Joe Smith had donned Mitchell's mantle and ran 'a going concern', that Gooch thought he could don Westbrook's mantle, and did, for the duration of the war, run 'a going concern'.

But there comes the time when it is necessary to start from base again, and, when that time came, the lack of basic practical aircraft production experience showed, and was heavily underlined when the three jet aircraft contracts carried out under his stewardship at Hursley ran up such a cost. A lot of this cost was incurred by his over-manning tactics, which I have mentioned.

At the South Marston end, Stuart Lefevre did not lack this necessary experience and, as previously mentioned, when the larger orders for some 185 Attacker aircraft arrived, they went into South Marston. However, to protect his position Gooch made a point of fostering Joe Smith's patronage and poured scorn on Lefevre in public, and in private. This set up a very nasty situation between the two areas — a situation, I hasten to add, which was not improved by the scorn Lefevre made openly about Gooch. Gilbert Taylor's weekly visits were often to diplomatically smooth down some of the ruffled feelings, and he certainly did not encourage me to take either side — just get it right was all he asked.

How Stan Woodley stuck the constant feuding I have never understood, faced as he was with two men who really loathed each other. In my opinion he should have come to grips

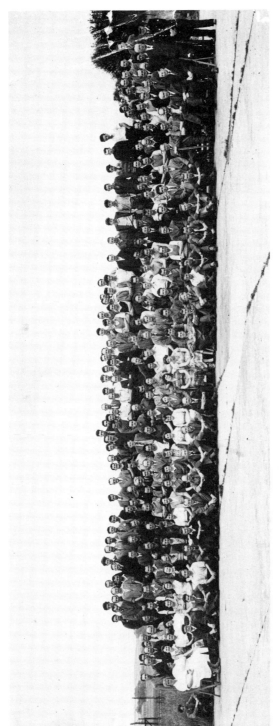

The staff at the Experimental Flight Hangar at Eastleigh, 1955. Far right seated, Bert Diaper the Foreman, and next to him Frank Perry the Experimental Manager.

and resolved the matter once he was firmly established in his position, but he failed to do so, and in the end his 'goodnaturedness' (and I believe it was that) partly became his own undoing.

Gooch, in turn, isolated by his inexperience, and lacking the good Production Engineers who had departed, relied on what comfort Joe Smith could provide whilst, one by one, the main core functions of ratefixing, estimating, and contracts had all passed to South Marston, and this caused him to adopt a manner of somewhat elevated stance to disguise his shortcomings. It was a great pity, as this attitude alienated those who were still trying to do the best they could, regardless of the circumstances.

With South Marston occupied with building the Attacker order, and the Southern Area's prototype work insufficient to absorb its full production potential, first the Swift, and soon afterwards the Scimitar, main component assemblies were allocated to Itchen, for their fuselages, and Eastleigh Main Hangar, their wings. The other, newer, Eastleigh Flight Shed was busy building Joe Smith's latest creation, a single-seater jet fighter with 'crescent' wings that had devolved from the testing of a wing style pioneered by Handley Page.

Whether this aircraft would have vindicated Joe Smith's reputation we were sadly never to find out. Duncan Sandys silly assertion, 'that the day for manned aircraft was over', killed it, just as it did advanced types in other companies. It was within a couple of months of its targetted first flight date. This aircraft, and the wings at Eastleigh, were practically no trouble for me, as the Senior Ratefixer at Eastleigh, Ron Hailey, was a very competent man who had years of experience, even some of it pre-war, and had he not been so closely associated with Gooch for so long, would most probably have had my job. But Itchen works, where I set up my base, was a different kettle of fish, not dissimilar to the Airspeed Christchurch situation, except that this time there was just enough time for remedial action.

Where incentive schemes go awry, is when the ratefixing responsibilities are suborned to shop supervisory staff or worse, union steward's pressures. At Itchen, it had got out of hand due to both factors. As a result, it was fairly obvious that a trial of strength would be a certainty, before long. First it was essential to sort out my own staff, and here I was advantaged by my own reputation going before me, as two left as I arrived and one more, who I found cheating an operator, I dismissed on the spot, which also echoed round the troubled unit in my favour.

I transferred the one man whom I had confidence in at Hursley Experimental Hangar when I was there, and made him the Itchen Senior Ratefixer, borrowed two from South Marston whilst I interviewed and engaged replacements, and reorganised the clerical section. Gradually we began to get times discussed, and agreed with the essential 'breakdowns' which we were now required to have signed by both the operators concerned and the Ratefixer.

However, there were some operations where the Ratefixer could not effect agreement, and in due time I tried to get agreement, on some occasions even getting Gilbert Taylor to go through the disputed jobs with me. Even this left a few jobs where agreement could not be obtained without us throwing away 'the baby with the bath water', due to the deliberate intransigence of politically-motivated persons. It was these few jobs — no more than three, and not causing any major upset in the shop — that Gooch heard of and decided to make as an issue to have me removed. It was a calculated move in which I suppose he hoped that, by discrediting me, he would be able to nominate a successor who would be more amenable to the wilder and increasing demands he had been making, which would have used the ratefixing system as a means of increasing payments without reciprocal higher production. His ideas were to say to groups of workers, 'Get this completed by so and so date, and we will pay you all double time.' This was the very tactic that had proved such a catastrophe at Hursley, especially when compounded with overmanning.

The reconstituted Ratefixing Department at the Itchen Works in 1956. Ted Sellers, the Unit Section Leader is in the centre.

Goodbye to all that: Ron Telling who succeeded me, on my right, and left, Ron Hailey from Eastleigh.

However, he struck without any warning and the first I knew of it was being asked to go to the Area Manager's (Bill Heaver) office at Itchen. There, sat behind the desk, was Stan Woodley, flanked by Gooch and an uncomfortable-looking Bill Heaver. Woodley was very fair. He asked me to explain in detail how we compiled our times, how and where we incorporated preparation and contingency allowances, the procedures for dealing with disputes, the method and approach we used to get the signed agreements, the number of agreements achieved so far, and even to the backgrounds and experience of the new staff which I had engaged. After that, he questioned me very shrewdly on my own opinions regarding the situation, and I told him that it was not necessary, or wise, to bring people in to time by stop-watch (a South Marston method) and that I was not exactly in favour of having an operator's signature to prove the time was agreed. These two items I had much earlier argued with Gilbert Taylor, who had conceded the stop-watch factor, but insisted on the signature.

In respect of all this, Woodley's own knowledge and personal experience was vastly more comprehensive than Gooch's, and he would have known immediately had I been evasive or guilty of giving him a load of 'bull'. This session probably took all, or more, of an hour, and all 'off the cuff'. At the end, he said quietly, 'Thank you Russell', stood up, turned to Gooch and said quite sharply, 'There's nothing wrong here Gooch — you can find your own way back' and, to my astonishment, as well as to the chagrin of both Heaver and Gooch, walked out and drove away, leaving Gooch who he had brought to Itchen in his car, stranded. It was one of the best demonstrations of displaying displeasure I have ever seen. That also gave me the chance to tell Gooch just what I thought of his tactics and that either I, or Gilbert Taylor, would have been quite willing to explain any facet of our business that he did not understand. Then I stalked out. I felt sorry for Bill Heaver who always had a high regard for Woodley, which I believe was reciprocated, but who, nevertheless, had to work to Gooch's instructions.

Late on the following afternoon Gilbert Taylor rang me from South Marston. 'I hear you're in trouble', he said, but the tone of his voice was far from serious. Playing his own game, because by this time we had established a good working and social relationship, I replied, 'Not to my knowledge'. 'A certain gentleman (Woodley) has had words with 'Lefty' (Lefevre's nickname). I'll tell you about it on Thursday', he added.

We met, as we mostly did, at Hursley Park for lunch in the spacious Senior Executives' dining room, and over our meal, with Len Gooch eating his lunch only a few feet away, he told me how Woodley had praised my exposition to Lefevre who, in view of his animosity to Gooch, was delighted to pass on to Gilbert.

As far as I was concerned Gooch never interfered with my job again, and later, when my initial anger had subsided, I saw no reason to bear malice and carried on as before, still giving Gooch the support to which he was entitled, and when the next major modification blew up, attended his meeting at his request which, as far as I was concerned, signalled the end of the matter.

We successfully completed the rating of the Swift and followed that with the Scimitar. The shop floor gradually began to accept that the old inefficient ways of ratefixing were gone, and that deliberately motivated disputes, generally for the benefit of one of the various Shop Stewards more than the operator, no longer attracted the Senior Management, and freed me for more attention to the outposts of my area.

Chilbolton Airfield was at its northern extremity, and where ratefixing was much more difficult to apply when dealing with test flights and the many adjustments that arose from them, plus the day to day servicing on aircraft that did not have the complete similarity of production types (the Swift and Scimitar production final assembly and flying was all committed to South Marston). As long as a reasonably free hand was given to the Ratefixer

151

The Itchen Works in 1985. Apart from its changed livery it is almost identical to the pre and post war Vickers factory. The low building in the foreground was the Canteen.

The end of the story. Where the Luftwaffe failed, the post-war demolition men succeed in the 1970s.

Southern Newspapers

The Mould Loft building in 1985. The ground floor was the bicycle storage park.

'Coffin' and hooded pall-bearers as design office 'dies'.

The 2nd Type 535 prototype, VV119. The 535 type led directly to the Type 541 — the 'Swift'. In the white overalls is Mike Lithgow, Chief Test Pilot.

Vickers

Another view of VV119. *Vickers*

there, and he could be relied on to use his discretion, no bother would result. Fortunately in Gordon Richards (not the jockey) we had such a man, and he worked closely with the Airfield Foreman; often essential when time was of the essence in their liaison with the test pilots.

My visits there were cursory and roughly once a month. As I have said, the wing production at the Eastleigh Main Hangar was in capable hands, although I made a point of going there at least once a week, as I believed that while responsible people liked to be given a free hand, they did not like to be left out in the cold. The Hursley Park Experimental Hangar and the Eastleigh Flight Shed were still both under Frank Perry's jurisdiction, and were the weaker links in the chain. However, as they were both engaged on experimental work on which our side had been improved, just by the fact of my return, which spoke for itself, I was also aware that sooner or later the Design Office, Experimental Hangars, and Chilbolton were scheduled to go to South Marston. Because of this, the simmering war between Lefevre and Gooch went on — although thankfully it did not touch me personally again, enabling me to concentrate on feeding the Ministry of Aircraft Production's Technical Costs Assessors information, so that no further mistakes like that at Hursley occurred again.

Although the general thrust of the production management left something to be desired, and because that defect, in my view, deprived Woodley in making the representations to Joe Smith that his equality of status should have entitled him to do, the Design Office steamed ahead on its own individual course, without the benefit of a more enlightened exchange of opinions that would have, and should have, been the norm between two Special Directors in the best interests of the whole company. I must admit that this latter is an assumption on my part, as Smith and Woodley dined together when Woodley was at Hursley. I cannot believe that Woodley would not have advised Joe Smith to adopt a different position than that which he was taking, in a friendly and shared-responsible manner.

As I have said, I personally always found Stan Woodley very fair, and even after all the time that has elapsed since, I have no reason to change that opinion, which leads me to the conclusion that either vital design information was withheld from Woodley, or that if it was known, his nature was to remain silent, to leave Joe free to seek his own resolution. Whatever the reason, events moved remorsely on to an unexpected climax.

The blow that was to cause the most damage was delivered as a result of the Korean War. The Americans decided to launch an 'Off Shore' arms-purchasing programme. One item on their shopping list was front line fighter aircraft, and among those seeking orders and having their interest were the Gloster Javelin, Hawker Hunter, Folland Gnat and Vickers-Supermarine Swift. It was obvious that the order would be worth a vast sum of money and attract world-wide interest and further sales.

Each of the aircraft was to be flight tested by American pilots, and one of their Air Force Generals would fly and make the final recommendation to his purchasing authorities. The big question was Swift or Hunter? The Gloster aircraft was not really good enough, and the Gnat, although highly-praised, was thought to have too narrow an undercarriage track, and its designer, Petter, refused to move it out to the wings, an event that eventually caused Follands to encounter lack of home sales, and ended when Hawker's bought them out from the impossible financial position they were in.

The Hunter and Swift had been competing against each other since their inception. When the Hunter set a new 'World Speed Record' over the measured mile, the Swift went along a few weeks later and topped it, so Vickers' hopes were, on this basis, fairly high. Those hopes were soon to be dashed in a most dramatic fashion. When the American Air Force General flew the Swift, he landed to report an instability at altitude in the upper speed range. My first intimation of anything wrong was an urgent summons by Gooch to a Hursley meeting on a Saturday — in fact I was in the bath at the time. The meeting was to activate an urgent design request to build on to existing Swift wings a stepped leading edge.

This false 'notched' forward extension, from a point roughly one third of the wing span from the fuselage, was to be fabricated and fixed over the existing leading edge with all speed, so that the Swift could be tried again for the 'Off Shore' order. The job was done in a matter of days, nothing being allowed to impede its progress; it was tested by Mike Lithgow, and then the U.S. General had another try, but it did not make the aircraft fly at the critical end of its flight envelope to his satisfaction, and his recommendation and the subsequent orders went to Hawker Hunter.

This must have been a grievous blow to the Vickers Board! With the 'World Speed Record' wrenched from their rival, a large order from the R.A.F. well-advanced in production and already in Squadron Service, how could an American turn the aircraft down on the grounds of a flight defect — and why hadn't our own test pilots reported it? Questions were asked that had to be answered! It is all too easy to be wise after the event, and there are still some parts of the mystery that are not at all clear — one obviously is, why wasn't the defect found by the R.A.F.? Or was it?

I can only tell you what I know, and of the events that followed this shattering blow, from which your own conclusions may be drawn. Firstly, there is no doubt in my mind that varying types of flight instability were found by our company test pilots and duly reported back to the Design Office from the Type 510 onwards. I am also certain that Joe Smith was informed. Why nothing more was done, or why he failed to inform Vickers' Board, or at least alert them to the possibility that his design might not obtain the 'Off Shore' order, I cannot pretend to know.

On the few occasions I had to be in the same company as Joe Smith I had always thought of him as a dedicated, clever, and polite man with a sense of humour that bubbled out as an after-dinner speaker. The only time I recall speaking to him personally was after his original Mitchell Memorial Lecture, when a point I raised was answered with his customary courtesy. I can only assume, and I put it no higher than that, he may have been beset by the pressures that all designers suffer in a highly competitive business, and had to freeze his design for production and commercial reasons, when, all the time, this dark corner of doubt in his mind he hoped could be eliminated under the usual modifications procedures.

In my opinion, and that is all one can honestly give, Joe Smith's action was intended to be in the company's best interests, and certainly not to deliberately obscure a design defect to protect his own reputation. For that error of judgement he paid dearly in the traumatic days ahead. Almost as soon as the information became common knowledge, actions followed as fast as the aircraft's name.

The production order was cut at about the major component assembly state of the time, and worse, the Swift was downgraded by the R.A.F., to eventually become a low level photo-reconnaissance aircraft; a role in which, strangely enough, it achieved a remarkable amount of success. This latter-day success partly explains why the Swift had taken the 'World Speed Record', as the runs to establish that were at low level at El Adem in North Africa, and clearly indicated that the flight instability was only present at altitude in thinner air. With the production order cut to less than half — the figures were approximately 500 ordered, and cut off at 190 — and the adverse publicity that resulted, the main Vickers Board of Directors were obliged to enquire and adjudicate.

At the following year's Annual General Meeting, the Chairman included in his statement to shareholders words to the effect that regarding the Swift, he was taking steps to ensure that such an event would not occur again. Those words clearly eliminate any 'political'

156

reason, but at the same time they spelt out the inglorious fate of the Supermarine name in the Aviation Industry.

The order for the Scimitar, a large ungainly aircraft in the role of a Naval fighter, had its 100 order cut off at 76, and as the work began to wind down to its end, so the moves to South Marston began in earnest, accelerated by the early death of Joe Smith in February 1956. I cannot but think that here the events connected with the Swift took their tragic toll. The writing was clearly on the wall for all to see, and it was a time for individual choices to be made.

I must admit that the South Marston factory had little appeal for me, and when, as part of the reshuffling of top positions, Gilbert Taylor was made Deputy to Stuart Lefevre and handed his position over to his second-in-command at South Marston, I must confess to feeling a little peeved, but Gilbert, ever the frank man I new him to be, came to Itchen to tell me personally before it was announced. What he did not tell me, as his negotiating was at an early and delicate stage, was that he was in the process of obtaining Woodley's approval to my becoming Production Controller at South Marston. As a result, my own prospects looked rather dim as I saw them, and having been approached and offered a Works Manager's position with a smaller engineering firm, I decided to accept it. It was when I handed Gilbert my resignation he told me that his efforts on my behalf as Production Controller had successfully borne fruit. By then I had committed myself to the Works Manager's position in an area more to my liking than Swindon, and this time I felt I could not go back on my word. So I left at the end of March 1957.

After Joe Smith's death at 58 years of age, the Design Office move to South Marston, was made easier. Alan Clifton was appointed Chief Designer, but he must have known it was more or less a caretaker posting, and at about the end of 1957 the Design Office, and those members of it who chose to go, were transferred to South Marston. The Hursley Experimental Hangar was closed and the Hursley House and estate was abandoned, eventually to become the British home for I.B.M. Frank Perry went off to a Works Manager's post with another South Coast company, and the last I heard had returned to Vickers at Hurn's Mould Loft.

The Chilbolton hangar was closed and the test pilots team disbanded. One tragic outcome from this was that Mike Lithgow, who had transferred to Vickers at Weybridge, was killed while testing a B.A.C. 1-11. Les Colquhoun, who had won the George Medal for bringing home safely an Attacker with one of its wing folding portions having 'folded' in flight, went on to become an expert on hovercraft handling, but what happened to 'Chunky' Horne and Dave Morgan I do not know, but I hear that 'Pee Wee' Judge was killed whilst flying a 'gyrocopter at Farnborough in 1970.

There is one memory I treasure of this band of intrepid 'birdmen', which has nothing to do with flying. It was the company's practice to give its Executives an annual dinner and entertainment — purely a stag do — once a year. It was, by custom, usually held at a different area venue each year. The venue in this case was South Marston, and to ensure that our enjoyment was unconfined by driving worries, they provided coaches for almost door to door transport. On the return journey our coach included in its passengers all the pilots mentioned above who, led by Mike Lithgow, and as many of us who were sufficiently well-oiled and consequently daft enough to be persuaded by Mike, congregated at the very rear of the coach — beyond its rear axle — and on his order, jumped up and came down together, which according to Mike should lift the front wheels off the ground. It did — and one very irate driver, who had just had the fright of his life, let us all know just what he thought of such idiotic behaviour. He had every justification to do so, but I can never forget the boyish fun and craziness of those men who, within a few hours, would be solely responsible for an aircraft that probably cost a million pounds or more.

A more macabre event took place at the Design Office Christmas (and farewell) Dance on Southampton Pier in 1957. During the half-way interval, a solemn group of masked pall bearers brought into the dance hall a black draped coffin, suitably inscribed to indicate that this was the burial of the Design Office, and after parading it round for the senior management guests present to see, 'laid it to rest' in the centre of the dance floor. By this time I was an onlooker from outside the company, but my old interest and associations still ensured that I watched or noted the final winding down. My old area closed, unit by unit, the last being Itchen, and with that the link between Southampton and Supermarine's was finally broken.

The grand new office block of 1937/8 was used by a small engineering company, and later as the manufacturing site of chicken-plucking machines, but somehow nothing of any permanence stayed. Finally it was bought by the County Council and, once the new Itchen Bridge was built, the office block was considered unsafe and demolished. The old Mould Loft-cum-cycle shed is still in evidence; the cycle shed portion now suitably floored and windowed, it continues life as Vickers Marine office.

By far the grandest reminder of those days of yore is the Itchen works building; now proudly resplendent in its pale blue paint it houses Vosper-Hovermarine. Across the road the railway embankment is covered by a mass of small trees and bushes with no visible signs of that fatal tunnel to the air raid shelters. On the embankment's far side, the land was used for years as a dump, until now it is almost at the railway line height and, in its reclaimed form, is a public park with seats, and children play over what remained of the shelters twenty feet below.

An what of our personalities? With Joe Smith gone, only a skeleton design team under Alan Clifton saw out its dying days at South Marston, and finally ceased. Stan Woodley transferred to the Vickers Medical Equipment works and later wisely, in my view, took an early retirement. Leonard Gooch was similarly reposted, to the Vickers Office Equipment works at Dartford, where he prospered, eventually becoming Chairman and Chief Executive of Vickers Automated Systems Ltd., dying in 1976 before reaching his retirement.

I met him a number of times after 1957 — we both shared a common interest in the Southampton Football Club — but after his move to Dartford we met but once more. He had been to a meeting at Vickers House in London, and I was returning from a Ministry meeting at St. Giles Court. We shared a compartment on the Waterloo to Southampton train and this was in 1971. The strange thing was that although he recognised me, he did not seem to know where from, and he rambled on about his achievements at Supermarine's, talking with his eyes seemingly fixed about a foot over my head, looking into space, a mannerism he adopted when expounding about himself and giving me, in effect, exactly the same contribution that he made later to the 40th Anniversary of the Spitfire Prototype's first flight Symposium, held at Southampton University in 1976, barely three months before his death. The proceedings of that Symposium were subsequently published, and there is his contribution for all to see.

He undoubtedly told the same story to others, but in my case had obviously forgotten that I was present at the time the events occurred. I am inclined to suspect he was relating an account of what he believed had been his role, and what he wanted others to believe. The danger in this is that historians may latch on to his fantasising, and then we shall unfortunately have to agree with Henry Ford's dictum that 'History is Bunk'. Fortunately there is still time to make amends, although at the time Gooch gave me his version, I had no idea that it would be widely circulated subsequently, and, as on that evening his account appeared to make him feel important and happy, I did not have the heart, or even the desire, to challenge it.

I was in hospital at the time of the Symposium, otherwise I would have attended, and certainly have made my objections to his statements in open forum, but by 1976 I had already been relegated to the sidelines for four years by crippling arthritis, and it has only been due to a partial remission in my condition that has permitted me to write this account.

Before moving on to the events at South Marston I must record that Bill Heaver collapsed in his office at Itchen before its closure, and died very shortly afterwards. Here again I am sure the strain and uncertainty of his future must have contributed to his death. As the Foreman who gave me my start in 'K' shop, guided my way during my youthful years, shared with us all the bombing and dispersal that followed, and ended with his protegé sharing the Executive Dining Room he presided over at Itchen, it saddens me that his latter years were less rewarding than I believe were his due. At least he will remain fondly remembered as long as I live.

And South Marston? It still belongs to Vickers, and there is a real Spitfire displayed in its grounds; but with the cessation of aircraft building and design, their work gradually became more of a general engineering nature. Vickers sent in one of their Engineering Managers to replace Woodley; Stuart Lefevre, who was badly upset by a car accident which killed a young man, and no doubt contributed to his early death. Gilbert Taylor took over Lefevre's position and grimly struggled on towards the necessary transition to the new work, but the team he had successfully built for aircraft construction was not, in my opinion, up to the new tasks required of them.

Eventually Vickers stepped in and appointed Leonard Redshaw (now Sir Leonard), a very experienced Ship and Engineering Manager, to manage the factory. He gave it the shake-up it needed to get some commercial sense instilled into its workings. As so often happens in these cases, changes in top management have to be made and one of its casualties in this instance was Gilbert Taylor. I was particularly sorry about this as, by that time, I was no longer in a position to help him. Had I been in my last post I would have grabbed him as either Chief Ratefixer or Production Manager — not solely because of his previous kindnesses to me, but because I knew his worth and his capabilities in aircraft manufacture.

So it was that the name 'Supermarine' disappeared from the industrial scene; an inglorious and sad end to a name that had brought lustre, fame, and quite possibly in the final analysis, freedom to the land of its birth. Perhaps Charlie Burgess at B.E.A. struck the right chord to the firm's pre-war reputation when he told me how I had been selected for the Northolt post. 'If you come from pre-war Supermarine's, you can get a job anywhere', he said, and that just about sums it up.

My 'odyssey' had lasted, all told, with the two short breaks, a span of 21 years — over half my working life — and at the end of the day, with all its ups and downs, I would not wish it changed, neither would I have missed it for anything. It had lasted almost completely the active life of the Spitfire, as some foreign air forces were only discarding them in 1957. With the immense technicological changes since that time, it is pretty certain we shall not see its like again. Should you — young or old — have an opportunity to see and hear one of the few remaining flying Spitfires, do look up at that distinctive elliptical plan wing shape, the classical proportions of the body, and tail unit, and listen to the equally distinctive sweet engine sound with its propeller whistle, for you will be seeing and hearing a remarkable piece of history which, thank Heaven, was not 'bunk'.

Fortunately, the opportunities for seeing a flying Spitfire are better now than even just a few years ago. Due to the resurging interest that is growing, rather than diminishing, after forty odd years, and the current sale prices obtainable for flight worthy survivors (one recently went for £260,000), efforts are being made here, and abroad, to retrieve and repair any that can be found. In Sussex, there is one young man who is currently rebuilding four, and actually employs a small team to help him. I wish them luck. Those Spitfires are a fitting memorial to the genius who designed them and all who contributed to their construction.

ACKNOWLEDGMENTS

Although this book has been ten years in compilation and research and the opinions expressed my own, I have been fortunate in the aid and encouragement in various ways by the following: the late Tony Brode — Literary Editor of the Southern Evening Echo; Elizabeth Cathie — for arranging the photo-copying; Bob Culley and Bob Pearce — two ex-colleagues; Mavis Dominy and Susan Wallis — for translating my arthritic scrawl into a reasonable typescript; Gerry Gingell — Secretary of the Swindon Branch of the R.Ae.S. and retired member of Supermarines and Vickers; Irene Pilson — Author of MEMORIES of BITTERNE for her guidance; Jeffrey Quill — Author of SPITFIRE — A Test Pilot's Story; Dennis Stevens — Editor of the Hampshire County Magazine; Southampton City Council — City Archivists Department; John Vasco — Author of ERPROBUNGSGRUPPE 210 — The history of a Luftwaffe fighter-bomber unit in the Battle of Britain; Brian Wexham — Head of the Photographic Department, Vickers Ltd.; Mrs K. Southwell — past Secretary to S. Lefevre, and Leonard Redshaw, at South Marston.

Bibliography

Aircraft Production. 1949-1952. (Monthly magazine; now no longer published).
Aeroplane Monthly. Published by I.P.C. Transport Press Ltd.
Battle over Britain, by F. K. Mason. McWhirter Twins. 1965.
Fighter Pilot: A Self Portrait, by George Barclay. William Kimber & Co. Ltd. 1976.
Finest Hour: Winston Churchill 1939-41, by Martin Gilbert. Wm. Heineman. 1983.
Flying Magazines 1933-40. (ceased publication 1940).
German Aircraft of the Second World War, by J. R. Smith & A. Kay. Putnam. 1972.
Luftwaffe Encore, by Ken Wakefield. Wm. Kimber.
Night Bombing, by Hector Hawton. Thomas Nelson & Sons. 1944.
Supermarine Aircraft since 1914, by C. F. Andrews & E. B. Morgan. Putnam. 1981.
Sigh of a Merlin, by Alex Henshaw. John Murray. 1980
Spitfire: A Test Pilot's story, by Jeffrey Quill. John Murray. 1983
The Rolls-Royce Magazine. (house magazine of R-R Ltd.)
Wing Leader, by Group Captain Johnnie Johnson. (now Air Vice Marshal, rtd.) Chatto and Windus. 1956.
Spitfire 40th Anniversary Brochure and the Report on the Symposium of 1976. Both published by the Southampton Branch of the Royal Aeronautical Society.